Praise for *Rising from Existential Crisis*

A major contribution to thinking and writ
phenomena on the bodies, minds and souls of
in Britain for many years, Emmy van Deurzei
Brexit. She is transparent about what she wen
also considers the Covid-19 pandemic in terms of an 'existential crisis'. Here, she
is careful not to fall into the trap of assuming everyone has been equally affected
in identical ways. These deep reflections demonstrate how the public and the
private interweave. We see this in our consulting rooms – but those places are
also microcosms of general processes that many people endure. Hence, Emmy
has produced something that speaks not only to practising therapists, but also to
clients and, beyond that, to all citizens. The book has the potential to break out
of the therapy cloister because it shows what therapy thinking – done well – can
contribute to wider political, social and cultural conversations.
Professor Andrew Samuels, author of *The Political Psyche* **and** *A New Therapy For Politics?*

The term 'existential crisis' has been coined by numerous commentators
recently. In this book, van Deurzen makes a compelling and highly readable
case for an existential perspective on the ills that currently beset us. A
foundational truth of existential philosophy and therapy is that nothing is
fixed, everything changes. This understanding of the human condition is
urgently needed in the midst of pandemic, the ongoing concatenations of
Brexit, the erosion of democratic values, climate change, and so much more.
If we despair of finding firm ground on which to go forward, this book points
to it, and instils us with the courage to begin to make sense of what might
otherwise appear as chaos, while summoning responses that will help us
survive, even flourish. Existentialism is essentially a practical philosophy; van
Deurzen shows us how to use it just when we need it most.
Professor Simon du Plock, senior research fellow, Metanoia Institute, London

A compelling read, written with a humbling yet robust voice, to instil hope
and meaning when navigating the paradoxes and vicissitudes of current times.
Contextualised in current politics, such as Brexit and a global pandemic,
the book weaves through collective questions that have occupied people for
centuries, commending the courage, resourcefulness and resilience discovered
in our choices. This book calls for 'new flexibilities' in our ways of dealing
with crises, demonstrated by vivid personal examples of the author herself and
those of other migrants who have experienced the emotional and existential
exile, alongside identity shifts and questioning one's belonging. As an EU

citizen and an existential practitioner myself, who accompanies others in their quest, I found resonance in these pages towards reclaiming meaning, finding new ways of connection and 'rising' beyond adversity. This is a book for a wide audience, inspiring us to live with existential courage and use any challenge towards healing and growth.

Dr Fevronia Christodoulidi, senior lecturer in counselling and psychotherapy, University of East London

From the moment I steered into the introduction to this book, I was transfixed. With a rare blend of audacity and authenticity, the author acknowledges the genuine anguish that arises when lives fall apart, whether through extreme personal adversity, system-shattering socio-political events or an ineluctable and impersonal global pandemic. But, she argues, in embracing the pain that attends such pivotal periods, we can find the clarity and courage to reclaim and reconstruct a life of meaning. In artful but accessible prose and through riveting and relatable case studies, this book provides welcome signposts in a terrain devastated by loss, and wise companionship on the journey. In lives that are over-full with demands of every sort, Emmy van Deurzen's book comes as a wake-up call, amid the rumble of the mundane, to reclaim our lives from the cosily settled conventions and compromises that distract us from acknowledging and using crisis. My advice is simple: put this gem of a volume in your shopping cart, and add a few more copies for others you know whose lives also have been razed to their foundations. In this age, rife with challenges to our psychological and physical wellbeing and our very identities, this ultimately includes all of us.

Professor Robert A. Neimeyer, Director of the Portland Institute for Loss and Transition and Editor of *New Techniques of Grief Therapy: Bereavement and beyond*

How have EU citizens in the UK experienced Britain leaving the EU? Many felt thrown into an abyss, like Alice in Wonderland, pushed over a cliff edge and into a sea of anxiety. Despite campaigns to secure rights unilaterally, the government chose to leave EU citizens in limbo for more than two years, treating them as collateral in the Brexit negotiations. Many EU citizens also stumbled into the recesses of their own minds. Emmy van Deurzen's expert case studies of how Joan, Lucie and others found a voice and recovered teach us a great deal about human suffering and how to confront it. The stories contain a universal message of hope, resilience and overcoming in the face of adversity. Whatever happens to you, it's what you do next that matters. Learning how to respond and not just react to the crisis is the key to self-understanding and empowerment.

Roger Casale, Secretary General, New Europeans

RISING FROM EXISTENTIAL CRISIS

LIFE BEYOND CALAMITY

EMMY VAN DEURZEN

PCCS
BOOKS

First published 2021

PCCS Books Ltd
Wyastone Business Park
Wyastone Leys
Monmouth NP25 3SR
UK
Tel +44 (0)1600 891 509
www.pccs-books.co.uk

Rising from Existential Crisis: Life beyond calamity

British Library Cataloguing in Publication Data
A catalogue record for this book is available from the British Library

ISBN   pbk – 978 1 910919 85 9
         epub – 978 1 910919 88 0

Cover design by Jason Anscomb
Printed in the UK by Short Run Press, Exeter.

Contents

Dedication

To Ingrid, for the gifts of grit and resilience.

And to all those who have been disenfranchised or shattered by existential crisis. May your vitality light the way to your rising.

About the author

Emmy van Deurzen is an existential psychotherapist, philosopher and counselling psychologist. She is Principal of the New School of Psychotherapy and Counselling at the Existential Academy in London and runs her own private therapy practice, Dilemma Consultancy, in London. She is a visiting professor with Middlesex University, for whom she directs several doctoral and master's programmes. She has published 17 books on existential therapy and the challenges of the human condition. Her work has been translated into more than a dozen languages and she has lectured worldwide in more than 35 countries across all continents.

Acknowledgements

The first person I want to thank is my editor, Catherine Jackson, who was savvy, professional and deft in shaping my overly long manuscript into a much more compact and coherent book on existential crisis than it would otherwise have been. When she judiciously challenged my writing and cut a third of my words, I felt a little bruised at first. But it reminded me of my first editor in the early 1980s, who taught me that accomplished writing requires us to 'kill our darlings'. I was never very good at doing so myself and felt a sense of immense relief when Catherine scrapped all the unnecessary stories and sentences. I trust that she kept the ones my readers will actually enjoy reading. I apologise to the people whose wise words are not now included.

Second, I feel deeply beholden to Joan Pons Laplana and Lucie Dun for having given their time so readily and for having been so generous and genuine in reflecting on their life experiences and allowing me to include their extremely poignant and evocative stories in this volume. The pain they went through in their time of crisis led to much learning and understanding, which others may now benefit from. I know that many people will take great comfort and courage from their shining examples. I am also grateful to everyone else who shared their personal experiences with me over the months and years and who gave me permission to use their statements. This is especially true for Laure Ollivier-Minns. I want to thank Helen de Cruz, Elena Remigi and Véronique Martin for their tireless documentation of the feelings of the five million EU citizens in the UK and the million and a half UK citizens in Europe resulting from the Brexit referendum. I want to thank my colleagues, especially Neil Lamont, Jo Molle, Joel Vos, Sasha van Deurzen-Smith and Digby Tantam, for their work in the Emotional Support Service for Europeans at the Existential Academy, and to my friends in Voices for Europe, for keeping hope burning throughout these dark years.

Third I want to thank the colleagues whose research I have built on in this book. I am very proud of the phenomenological research of all our New School of Psychotherapy and Counselling students and graduates, but on this particular occasion I want to salute Dr Nancy Hakim Dowek, Dr Susan Iacovou and Dr Armin Danesh for contributing their research findings, which helped me to reframe and reformulate some of my own thinking.

Fourth and foremost, I want to express my profound gratitude and appreciation to my husband, Digby Tantam, who is my daily companion, both in our private and professional lives. Our continuous process of exchange and debate is always a loving struggle that leads to resolution and new inspiration. We are committed to getting through our existential crises together, each much stronger for sharing them with the other. Digby has been instrumental in helping me let go of past losses and disappointments by listening patiently, enabling me to refine and define my understanding of what I could learn from these setbacks. I am in awe of the love, support, attention and care he lavishes on me, validating my existence on a daily basis.

Preface

You may write me down in history
With your bitter, twisted lies,
You may trod me in the very dirt
But still, like dust, I'll rise.
    'Still I rise', Maya Angelou (1978)

When crisis strikes

A crisis is an event that usually happens out of the blue and strikes you down like a bolt of lightning. We may spend many years trying to avoid such events, protecting ourselves or staying in hiding. But, when crisis touches us, we are stirred to the depths of our being and we are always changed by it. Because of this, an existential crisis is an event that brings truth and new depth to our lives. We are shocked out of complacency, as everything we took for granted is suddenly in question. We must descend to the rock bottom of life, where we have to deal with unexpected and inconceivable losses. We are plunged into an existential reality that is stark and undeniable and usually completely outside our control. Somehow, we have to find a way to cope with this.

Why this book

This book is about the experience of going through an existential crisis, and it will explore and show how we may survive and rise from such a difficult challenge. What I have written here is deeply rooted in my own encounters with such watershed moments. It is my aim to demonstrate how each of us can learn to respond better to these sudden confrontations with emergency situations. We will consider together how we can meet such times of catastrophe with courage and creativity in order to turn them into moments of affirmation that transform the crisis into an opportunity for greater understanding and fortitude.

How do we meet the kind of existential crisis that revolutionises our lives and that we cannot hide or run away from? As turmoil turns into turbulence and our lives become unstable, we sense that everything has become irretrievably and irredeemably altered. We know in our bones that life will never be the same again. So how do we find the resolution and resilience to deal with this?

When everything trembles and we no longer feel physically safe, we often start doubting ourselves and other people. We may have been treated poorly by others and have, at least temporarily, given up on them. In addition, we often also lose our self-confidence and struggle to keep our head clear, as we feel quite overwhelmed and out of sorts. Our inner balance becomes disturbed and our mental and emotional wellbeing are affected. Our spiritual beliefs are also in question, for everything becomes chaotic and is thrown out of kilter and harmony. The entirety of our lives is stirred and shaken and, in the middle of all this commotion, we somehow have to find a rational and adequate response. People in crisis often report that, once they find themselves in such tumultuous times, they encounter a sequence of catastrophic events, with one thing after another going wrong for them. That is enough for many of us to start panicking or despairing, to lose our very trust in ourselves and the world around us. When we begin to find our calm again, we can see how to steady the situation so that further damage can be avoided and stability can be re-established.

Crises are always more sudden and more upsetting than we imagine they would be. Most of us experience several intense personal crises during our lives, but natural and social disasters may also come to strike us out of the blue. Sometimes events arise that hit a whole group of people, or even a whole community. In the case of a political event, it may affect an entire nation. In the case of a pandemic, it may concern and affect the entire world. Some crises are long in the making and we can begin to see them foreshadowed in our lives ahead of time, giving us some opportunity to prepare for the misfortunes they herald. We are currently facing quite a few of such crises across humanity, as we are slowly waking up to the climate emergency, the threat of the increasing world population, the mass destruction of biodiversity and the consequences of a potential nuclear catastrophe. All of these things menace our planet as a whole, rather than just a few human beings. We have lived with the knowledge of such things for a long time now, in the same way that previous generations lived with the constant fear of wars, famines, plagues, revolts and revolutions.

Concrete experiences of existential crisis

Yet, the entire world went into shock when the Covid-19 pandemic struck country after country in 2020 and continued through into 2021 (the time of writing this book), putting us into lockdown and changing all of our habits. It left us reeling and having to think about the world in a new way. Some people fell ill and recovered, but many millions died – in hospital intensive care, at home and in nursing and residential care homes. Many of us became frightened for a while that we would not survive if the virus struck us. We had to face the possibility of our own demise in a very intimate fashion. Many people found themselves made redundant or furloughed. Financial problems loomed on the horizon. Shops closed. Businesses went bust. Investments and pension pots were diminished. Our safety and our future were in question and our lives were brought into new and sharper focus. We were forced to think more carefully about our lifestyle and the future of our society and our planet. While some people withdrew and tried to distract themselves, others collapsed into apathy. At the same time, we saw many good people rising to the challenges, either because they were key workers and had to keep our world turning or because they found meaning in helping the most vulnerable among us.

It was disturbing and upsetting to hear about so many elderly people dying in care homes. It raised moral questions about our world and our politics. It was worrying to have to stay isolated for a long time, although it was also strangely peaceful on our streets and our air quality improved temporarily without all that traffic. The world was suddenly on pause, without its rat race, its rush hour and its predictable nine-to-five wage slavery. We watched the political landscape shifting and the different responses evolving in different countries. The authoritarian governments made many wrong decisions that would have terrible consequences for their citizens. They were careless and nonchalant about people's wellbeing. Despite their boastful proclamations, the US and UK governments were exposed as being behind, rather than ahead of, the curve. Questions were asked about this. Brazil seemed to lose control over the virus entirely. Capitalism itself was faltering and failing in front of our eyes. We could imagine the Western world on the brink of disaster. We could see and feel that it was wrong to put the economy ahead of vulnerable citizens and yet we were also acutely aware that we could not just stop producing food and vital products. Survival depended on carrying on. Denial and deception of the public were rife in the countries that did poorly, and transparency was greater in countries such as South Korea and New Zealand that were resourceful and resilient, managed to protect their citizens effectively and thrived. We learnt many lessons.

It was clear that this pandemic was not just a physical threat. It was intermingled with social and political issues, and it had considerable personal impact on many of us individually. People's personal lives were revolutionised; couples and families were thrown together or torn apart. We all had to face new relational pressures. Rates of domestic abuse went up alarmingly. Our beliefs and opinions were put to the test. Our chances of staying safe depended greatly on how our government responded to the pandemic but also on how we ourselves adapted and showed our resilience. It wasn't a foregone conclusion that our state would or could protect us. Seeing the way in which some politicians used the media to deliberately mislead and misinform was an education for many. It had never been so obvious that our wellbeing is determined and limited by the way in which our governments choose to protect or undermine our rights as citizens.

There is no doubt that many people who are facing such threats themselves go into denial and turn to wishful thinking. When we are afraid and find it hard to deal with difficulties, we all tend to stick our heads in the sand for a bit. We have to do so. We have to cocoon ourselves, cradle ourselves back to security. We hide to try to re-establish some safety and serenity. We learn to value the role of sanctuary. We learn to find solace in the things that truly matter. Unfortunately, our self-protectiveness can also backfire. We can become passive and willing to accept things that are not really good for us. We let others take over who do not necessarily have our best interests at heart. We have to learn to balance courage and determined activity with self-care and compassion.

Responding to crisis

In this book I will explore how people respond to crisis and how we can learn to respond in ways that are more beneficial and less destructive for us. There are, of course, many forms of crisis. Some are created by health issues, others by family or relationship issues. In these pages, I will focus on events that are sudden and feel catastrophic. I will look particularly at the human, personal and psychological impact of political and world events on us as individuals. I will ask how people cope and overcome such crises. I will consider why and how some people find ways of rising from crisis that seem to demonstrate greater strength than others can muster. I will highlight how some people learn to thrive on crisis and the lessons we can draw from this on how to rise to the challenge ourselves. I will not consider any crises that are purely internal or relational in nature, although you may find that my observations apply to such situations as well.

I will look at the kind of crisis that is caused by a sudden calamity that changes lives, especially where we feel particularly helpless and victimised by it. When people are caught in the crossfire of events beyond their control, this has a particularly strong impact on them. Wars and other political events that cause distress are especially hard to deal with. I will not just look at the Covid-19 pandemic but also at the impact of the Brexit referendum – the political swing in the UK in June 2016 that brought the country to a halt and created a deep divide between us, as it heralded the end of the UK's membership of the European Union.

The Brexit referendum led to years of turmoil and bitter conflict, splitting the nation and creating major unsafety for particular groups of the population. It was almost like a social experiment carried out on an unsuspecting public, and one group of people was impacted so strongly and so negatively that they felt completely disempowered and diminished by it. These were the estimated five million EU citizens resident in the UK, who were not given a democratic vote in the referendum, even though their lives were directly in the firing line, and even though their rights to their homes and to safety in their adoptive country were under threat and their future was in the balance. The Brexit years bled seamlessly into the unexpected hazards of the Covid-19 pandemic, and the combined effect had a demoralising impact on many people's lives. At the same time, these years of continuous challenges taught some people how to handle such situations better, and I will take a look at that too. I will provide some in-depth case illustrations from which to draw lessons about the way in which people were able to respond constructively to these tragedies.

Outline of the book

I will look at existential crisis from a number of different perspectives. In the introduction, I will seek to define existential crisis to understand it better. In Chapter One, I will look at the experience of crisis and how it shifts the parameters of daily existence, leaving us feeling quite crushed by what is happening to us. I will give an example from my own life to illustrate how the initial shock of crisis may slowly transform into a new flexibility and ability to cope that may allow us to change destructive habits and redirect our lives with greater clarity. Crisis indeed opens our eyes and may reveal truths about our existence that were previously hidden.

In Chapter Two, I will turn to the experiences of the five million EU citizens in the UK whose lives were upturned by the Brexit vote. I will attempt to explain why their plight was so terrible for them, even though, or perhaps because, this was hidden to most other people in the nation. I will look at the difficulties and upset experienced by people who found their security and safety suddenly in question when it was made clear to them that they no longer belonged in the country where they had built their homes and families.

In Chapter Three, I will take a close-up look at the actual experience of one of these people, whose expectations of the world and of himself were shaken by what to him felt like a calamity. I will demonstrate how his struggles ultimately led to him finding new determination to contribute something good to the world. I will seek to understand why someone who was previously so strong and resilient nevertheless had a breakdown because of what was happening to him. I will look at his story as he wrote it himself and go on to quiz him in more depth in order to examine his personal experience carefully and learn from it.

In Chapter Four, I will have an in-depth dialogue with a woman whose right to stay in her home was put into question by the Brexit vote. She initially felt quite distraught and could barely manage, but she didn't give up and made sure she would not be destroyed by her experience of disenfranchisement. This sensitive and artistic young woman found her own ways of coping with the situation and her experience will provide further precious information about how people rise from existential crisis.

In Chapter Five, I will consider how people learn to make sense of life and the losses it inflicts on them in a crisis. I will look at what we learn in a crisis and how we can muster our resources and find a way to contend with the difficulties thrown at us. I will look at some of the concrete and practical possibilities available to us in surmounting our crisis.

In Chapter Six, I will introduce some ideas from existential therapy to help us understand the plight of people in crisis. I will discuss some more general philosophical ideas about life and some specific concepts that apply to existential crisis in particular, derived from existential practice. These show us that crisis is not just inevitable but essential to human existence, and perhaps to life in general, and is part of our life-long development. Having a map of life to find our way in such circumstances can be very helpful.

In Chapter Seven, I will focus on what happens to people when they are struck by an extreme and bewildering form of existential crisis. I will look at what we know about people's responses to such tragedy, loss and trauma. I will illustrate this with some very serious examples of situations when people's lives were affected by active combat in war or by being forced out of their home country. I will look at those who survive such situations and how they do or do not manage to make sense of it.

In Chapter Eight, I will take a look at the emotional impact and human cost of the global Covid-19 pandemic. When the entire world went into a state of shock and crisis, how did people fare and how did they cope mentally and emotionally? I will explore why, although we were all under threat from the virus, not everyone was in the same position or had the same vulnerability or response to it.

In Chapter Nine, I will provide an overview of the many ways in which people learn to mitigate experiences of existential crisis in practice. How can we make sure that we come out stronger from our disasters? How can we learn to rise from crisis and even to thrive on it? I will draw on some of the lessons outlined in the previous chapters to draft a blueprint for living with existential courage.

In this way, throughout these pages, we will together figure out, step by step, how the theory and practice of existential courage link to illuminate our lives when we feel lost and in the dark. My aim is to show that, if we want to live life to the full, we must seek to understand how meaningful struggles create new, stronger but also more flexible structures to secure our daily existence. Existential therapists and philosophers have a great deal to bring to the table on these issues and there will be contributions from many authors throughout these pages.

Mostly though, the book will draw directly from human experience, distilling the essence of what has worked for people in practice. Our conclusions will show that we can find strength and wisdom in adversity without becoming negative, despairing or bitter and without letting our suffering and shattering destroy our capacity for kindness, collaboration, courage and humanity. For, in the final analysis, our encounters with misfortunes will remain a core part of our lives, no matter how good we become at facing them. What we need to understand is that these times in life can create fertile ground on which we can cultivate reliable strength, alongside a new sense of humility and a profound commitment to our fellow human beings.

Introduction

Politicians and journalists around the world have been liberally using the term 'existential crisis' in the past few years to refer to situations that represent a threat to the life of a nation, a group of individuals, an institution or an idea. They have started to use the term 'existential' as if it meant 'terminal', 'mortal' or 'critical'. But the word 'existential' doesn't mean any of these things. It simply means 'related to existence'. Going through an existential crisis is to go through a crisis of one's whole existence – a crisis that affects everything. This means that we enter into a phase of acute instability, during which we become aware that life is precarious and our situation perilous. Clearly, this would be the case if our life were threatened and the situation were desperate, but it can also happen when we are going through a process of serious transformation and change that is not directly related to an immediate threat of death.

People who have a mid-life crisis, waking up to the futility of their existence and wanting to shift their entire world to begin anew, are having an existential crisis. Women who give birth to their first child often find that their existence is thrown into turmoil and everything is altered. This too represents an existential crisis for them, as it revolutionises their every moment and the very core of their identity (Arnold-Baker, 2020; Adams, 2018). Similarly, when people lose their job or are faced with divorce, this is frequently experienced as an existential crisis. When people migrate to a new country, this represents an existential crisis, as they have to re-orientate to an entirely new culture and often to a new language. When people are denied safety in their home or place of residence, this also leads to an existential crisis. People who become homeless certainly experience it as a disaster. And, as the whole world discovered in 2020, when we as a human race are exposed to a viral pandemic and have to completely change how we live, work, learn and interact with one another, this can also lead to an existential crisis, especially if our personal survival is in question. I would conjecture that most of us, if not all, have recently been confronted with an existential crisis of some kind or another, and it has become vital for us to understand this experience better.

How does it affect people when they realise their lives are on the line and are in a process of utter change and total transformation? Rather than concluding that an existential crisis is simply the end of something we know, which it usually is, we need to consider how we go through such a crisis and how we can emerge from it with the capability of building a new future. Moreover, instead of fearing the experience of existential crisis, we need to understand that we may be able to learn something of great value from it. This all depends on whether we succeed in figuring out how to retrieve something positive from a disaster instead of being buried under negatives in despair. The Chinese word for crisis, *weiji*, is formed of two components. The first, '*wei*', means danger; the second, '*ji*', means 'a turning point' – a point when change happens. The English word 'crisis' comes from the Ancient Greek word κρίσις (*krísis*), which means 'decision', or 'judgement', and also 'turning point' in the context of an illness. It in turn stems from the verb κρίνω (*krínō*), which means to judge, discriminate, choose or decide. A crisis, then, is a critical moment when we have to make important decisions about what to do and which way we go in response to the threat of danger.

In this book, I shall look particularly at the way in which political and social events can affect individuals and provoke an existential crisis in their lives. I will consider how such situations can revolutionise people's lives in such a way that their entire existence is in jeopardy, not just physically but also emotionally, mentally, socially, culturally and spiritually. I will look at the experience of existential crisis on all those dimensions and trace carefully how a person's life can be profoundly affected at all those levels by external circumstances that undermine their previous sense of internal integrity.

How does it feel to go through an existential crisis?

An existential crisis usually feels like a catastrophe that comes upon us out of the blue, like a bolt of lightning, striking at the very heart of the life that we have previously enjoyed and have taken for granted. We all experience daily difficulties that we take into our stride with more or less ease, and some of us may get very good at solving problems on a regular basis. However, we can never be fully prepared for the sudden and complete upheaval that follows an apparently catastrophic event. Such an occurrence gets to us, because it strikes at the very foundation of the connections and meanings we value and have built up carefully over the years. A crisis is exactly the kind of episode that we cannot completely prepare for and that attacks the ground of our existence.

Existential crisis can happen to us unexpectedly through a physical event, like an accident or a natural disaster, or through the sudden, violent death of someone close and dear to us – a child, a parent or a partner. This kind of existential crisis can also be experienced, very poignantly, by people who are given a cancer diagnosis or who find out that they have lost a much-loved job, their home or a large amount of money. Interestingly, it can also apply to people who suddenly win a lot of money or are promoted into a job they feel unprepared for. When our lives are precipitously altered, we immediately experience everything as unreal or out of kilter. This is the hallmark of an existential crisis. Our usual homeostasis is suddenly disturbed and we find ourselves battered, struggling between a feeling of victimisation and an awareness of the importance of taking action and shouldering responsibility.

Existential crisis visited upon us by physical or natural events can feel like a low blow dealt by unseen forces, and it may make us briefly lose our trust in safety, in the planet, in our god(s), in fate or in fairness. But when existential crisis is visited on us through social or interpersonal events, like being sacked from a job, disinherited by one's parents or served with a court order, the consequences may be even more dire, especially if we don't feel we had any responsibility in the matter. We may temporarily feel as if we have been hit by a truck, as we literally reel from what has happened and try to regain some basic sense of equilibrium. Prisoners who have been wrongly accused of the crime for which they are serving time report the same type of mind-bending experience of incongruity. They realise that everything is out of synch, nothing can ever be the same again and nobody can ever be fully trusted. This experience of absurdity and oddness is very well described by Kafka in his book *The Trial* (Kafka, 2009).

Whistleblowers similarly find their trust in society shattered after their revelations are held against them and they become victimised and shunned (Field & Lamplugh, 2010). The defining characteristic of the crisis here is the shattering of our basic framework of meaning when it is invalidated by the world around us. This leads to us becoming mistrustful of society, or even of humanity itself. Not being able to feel at home in the world is very much part of it. It can lead to suicidal feelings as we feel shut out of the social world and experience ourselves as unwanted outsiders. Many people who bring disasters upon themselves through substance abuse started this behaviour in order to soothe themselves from some other catastrophe. They seek to experience a sense of harmony, wholeness and connection by using the substance they turn to, but often find instead that it cuts them off even further from the world. I have worked with numerous people whose lives were shattered when they ended up with psychiatric diagnoses because they could not cope with important changes in their lives and found themselves in a double bind. R.D. Laing wrote about this experience of existential crisis in great detail (Laing, 1959, 1961, 1967). Unable to find the strength to stand up to events or to the system they are caught up in, ordinary people may find themselves weakened and end up being given a mental illness diagnosis, which then can lead to catastrophic outcomes (Johnstone, 2000, 2014; Watson, 2019; van Deurzen, 2018a, 2018b, 2019a, 2019b). There is always a risk that, if we are not able to sustain our passage through an existential crisis, it leaves us exposed to deep-seated emotional problems.

Impact of existential crisis

This makes it even more important that we learn to understand how to face existential crisis and ensure that we can resolve the inner conflicts, hurts and vulnerabilities that result from it. If we do not understand how this works, we may find ourselves blindly making things worse. People can all too easily ruin their lives by stumbling from crisis to crisis and never really getting a grip on their lives again. For most of us, moments of self-doubt are generated when we go through normal personal transitions, like those of puberty or marriage, starting full-time work, giving birth or experiencing the death of a parent. The new situation may sever so many old and familiar connections in our network of meaning that an all-encompassing sense of futility or emptiness ensues. It is literally as if the world has imploded, caved in, and we are left with a vacuum, a great emptiness inside of us, as well as all around us. A person may feel as if their identity and the core of security in their life have been removed. Laing spoke of this as the rupture of our 'ontological security' (Laing, 1959). Some people may experience this as a personal breakdown or a psychiatric emergency. Many people these days would describe it simply as an experience of depression, melt-down, panic or anxiety. The popular vernacular on these events is flexible.

Sometimes, such moments of emotional crisis occur because a person feels as if everything is suddenly in question because of a spiritual crisis or a crisis of meaning. This might happen when a long-held set of beliefs is suddenly shown to be untrue or unreliable. The entire meaning of life is in the balance because the purpose of life was to serve those principles or ideals. This is the existential crisis experienced by the nun who is working as a missionary and whose observations of child death all around her bring her to doubt her faith. It is also the existential crisis of the person who has striven to be good all her life, only to find that those who are not so committed tend to win the economic race for survival. I have known many people driven to despair after finding that those who cheated bagged the prize or those who harmed people won the popularity contest. Many a good person with a clear conscience has felt like giving up because they discovered that the dice of life were loaded. Unsurprisingly, such experiences become more common when we find ourselves in a situation of war or social upheaval.

Being realistic about people and politics

Part of the learning we gain from living through crises is that we should be modest in our expectations of the loyalty of other people. It took me quite a few crises to begin to understand that we cannot expect other people to truly understand what we are going through. Most people will only jump into the breach for others if they are able to protect themselves. A good swimmer will jump into the river to save a drowning child, but one who doubts his or her own swimming ability may stand by and do nothing, or perhaps will run to get help. It's logical and we must remember that most people feel out of their depth when trouble comes. Most people are bystanders in somebody else's crisis. This doesn't make them bad or immoral, just normal. It took me a long time to accept this.

I grew up in the Netherlands in the years following the end of the Second World War, when the whole country was still reeling from the effects of the Nazi occupation and the fighting. For decades I couldn't understand why people had let this happen: why nobody had stood up to Hitler and why the Jewish people, the gypsies, the intellectuals, the disabled people and the communists had not received loyal support. Now I can understand how the German people turned a blind eye as the war machine cranked up and eventually exploded into mayhem. When Hannah Arendt spoke about the banality of evil (Arendt, 1964, 1973, 1951/1979, 1958/2018), she didn't just mean that bad people get used to doing bad things and become casual about it. She also meant that many good people start accepting bad things that happen, as they simply become used to them and pass them off as trivial and inevitable.

More recently, we all witnessed what happened in the US when Donald Trump was elected president, and what happened in the UK over the vote to leave the European Union. Nations were artificially divided and tensions mounted. I understood for the first time that whole nations can be lied to and soothed into condoning things that will ultimately be bad for them. I have seen politicians appease right-wing ideas, turning a blind eye to what were very worrying steps towards totalitarianism. It was the same with Hitler in 1930s Germany: evil grows slowly, bit by bit, step by step. It is only when people realise they no longer have any control – if they ever really did – that they begin to see what has happened. By then, it is often too late to amend the situation, and crisis will inevitably follow (Albright, 2018).

When the 2016 Brexit referendum unleashed a nasty tide of xenophobia, racism and bigotry in the UK, in a way that I had never imagined possible in the country I had adopted because of its gentleness, openness, fairness and progressiveness, I began to understand the reality of what my parents had warned me about in my childhood. For the first time, I truly grasped the lessons they had learnt: that division, segregation and discrimination are terrible things and that they lead to worse things downstream that can rarely be stopped because good people do nothing about it for far too long. Never in my worst dreams had I imagined that I would find myself at the receiving end of such treatment. Yet I was among the five million EU citizens who, having lived in the UK for many years and built a life, a home and a family there, found ourselves having to apply for British citizenship or for settled status, in some cases in vain.

This book grew out of my personal experience of the impact of Brexit. My passion about this comes from my deep, personal commitment to keeping the peace in Europe, based on what happened to us all in the Second World War. My professions of philosophy and psychotherapy contributed a great deal to my being able to make good sense of what was happening. I knew I had to document it and write about it: we have to keep learning; we cannot afford to be complacent about our future, as both Brexit and the Covid-19 pandemic have shown us. We must continue to understand what happens when people think that equality, diversity, fairness and co-operation can be taken for granted – or, worse, that they don't matter. We must never forget that life is fragile: that things happen in the world that can bring the whole human race face to face with extinction. If we stop supporting and protecting each other, we not only create hell on earth for others; we create hell on earth for ourselves.

The purpose of the book

This book is my offering to all the people who have been deeply affected by existential crises. The Brexit experience was a tragedy that befell the UK and has adversely affected the lives of millions. The Covid-19 pandemic is another tragedy that has touched us all, one way or another. I believe we can learn important lessons from considering how we coped. It is clear that many people have found themselves confronted with terrible situations. They may have experienced the terror of suddenly discovering they have no 'home' anymore, and that they are no longer wanted where they thought they belonged. Or they may be among the millions who have found their futures dashed by the impact of the pandemic on their work, jobs or business, or who have lost dearly loved parents, partners or friends, and have seen their assumptive and known world shattered or dashed from their grasp.

I believe it is more important than ever to document how people cope and survive, how they surmount and transcend such difficulties. None of us is exempt from being hit by crises. Every human being will experience some crisis during their life. What we need to know more than anything if we are to keep going forward is how human beings adapt to such challenges: how we find our inner resilience, overcome pain and suffering, rebuild our lives and survive to live another day. This book is about rising from our crisis and finding new strength in it. It will consider how we may actually learn something new from going through the fire of our challenges. But in order to understand how we can learn those lessons, we must be prepared to plunge deeply into the experience of existential crisis and consider how it shakes and shapes people.

If there is one thing we have learnt during the beginning of the 21st century, it is that crises will hit us, no matter how well prepared and safe we think we have made ourselves. Fate does not deliver any exemptions. We must all be aware that hardships cannot be avoided and that each of us will be faced with times of insecurity and uncertainty. It is therefore a great asset in life to know a bit more about such situations and to learn to face up to our adversity when it happens to us.

It may seem that you are on a dark and lonely journey, but if you are willing to come to grips with your trials and tribulations, you will find much to cheer about and hold onto during such troubled and difficult times. You will undoubtedly recognise much of what I explore in the following pages, but the ideas that we formulate may help you articulate the wisdom that can be derived from such difficulties and should enable you to feel invigorated, instead of weakened, by your experiences.

1

The experience of existential crisis

There are good reasons why I became interested in making sense of existential crisis and why I chose to study existential philosophy, psychology and psychotherapy. They are the same reasons I chose a career in which I could support those who find themselves in difficulties or dire circumstances. As I have mentioned in my introduction, my early years were marked by growing up in a country struggling to emerge from the overwhelming existential crisis of the Second World War. In a country that had been occupied, bombed, plundered and starved for five years, there was very little infrastructure, and throughout my early childhood the evidence of great suffering and ongoing struggle was all too evident. I grew up acutely aware of the dangers in the world, and for a long time I expected the Cold War to turn into a Third World War. During the war, my parents had been through a winter of starvation and my father had been hidden from German deportation, while my mother nursed children dying of the consequences of malnutrition and deprivation. They counted their blessings for having survived and for eventually finding a very small, rented apartment to raise their family. They never complained but were clearly deeply marked by the disturbing events that had marred their early adulthood. I could list many specific events in my life that led to my choice to care emotionally and mentally for other people, but it came largely out of observing and experiencing the oppression and suffering of people around me as I grew up.

My bolt-of-lightning moment

Beyond the overarching impact of the suffering of the Second World War on my life, I was catapulted into acute awareness of my own existence and responsibilities when I had a serious traffic accident at the age of 10. This was the bolt-of-lightning-out-of-a-blue-sky moment that altered my entire life and redefined who I was and would become. Sometimes it is hard to know whether the events themselves are what bring on the crisis or whether the crisis has been brewing for many years beforehand and has created a breeding ground for catastrophe. If there was something that led up to this childhood crisis, it was the fact that, living as we did in a tiny flat, I had to seek my own space and freedom from an early age, to get away from the explosive pressure-cooker atmosphere, where tempers often frayed and flared. I had become used to making myself small, crying by myself in the toilet. I had learned to be an observer who tried to stay out of trouble and who hid in her own world. I was quite introverted and a great reader (and an early writer of poetry and short stories). But I also liked to go out into the world, and I did a great deal of cycling, often through the dunes of The Hague, since we lived right on the coast. I found a lot of my safety in the coastal trees, the beach and the seagulls flying across the low skies over the grey North Sea. I also cycled the long trip to the library every week, after my folk music class or my work on the school allotment, to feed my reading habit.

Because we had so little in our household until the mid-1960s, I had to share my sister's bike. My sister was nearly three years older than me, and in truth she hardly ever used the bicycle. Every week, I relished getting my seven-book allocation (two novels and five non-fiction books) from the library. I had been allowed to borrow from the adult section for quite a while and I was reading books across a wide spectrum, avidly absorbing as much knowledge as I could. The books and the bike were both lifesavers. I was a careful child, as I was acutely aware of the dangers in the world, and I was also a very experienced and cautious cyclist, having passed my official school cycling test a year earlier. Nevertheless, on that spring afternoon in April 1962, on my homeward trip, I didn't notice another bike racing down the hill towards me as I took a sharp left turn towards the school. I do remember arranging my books and my musical instrument carefully on my bicycle after visiting the library, but all memories of the rest of that trip are gone.

I was struck off my bike and went down violently on the cobble-stone street. I was knocked out like a light and woke up around four hours later in the children's hospital x-ray department, where a grumpy middle-aged female radiologist, dressed in leather, was taking pictures of my skeleton and skull. I was tied to a gurney and I very rapidly became aware of a sharp pain in my head. I was bleeding and vomiting and crying and could not make any sense of what was going on or what had happened to me. My parents, who had somehow been located by the police, presumably through my library card, had already been brought into the hospital when I woke from my coma. After the x-rays were completed and I was in a woozy, semi-conscious state, I was finally told by a team of doctors and nurses that I was seriously injured; that I had 'small fractures at the back of my head' that had to heal completely before I would be allowed to stand up or walk again.

It was very frightening and disorientating and I felt lost and dismayed. It took me a long time to get used to the idea that my entire life had just changed, that I could not go home and that I had to remain in the hospital for the foreseeable future. My stay was to last for numerous weeks, and I had to rest in bed at home for many more after I was discharged. The accident happened in April and I was not allowed to walk again until July, just before we went on our usual annual family camping holiday to Scandinavia. I didn't go back to school until September.

It was as if a bomb had exploded, blowing a gigantic hole at the core of my existence. When I woke up, reluctantly, from my nearly four-hour coma, I could hardly understand the meaning of it all. I had no recollection of the collision but, oddly, had lurid flashbacks of a near fatal accident that I had witnessed happening to one of my friends, years earlier. I was terrified that, like her, I too would need an operation to have a piece of plastic inserted in my skull where it had cracked open. I could not comprehend and certainly could not remember where and how I had been injured. I was in shock and my body was trembling, as if it had gone stone cold. It was like coming out of the North Sea after a swim on a cool spring or autumn day. My teeth were chattering, and I experienced my body as being out of control. I found my consciousness flying all around the room and up to the ceiling, from where I watched people looking after me. I also had visions of my sister watching me as I lay injured in the road; I could even hear her chiding me for being such a 'stupid idiotic child', which I seem to remember was her favourite insult for me.

I was sick repeatedly, but when I tried to sit up to vomit, I discovered that this wasn't really possible because it produced a sharp and stabbing pain that deeply dismayed me. I felt so tired, groggy and dizzy that I kept passing in and out of consciousness. The only thing I asked my parents, when they were briefly allowed to come into the room to speak to me, was when I could go home. As I spoke, I could see the doctors and nurses shaking their heads at me and I understood I was no longer under my parents' authority. I remember crying because I would not be able to go on the school trip in May, which I had been longing for since January. The doctors told me straight away there was no question of me going to school or on any trips for the foreseeable future. I felt deeply bereft, as if my life was over, but I soon gave up crying when I realised it made my head hurt more. I was told I was running a fever and had vomited blood, which meant I had to be very calm and very careful.

I began to set my expectations a great deal lower when my parents were asked to leave, and they obediently abandoned me. I understood the seriousness of the situation I found myself in and started counting small blessings. I was pleased and hugely relieved when I finally finished a second bout in the x-ray department, which seemed to go on forever. I was rolled on a hospital bed through the now darkened and silent hospital, which seemed empty and eerily spooky without my parents by my side. It was all very unexpected, scary and disconcerting. I became very quiet as I listened to the doctors arguing about my x-rays, discussing the different types of skull fractures. I knew and accepted that I was in deep trouble. I was not responding well to my neurological tests either and this registered in my mind like personal failure. It seemed to me that this was all my own fault, and I was failing the test of being a healthy and well-functioning child. I had messed up and was not doing well.

They kept shining bright lights into my eyes and testing my foot reflexes. I could tell that they thought there was something seriously wrong with the way I responded to these tests, and it felt damning and catastrophic. I was trying to work out how I might give them the correct response. I wanted to pass the test and started moving my feet and legs in different directions when they scratched me. They just told me off and admonished me to relax. I wished I knew what it was they wanted from me but couldn't work it out and could not produce the desired result. When I threw up some more, a nurse was made to check for blood in my vomit. At one point I passed out again, perhaps after an injection, and woke up, alone, in a cubicle with curtained glass windows on all sides.

I was to spend the next few weeks in that small but safe shelter that became my sanctuary, lying motionless on my back on a hard board in a small bed with iron railings all around it. I was all by myself most of the time and I was not allowed to move or read, sit up or even go to the toilet. I got used to having bedpans shoved under me. My only visitor was my mother, who knew the head nurse, with whom she had worked in that same hospital during the war. She was allowed to visit me occasionally and briefly. But when she failed to turn up for a visit on the first day of my stay, I felt frightened and abandoned and cried all afternoon, until my fever made me sick again and the doctor was called, which led to me being given another injection. The doctor berated the nurses for not having shut the blinds against the sun, but nobody understood that what I really needed was quiet companionship and reassurance.

Learning to cope with the crisis

I remember the discomfort of lying on my hard board in that tall, narrow, metal bed without a pillow. I protested fiercely when they first stuck needles into me, but soon gave in to the medical interventions. For the next weeks, I lay there, silently, passively, in isolation, accepting my fate, dozing a lot of the time and learning slowly to enjoy rather than fear the visits from doctors and nurses. It was a good day when my curtains were eventually opened and I could see beyond my cubicle to other cubicles. Now I could see other bandaged, mute children, hooked up to machines, some recovering from major surgery, none of them ambulant or in any state to communicate. I heard their occasional cries and complaints. My cubicle was my safe place, and I became greatly attached to it. I learnt to relish my solitary state and to make the most of it. I had never had a room of my own. In our flat, I shared a tiny boxroom with my sister and one bed had to be pushed under the other every morning to make room for us to get up and get dressed. My hospital cubicle was palatial, by comparison. This new space and privacy were a precious luxury, not a deprivation at all.

When picture postcards started arriving for me from school mates, teachers and my family, I began to feel as if I had become rather special and privileged. I started growing in my suffering. My father's young colleague sent me a luxurious bouquet of my favourite flowers: multicoloured sprigs of sweet peas, ranging from almost white through the whole spectrum of lilacs and pinks to dark reds and deep purples. It was magic to me to be given such a gift. I spent much of my time looking at these flowers, inhaling their fragrance and deciding which were my favourites. As I wasn't allowed to move, studying these blooms carefully for hours, admiring the individual character of each petal, became my first phenomenological observation. I discovered more and more about the nature of those sweet peas. Later, after the flowers had faded, I received a small bottle of 4711 Eau de Cologne from my favourite grandmother and started furtively applying tiny drops of this magic liquid to my wrists and neck (a kind nurse secretly showed me how) whenever I was bored, worried or unhappy. That particular brand of cologne continues to hold a special healing power for me to this day, and I keep a small bottle of it in my consulting room. I am still fond of sweet peas too, and like cultivating them in my own garden.

These gifts were extraordinary to me. I'd never been much spoiled and was used to owning only a very few things that had not previously belonged to my sister. Such gestures signified that I was loved and cared for in a way I had never known. They also helped me hang onto the idea that I still belonged to the world outside of the hospital. They gave me hope for a better future and each of them was to me like a mystic talisman. I adored my grandmother for having been so kind and thoughtful. It was wonderful to know that I mattered to her. Up to then, I had always felt invisible to her; I was the youngest of her eight grandchildren and I had assumed I was less important than the other seven, who were all so much more accomplished and grown up than I was.

My grandmother was not well, and she was to die a year later, leaving me feeling deeply bereft in a way I could not communicate to anyone. While I was in my hospital bed, she stopped me feeling like an outcast by sending me picture postcards every day. She knew how fond I was of animals and how I longed for a dog of my own, which I would never be able to have as long as we lived in that tiny flat and my dad struggled with asthma, so she sent me pictures of puppies and foals and kittens. I had quite a collection of them by the time I went home. They were displayed on the chest of drawers next to my bed and I named every animal and was able to play imaginary games with them, making up stories about them. I created an alternative world in which I was surrounded by all these new animal friends.

Even so, not being allowed to move or read became a big problem as my condition began to improve and I started having an appetite for life again. There were young, disobedient nurses who started smuggling children's books to me from the hospital library, seeing how bored and lonely I was. They were meant to read them to me, but I ravenously devoured each book I got hold of, hiding them under my covers when people passed by my cubicle. Some of these books were romantic novels for teenage girls, but for some reason there were also quite a few boys' adventure books, which I had never read before, and so I began to have fantasies about spies and detectives and became rather obsessed with them. I ended up reading a few Edgar Wallace books too, when the nurses realised I was a quick reader who liked bigger challenges. No wonder that I conjured up an imaginary friend for myself – a private detective named Dick Martin, who became my trusted companion for the next few years. He turned out to be one of my best allies as I tried to hold my own in my tight-knit family, where I was often under great pressure. I also much enjoyed a more childish detective book, Erich Kästner's *Emile and the Detectives* (1928/2015), which I could fully identify with, having always been a bit of a tomboy. But it was another book by the same author that was to transfigure my life in my solitary confinement.

The transformative moment

My mother brought me this novel by Erich Kästner; it was titled *Lottie and Lisa* in its English translation (Kästner, 1949/1985), although its actual title in German and Dutch translates as 'The Double Lottie' (*Das Doppelte Lottchen*). It is a story about twin sisters who are in many ways each other's opposite. It was a special get-well present and had been recommended by an insightful aunt. This aunt was clearly aware of my struggles within my family, as I will explain below, and was determined to give me some help. I understood this instinctively and was so grateful for her kindness. I felt she had seen beneath the surface of my existence.

The book is about twin sisters who get separated at birth after their parents' divorce; each parent takes a twin to live with them in different cities and different countries, one in Germany and one in Austria – two countries I had travelled in. In the story, all communication between the two family units is severed and the girls don't know of each other's existence. When they meet by chance at a summer camp, they are puzzled by their striking resemblance. When they figure out that they are twins, they plot to find a solution to their awkward situation and secretly swap lives, returning to each other's existence and their unknown other parent. The rivalry and tensions between the girls and their divorced parents were straight out of the book of my own life. The story went right to the core of my preoccupations with my very problematic relationship with my sister, Ingrid. People often thought we were twins in those days, because I had shot up rapidly and had caught up with her in height, although not in substance. I was tall for my age and lanky and weedy, while she was pretty and petite and, at 13, had acquired a shapely feminine figure.

Ingrid had enough of a problem with me already because she had to share 'her' room with me, but me catching up with her in height was, understandably, annoying and upsetting to her. She had a fierce, determined and strong character and was highly active, dynamic and temperamental. She was used to being number one. She had no difficulty in keeping me in my place as her little sister and found it extremely easy to boss me about and outshine and outdo me in everything. She was top of her class, top in gymnastics, top in swimming, top with the boys and got all the best parts in school plays. I was none of these things and, at first, looked up to her and was filled with admiration and pride in being her little sister. I imitated her, colluded with her in mischief and did her bidding. But by the time I was four or five, I had become frightened of her temper. In that tiny room, where I was only really welcome at night, I felt unsafe. I had regular nightmares.

She bullied me mercilessly when my parents weren't within earshot, and she was a dark shadow looming over my childhood. Every one of my birthdays became a drama, as Ingrid begrudged me getting presents or being the centre of attention. I came to dread them. Most of the family were aware of the problem, as Ingrid frequently lost her temper and could sometimes be as ferocious with my mother as she was with me. There were rows and physical fights on a daily basis. It was obvious to me that my mother had lost control over Ingrid a long time ago and that she feared her. It goes without saying that this also meant that my mother was incapable of keeping me safe. My father kept out of matters of education and family, and for a long time refused to see or deal with the problem. He also adored Ingrid. He used to smile at her mischief, calling her a 'ball of energy' or a 'true force of nature'.

Ingrid was frequently held up to me as an example of enthusiasm, energy and ambition. I was more inclined to withdraw, preferring to create a dissociative bubble for myself, sprawling on my parents' beds, or curled up in an armchair, reading a book. I was what my dad dismissively called a 'daydreamer'. He often berated me for being weak, slow and over-sensitive. I was inclined to cry easily, even though I bit my lip or cheek to stop the tears from flowing. I was not good at standing my ground with my sister. I was absolutely no match for her. I was the prototypical introvert with skinny legs, freckles and an overbite. I was a good and kind-hearted compliant child and I tried to please and be obedient. I had none of my sister's charm, high-octane energy and multi-talented genius. Or so it had always seemed to me. I expected to have to earn affection by doing things for others, behaving myself and staying in the background.

But I also felt I was a good person, and I didn't really want to change myself to become tougher and meaner to compete with Ingrid. I compensated for feeling weak and inferior by being a 'good girl' and my mother's little helper and 'guardian angel'. The main gain was that I became a calm presence for my mother – a peace-making counsellor when she had a hard time with my sister. Every day, when I did the drying as my mother did the washing up, she was in tears and complained of headaches. This is how I learnt my profession. I was trained early on to empathise. It was constantly reinforced, as I got plenty of praise from both my parents for being the modest, kind, thoughtful and helpful child in the family. Unfortunately, however, it was obvious to me that I was runner-up to my sister, who held centre stage, wowing everyone with her amazing accomplishments. It seemed to me that she was the real daughter, whose achievements I would never be able to replicate. All I could do was endear myself to people. Both of my parents called me 'sensitive' and 'vulnerable', and it was obvious that they thought me too delicate and susceptible. They admonished me not to let my sister get the better of me, but she always did. For a long time, I had no idea what it was like to be in my sister's shoes, but that changed as I lay pondering our family situation in my hospital bed.

Solving the crisis by gaining new insights

What became clear to me, having read the Kästner book a few times, was that our family was divided. I could see how alienated my mother was from my sister and how she had lost my sister's trust and affection. I sensed also that my mother had deftly subjugated me so as to have at least one obedient and subservient daughter. She could not have tolerated having two rivals in the home. I could see how she had harmed herself by living for and through her daughters and how this led to her ongoing battles with Ingrid, who would never accept her lead and admonishments. For the first time I understood that my sister's position was no better than mine. Both of us had our strengths and both of us were lacking in something important. She lacked peace and I lacked energy. She lacked boundaries and limits and I lacked confidence and space. It was all described so clearly in Kästner's book, and I knew then that I would have to learn to assert myself if I was to make myself more whole and less submissive. I needed to detach myself from the far-too-close alliance with my mother and I had to learn to stand up to my sister.

For the next eight years, after I got better from my accident, I assiduously tried to create a better position for myself in the world. I kept my head down in the family but prepared for my independence, as it became increasingly obvious to me that there was no room for me in the Netherlands. I left home at the age of 18, immediately after my final exams, never to return to live with my family again. I lived in France for seven years, where I studied, worked, trained and got married, and after that I came to the UK. So, twice I gave up my established routines, my friends and my identity to start all over again. It was as if I had to keep doing this to prove to myself that I was free to be what I wanted to be. But my escape would never have happened if it weren't for the existential crisis I went through at the age of 10 when I made the decision to change myself. This was when it became clear to me that I was independent and capable of overcoming my own challenges, and I was insightful enough to see that it wasn't my fault (or anyone else's, for that matter) that everyone in our tight-knit family was suffering; it was all about the after-effects of the war and the impact this had had on both my parents. It was also about the lack of available living space and the pressure this placed on all of us.

My mother was heartbroken when I left to live abroad, and I carried a burden of guilt for the existential crisis this caused her. She soon transferred her affections onto my eldest nephew, Ingrid's first child, born just a couple of years later and whom my mother looked after during his early years. My family never fully understood why I had left the Netherlands, and it took me a long time to understand it well enough myself to explain it to them in a way that wasn't reproachful or hurtful to anyone. I just knew in all my bones and sinews that it was vital for me to get away from the intricate and complex network of mortifying affections and connections that had held me in a stranglehold for the first 18 years of my life. I felt like a bird escaping from a deadly trap, or an insect detaching itself from a sticky and suffocating spiderweb. My migration was necessary to my survival, even though I was initially deeply wounded by it and had to build my strength slowly but surely after I made the move.

But I would not have had the independence of spirit necessary to make these later life choices if it weren't for the accident and that time in hospital. The Kästner book was a revelation. It articulated everything I had felt but had been unable to speak about. It provided me with concrete descriptions of a family situation in which the parents had similarly divided their children: Lottie was her mother's little helper and Lisa was her father's adored daughter and mischief-maker. To me, in that hospital sanctuary, this book provided me with deep insight and much needed therapy. The beauty of the book was that the author was able to reveal the underlying emotions I had never been able to name before, while providing perspective and clarity on what was happening and tracing some solutions to the problems. He didn't deride either of the parents or the girls and he didn't take sides with or against any of them. His even-handed descriptions of what had happened to these girls with such different characters gave me both more respect for my own role in my family and a deeper understanding of my sister's battles. It became an immediate inspiration to me for how I might be able to alter my family situation and my own role in it.

Here I was, in my safe haven, having been removed from all these struggles and with plenty of time to make sense of it all. It was the first time that I went deeply into the persistent effort of self-reflection instead of going further and further into my imagination, escapism, self-pity or peace-making. In the benevolent silence of my little hospital cell, I began to process thoughts, feelings and memories. I became aware that I had been craving this kind of privacy and shelter where, for the first time in my life, I could weep for hours without my father becoming angry and upset, my sister ridiculing and mimicking me or my mother matronising and belittling me. The freedom to cry made me very happy, because for the first time in my life I felt what it meant to live without oppression and tension. I relaxed.

But the book didn't just provide me with an experience of catharsis. It also showed me the way to creative change. It dealt with the two topics that had scared me the most: parents fighting, disagreeing and divorcing and children struggling with each other for survival. My sister's threatening presence had always been a dark cloud over my existence and, until now, I had felt victimised by it. She exerted power over me in a way that was invalidating and nihilating. I had sometimes hoped that my parents would do what they said and send her to a special boarding school for difficult girls. But now I knew that I was also afraid of losing her. She was my best ally as well as my fiercest foe, and I could not imagine becoming my mother's sole object of attention. I began to understand all this as I lay there in hospital and faced up to the real crisis in my life: that of my conflicted family. Kästner articulated it for me to perfection. He set me on a new trajectory.

The crisis was the catalyst for a transformation that was long overdue. As happens so often, it smashed all habits and routines and created a space for a change of direction. I knew for the first time in my life that I was going to have to get braver, learn to stand my ground and face up to all the things that I feared, including my mother, my father and my sister. I became aware that I no longer wanted to be so good, so tame and so compliantly lame that I was nothing more than my mother's guardian angel. I wanted to be strong and grown up and have some adventures of my own. It was clear that I was getting better. I felt new impulses and vitality inside of me. My first act of self-assertion and disobedience was to finish reading the book on my own and tell my mother, rather brazenly, that I had done so.

Making sense of the transition

During my adolescence, I discovered philosophical and existential ideas, which came as a salve on my wound. I felt met and understood by these authors. Here was a whole discipline and specific movement dedicated to describing the world as I was experiencing it. On the one hand, these authors resonated with my sensitivity; on the other hand, they provided a toughness in their approaches to living that I badly needed and craved. I discovered about having the courage to live despite vulnerability – or better still, because of that sensitivity. It became my objective to be brave. I became aware of how precious life was and how important it was to make something of it. I puzzled a lot about my role in the family and knew I had to become stronger and not be the butt of my sister's jokes or the object of her scorn and vilification anymore. I learnt to be self-sufficient and to take into my stride what had initially felt like a complete calamity. I became more self-aware too and recognised that I was different to many other children and certainly very different to my sister. I became aware that my injuries and my traumatic experience did not have to damn me to insecurity or diminution but could be overcome and risen above. I was beginning to see that I might be proud of having survived my plight. I learnt to value my scars.

The hardest bit was to fit back into the normal routine at school in September, after having been away since early April, but I gradually caught up with my classmates and was moved to prep class for secondary school the next September. Once in secondary school, I did well enough to be picked out with only two others from my class to transition to the classical stream of education, the 'gymnasium'. All of this happened without great dramas or setbacks, despite the death of my grandmother, which also greatly affected me. Somehow, my traumatic experience had forged a new valour and determination inside me, and I was able to keep going and pull through these new contretemps with relative ease and determination. I had become purposeful.

Going into my classical education was a new and important marker, because it set me apart from both my parents and my sister, who had never learnt Greek or Latin. It was also when I was introduced to reading philosophy, carefully and slowly, especially Plato. This was like a homecoming for me, as the Socratic dialogues spelled out what I had myself been trying to formulate and affirm in my life. Socrates' audacity and his ability to stand alone and hold his own against the rhetoric of his opponents became a shining light and example to me. It felt good to despise the sophists and to join with Socrates in looking for truth and wanting the Good. I also took a liking to the Stoical aphorisms that we read in Latin class. And I began to take heart from knowing that I knew, unlike many others, that it was important to 'memento mori' – to remember that we all must die. I had come close enough to death to really know it. I also loved the dictum 'Sol omnibus lucet' – the sun shines for everyone. It reminded me that I was entitled to my place in the sun too and I did not have to hide in the shadows. It is undoubtedly why I chose to move to Montpellier, in south-east France.

There is no doubt that my adversity gave me the measure of human existence: I knew what to expect and I would never take anything for granted ever again. This stood me in good stead, and I continued to rely on this understanding and its underlying resoluteness throughout my life. Over the next decades, with each difficulty, and there were many, I had the same immediate reaction: first, a feeling of fear and disgust at each new setback, in the recognition that life was full of problems, but then finding my nerve again and trusting I could and would get through it. I learnt to seek solutions and carry on regardless, always remembering that the new learning would take me further and make me stronger. I had learnt to be staunch and self-reliant.

2

Brexit: shattered lives and identities

I went on to encounter a considerable number of other crises in my life, not all of them full-blown existential disasters but each of them difficult and demanding enough in their own right. There was a whole range of them: being plunged into a new culture and language twice in my life, suffering a serious infectious illness at the age of 20, and losing my precious and much-loved first dog in a spate of local pet poisonings in the French countryside. There was also the total flooding of my basement flat in London when my son was four months old and, two years later, the traumatic experience of a miscarriage after a violent physical assault when I was 16 weeks pregnant. Each of these things shook my life and forced me to re-orientate myself.

Ten years after the miscarriage, I went through a full existential crisis and a year of acute anxiety when I was unfairly dismissed from my job as head of the academic training institute that I had carefully built up, with my colleagues, over the previous 14 years. With it, I lost my place in the world, my income, my mission, my colleagues, my students and also my trust in fairness and justice. It demonstrated to me what happens to whistleblowers who believe they must stand up for what is right, only to find that they are bullied and victimised for it. My desolation was compounded by being a single mother at the time, with very little support behind me.

Then those who had sacked me took me to the High Court, to try to stop me setting up a new, independent school a few months later. My new office and my home were invaded by officers of the court, all my belongings were searched and computers were removed. I felt devastated to be falsely accused of wrongdoing. I wasn't allowed to speak to anyone about it, so was unable to challenge the way the situation was distorted by others. I won the High Court case, but for close to a year lived with a sense of continuous threat, dread, fear, impending doom and utter wretchedness, as I battled my way out of my terrible predicament, surrounded by solicitors and barristers. I learnt first-hand how vital it is to have the support of loyal friends and colleagues and to be believed when we speak the truth. To this day, I am immensely grateful to those who helped me sustain the new school throughout this episode.

Some crises take a terrible toll on our inner balance and confidence and cast a long shadow over our lives. It can take many years before we re-establish ourselves well enough to be at peace and hold our ground once more. Like everyone else, I had to learn many hard lessons about myself and my vulnerability and tendency towards martyrdom in the face of tough opposition. But, as is often the case in crisis, the situation also taught me much about the way the world works and made me stronger and more realistic. That process of disillusionment can take a long time before it can be turned into something constructive. I began to understand that we are not given the choice to decide how our lives will unfold and evolve. No matter how hard we work, how well we behave and how kind we try to be to other people, if we are out there in the cut and thrust of society, we will encounter numerous difficulties and suffer untold setbacks and hardships. We cannot demand harmony and tranquillity and should never expect it. If we try to force our destiny by avoiding troubles, life takes revenge by throwing a new curve ball at us. All we can do is to make the most of the situations that we encounter and stand strong when fate defies us. Our vigour and persistence will eventually pay dividends. Post-traumatic growth is a real phenomenon: we definitely grow stronger by suffering occasionally and we are capable of surviving far more than we ever think we are (Calhoun & Tedeschi, 1989, 2013; de Beauvoir, 1948/2018; Denham, 2008; van Deurzen, 2015a; van Deurzen & Adams, 2016).

We stay physically fit by taking regular exercise. Without this, our bodies cannot grow stronger and more flexible. We stay mentally and emotionally fit by engaging vigorously and regularly with society. Without this, we cannot develop new courage and resilience.

Nevertheless, after that last big existential crisis, it took me close to 20 years of assiduous commitment and hard work to re-establish enough stability in life to enjoy peace of mind and inner quietude again. For a long time, I felt I was in exile from the world I had previously belonged to. I have seen the same thing happening to clients who have been through the mill of existential crisis. Some are so broken by their misadventures that they find it almost impossible to rebuild a safe base for themselves and regain an appetite for the good things in life. But those who keep their nose to the grindstone and are willing to reflect on their experiences and let go of their grudges and grievances will eventually rise again. I felt very privileged to be able to work hard at re-establishing my position in society, to build up a team of loyal and hardworking colleagues and together have the satisfaction of contributing something of value to the world again. It is a case of continuously solving problems and creating networks, seeking to be of use to others whenever we can. Things will keep improving if we keep pushing, building bridges, creating new things and contributing our strength to those who need it most. The lessons we learn are about recognising who to trust and who to avoid, where to put our effort and where to make sure we protect ourselves. Putting in persistence and dedication in order to overcome and thrive after a crisis is vital. Sometimes it can take a long time before the new seeds we are planting grow into trees that bear fruit. And, of course, there is no guarantee that there will be no further difficulties and new crises. In fact, it is highly likely that there will.

And so, in 2016, came the Brexit referendum, and once again I was plunged into an existential crisis. It wasn't just that I was suddenly exposed to doubt about my residential rights in the UK; I was also directly confronted with the despair and doubt of thousands of others in a similar situation (Beech, 2020; Hatherley, 2019; Hinde, 2019; Home Office, 2020). It was incredible to me that a nation could suddenly turn against five million EU citizens in the UK, plus the 1.5 million UK citizens living in the EU, and sacrifice them to a hare-brained scheme that had not been fully thought through. It was particularly galling that politicians kept saying it was a democratic decision when none of the five million people whose lives were completely wrecked by it had a vote. I felt outraged that I did not have a voice, as did many others. For us, democracy had truly died when we were silenced and treated as if we were no longer part of the British population (Runciman, 2018; Stanley, 2018). I also felt disheartened and dismayed that the British people, who had been co-architects of the union that safeguarded our hard-earned peace in Europe, were prepared to simply walk away from it.

Dealing with the fall-out of that historic 2016 referendum took up much of my time and energy over the four years that followed. I felt I had to stand in the breach, shoulder to shoulder with my fellow EU citizens in Britain, and I tried to use my knowledge and experience to help those worse off than me in this situation. I began to see evidence of people collapsing in despair all around me and knew that I could never just be a bystander to this calamity (Clarkson, 2006). There was a sense of incredible solidarity among the five million. We shared the shock on 24 June 2016, when the realisation set in that our lives had changed overnight, drastically and dramatically, and that we had become surplus to requirements in the country we considered to be our home. From being honorary British citizens and honoured and respected equals, exercising our freedom of movement as citizens of the EU, we were suddenly turned into undesirable migrants. This led to a sense of loss and deep insecurity that was hugely traumatic for those who were unable to secure their right to residency immediately. It was most definitely a violation of their human right to feel safe in their home (Low, 2017) as we were literally threatened with deportation (Minton, 2016; Moran, 2020). We became targets for discrimination (Nelson, 2016; O'Carroll, 2020; Strangor, 2016). Like many others, I was stunned what was happening to my life and felt struck down with the Brexit blues (Powdthavee et al., 2019; Quinn, 2017). It took me a little while to gather enough confidence and insight to find the energy to deal with the implications for my own situation.

I had always felt secure in the knowledge that I had registered with the Home Office as soon as I arrived in the UK in 1977 and had renewed my registration annually until I was granted Indefinite Leave to Remain (ILR) in 1984. When, in 2015, the government started talking about holding a referendum on whether the UK should remain in the EU, I decided to take precautions. I began studying for the infamous 'Life in the UK' test and, as soon as I passed this, went through the intense, demanding and complex process of applying for British citizenship, which I did in January 2016, thinking there would be ample time to get it sorted out so I could vote in the June referendum. How could it be right that non-British EU citizens living in the UK were not going to be allowed to have a vote on a matter that affected us so fundamentally? Muting our voices at a time when our very security was at stake seemed dishonest and belittling; indeed, it felt like a breach of our human rights. I retitled the Facebook group I had created for EU nationals in the UK, calling it 'Voices for Europe'. I began to actively protest about our fate on social media and the group started growing.

Then, to my dismay, in March 2016, the Home Office rejected my application for citizenship. I was dumbfounded; it had been rejected because I did not have the newly created permanent residence card that the government had stealthily introduced in November 2015 (less than two months before I applied). I had been (rightly) advised that my ILR was a valid way to establish settled status and was amazed that the Home Office could have made such a mistake. I was confident that this would be swiftly corrected and promptly asked for my application to be 'reconsidered' (Home Office terminology for an appeal). I did this without consulting a solicitor as I was so sure it was a simple mistake made by someone new to the system. How naïve I was! I sent my appeal in mid-March and by June had heard nothing back. I realised I would now not be able to vote in the referendum and became angry and suspicious about what was happening.

The impact

When the referendum result turned out to be so damning for EU citizens in the UK, my anger at not being given my democratic rights turned into acute anxiety. I could see how badly all this might play out and how dangerous my situation was becoming. At this point, I contacted my then MP, Nick Clegg, in Sheffield Hallam, where I lived, and he wrote to the Home Office to ask them to provide a speedy response to my request for reconsideration of my application for UK citizenship. It had begun to feel as if normality had been replaced by something a lot more threatening and less reliable – Kafkaesque, indeed. I worried that I would not be allowed to continue living in the UK and became even more worried when I received a second rejection. This time I was told by the Home Office, in no uncertain terms and in writing, that this was the end of the matter. I would have to apply for a PRC before I could make a new attempt at an application for citizenship.

This just seemed outrageous: how could they require me to go through the same process I had already successfully gone through in the 1980s? I felt a deep sense of revulsion and betrayal. I had paid tax for 40 years, was married to a British citizen, had contributed so much to British society and had been granted indefinite leave to remain from that very same Home Office for 32 years and had the card to prove it. It seemed as if rationality had completely gone out of the window. It did not feel fair, right or understandable. I didn't recognise the fair-minded Britain I had come to live in 40 years earlier – a Britain I thought I knew and loved. My loyalty was not being repaid. But I was still far too afraid to feel outraged.

I realised I had to consult a solicitor and was somewhat calmed when she told me that she spent most of her time dealing with similar problems with the Home Office and that they were almost always wrong. She recommended that I ask for a judicial review. Strengthened by this legal opinion, I now joined several Facebook groups, most importantly the UK Citizenship for European Nationals group (UKCEN), led by Gloria Borgognoni-Holmes. The solidarity and support I immediately felt in this group gave me new hope and great encouragement to carry on. It was now obvious to me that my crisis of confidence was shared by thousands of other people in a similar situation. Everyone was recounting very similar and frustrating experiences. I was far from alone. I joined other groups too, including *the3million* pressure group set up by Nicolas Hatton and Anne Laure Donskoy to represent what turned out to be five million EU citizens living in the UK. I also joined the New Europeans group, set up by Roger Casale two years earlier to defend the rights of all EU citizens. I became aware that there were many immigration specialists who, like my own solicitor, were sure that the Home Office was not acting in good faith or in a fair or correct manner. Something was amiss. We were on the receiving end of the 'hostile environment' – that awful Home Office ploy implemented by Theresa May from 2012, when she was Home Secretary, to rid the country of immigrants.

I approached the Aire Centre in London, which specialised in supporting EU citizens in exactly these kinds of situations, and was generously offered free advice by its director, Matthew Evans, who was calm and kind and utterly aware of how badly the situation was affecting people. He eventually referred me to a specialist barrister, Colin Yeo, who was to set up the Free Movement website that became a guiding light for many EU citizens in the UK. He really knew his business and was able to quote chapter and verse from the relevant legal documents to show me that the Home Office had misinformed me and, indeed, wronged me. Far from the permanent residence card being the only pathway to an application for UK citizenship, there were in fact four ways to give evidence of settled status, and ILR was most definitely one of them. That was the law, and the Home Office had acted unlawfully in denying me my citizenship and my vote in the referendum.

On the strength of this new knowledge, I emailed the Home Office. Then my original application fee was returned to me, without them even informing me. It simply re-appeared in my bank account. I smelled a rat and got back in touch with Nick Clegg, asking him to write again to the Home Office senior official he had previously contacted. I gave him the detailed advice I had obtained from Colin Yeo and he conveyed it precisely to the Home Office, with some strongly phrased comments about the treatment meted out to EU citizens in my situation.

The hostile environment

There was no doubt in my mind that the UK was in thrall to a process that was not only undemocratic but also frankly and deliberately hostile to all foreigners. It wasn't hard to research this and to discover the official Home Office policy dating back to 2012 to create this 'hostile environment' for all immigrants. This now included EU citizens. I could feel the xenophobia not just in the Home Office but also on social media. Outside of the EU-citizen groups, and sometimes even in Remain groups, people said things to me like, 'Why don't you go home if you are no longer feeling welcome?' This utterly outraged me, since the only home I have had since 1977 is in the UK. There was no other place in the world to which I could suddenly move. Nor did I wish to do so.

I began to feel so incensed about all this that I threw myself into human rights work, joining the New Europeans board as well as continuing to develop the Voices for Europe group I had founded. This human rights commitment began to dominate my life very quickly. There were endless meetings and events to organise. There were hundreds of thousands of people in need. I had never been part of any political or human rights organisation before, but in December 2016 I found myself at Downing Street, with Roger Casale and

Nicolas Hatton, to deliver a petition for EU citizens' rights to be reconsidered by Theresa May, who was by then Prime Minister.

We were not invited in, but we were highly visible and were interviewed by ITN, ITV and Sky News. It was the start of many dozens of press interviews and articles for the newspapers that I contributed to over the following years. The campaigning work was a whole new use of my professional skills as an author and lecturer, which I enjoyed and relished but which also made me increasingly aware of the dangers of what was going on in politics in the UK and made me more and more motivated to do something about it.

I felt indignant on behalf of the five million people who were being treated so appallingly and became aware of the high levels of distress some were suffering. People were becoming insomniac, depressed, anxious and even suicidal. So, with Neil Lamont, Digby Tantam, Jo Molle and my colleagues at the Existential Academy, I established the Emotional Support Service for Europeans (ESSE). The more I heard, the more I was motivated to do what I could to set some of these wrongs right, out there in the real world and in the consulting room. It was all about helping people to rise to their existential crisis. ESSE was free to all EU citizens who needed emotional support and was staffed by us on a voluntary basis (Vos et al., 2020). We were able to find several other registered psychotherapists to join us and they each took on two or three clients at a time. We got referrals through New Europeans, Voices for Europe and another EU citizens action group, In Limbo, and worked with well over 100 EU citizens who were anxious, depressed or suicidal because of what was happening to them. We also published our research on the patterns of suffering and overcoming they shared (Vos et al., 2020).

Resolution

Meanwhile, my personal predicament was eventually resolved in January 2017. Out of the blue, I received a phone call from a Home Office official one Friday evening at 6.30pm, asking me if I would like to pay my application fee for UK citizenship again, since I might very well be successful this time. A month later, I finally received my letter of approval of my application for UK citizenship. It was almost an anticlimax after that whole year of shadow battles, but it was still a huge relief that changed my state of mind considerably for the better. I felt deeply grateful for the support that many good people had given me, most especially the people at the Aire Centre. It was a real victory for them too. The Home Office had now evidently accepted my application on the strength of my ILR certificate from 1984. Therefore, they had to promptly change all their application forms and the guidance on their website. This was indeed done within a week of my receiving my letter, and it led to many other EU citizens being able to apply for UK citizenship with an ILR certificate, even though some continued to be told this wasn't possible and further battles had to be fought to get them all through the system.

I was just so relieved that my particular nightmare was over. I was now able to look back at the experience to see how unnecessary and grotesque it all was. I had, for instance, been challenged on my fluency in English, even though I have a PhD in philosophy from City University and many books to my name. Showing my PhD certificate was not enough either; I had to get a new letter from the university to affirm that my English had been up to standard when I did my PhD. Such humiliations do have an effect. They make you feel as if you are not trustworthy, not equal to others and not respected. I also had to produce five years of tax returns and a complete list of all the times I had been out of the country in the previous 10 years. The latter in particular had really challenged me, as it was not easy to retrieve the information: both my parents had been ill and died during that period and I had made frequent brief visits to the Netherlands, sometimes going there and back in one day, and I had been travelling abroad to lecture up to 10 times a year for decades.

Compassion with the five million

I was stubborn and persistent in my pursuit of my UK citizenship because I knew I deserved it and had earned it by my hard work and long-term loyal commitment to the country. All along, however, I was aware of how wobbly this denial of my status made me feel and I could see that many other EU citizens, who felt less certain of their rights, were being bamboozled and terrified by the hostile environment. Knowing how vital it felt for me to guard my rights now that the UK was leaving the European Union, I experienced a strong sense of compassion and fellow feeling with my European compatriots who were unable to secure their residency status. I was deeply troubled by seeing so many of them giving up and leaving the UK. Thousands of them did so and every single friend that went left a vacuum behind.

All of this made me more committed to challenge the appalling state of affairs that was, and still is, affecting so many people. This is nothing to do with squabbles between Remainers and Leavers. It is about protecting people's human right to be respected in their homes and to be treated with common courtesy, decency, honesty and fairness. We should never dismiss other people in such a casual and damaging manner. Administrative pettiness and red tape are alienating enough in themselves, but when they are deliberately used to undermine people's status and confidence, something very sinister is at work. It is a well-known, deliberate tactic of dehumanisation (Smith, 2011, 2019, 2020). My previous experiences of being bullied, first by my sister and later by my employers and some of my colleagues, had prepared me not just to recognise the bullying but also to call it out and fight against it. I had learnt that, when faced with a crisis of other people's making, you must not victimise yourself or let yourself continue to be a target. You must stand up, speak up and be counted. You must state your case loudly and clearly and find allies. I adopted the motto, 'Zero tolerance for intolerance.'

A whiff of totalitarianism

I soon stopped thinking that mistakes were being made or that the Home Office was incompetent. It was abundantly obvious that these were deliberate strategies and that people were being treated disdainfully in order to encourage them to leave the country. These were not consequences of bureaucratic error but acts of oppression. Something had happened to turn the UK into an authoritarian, oppressive society that permitted itself to practise a hidden, obnoxious and toxic form of ethnic discrimination. When the Windrush scandal broke (Gentleman, 2019), here was another example of the cruel and unfair treatment meted out to a whole section of the population. A society that acts in this manner can easily slip into totalitarianism (Albright, 2018; Johnston, 2020; Klein, 2008, 2014; O'Toole, 2018).

We, the five million, were treated all along as if we were unimportant; clearly, our futures did not matter. We were pushed aside and muted. The letters we received from the Home Office around 2017 actually stated that we were 'negotiating capital' in the government's discussions with the EU. We were chattels. This kind of disdainful and harmful instrumentalism is entirely unacceptable in a mature democracy (Benedi Lahuerta & Iusmen, 2019; Hatherley, 2019; Hinde, 2019). It all seemed outrageous to me, but there was a lot of fear and trepidation among EU citizens. Nobody wanted to take too many risks or become too visible. It was hard to persuade people to make a stand and rebel. Whenever I spoke about the possibility of suing the government for denying us our rights, nobody was interested in supporting it. It felt like people were terrified, paralysed like animals caught in the headlights. I realised that my own arduous process of liberating myself from the situation had given me clarity, but that my privileged position in having obtained UK citizenship had also put me out of touch with where other people were.

However, when speaking to those seeking help from our ESSE support service, I was often reminded of just how horrified and frightened they were. It continued to shock me to watch people's reactions. They simply weren't expecting this kind of treatment. They were appalled and lost in it all. The extreme distress that I began to observe in some EU citizens was on a level with the distress I saw when I worked as a psychotherapist with survivors of concentration camps and with refugees from countries like Rwanda, the Balkans and Iran. The complete state of immobilisation some went into, combined with their chronic anxiety, depression, insomnia and terror, was akin to the distress experienced by war survivors.

There is no doubt that we can observe even more severe distress in people who have been tortured or maimed or who have seen family members killed in front of them, but the agony of suddenly finding your home to be unsafe and your residential rights in question is still deeply unsettling and upsetting. I spoke with hundreds of people about their mental state in response to the situation and exchanged endless emails and thousands of social media messages with people suffering in this way between 2016 and 2020. Some of them became so despairing that they were suicidal. This happened particularly to people who did not have their tax records or National Insurance contributions, which they needed to apply for their permanent residency.

I met many women who had been married to British husbands for decades and whose children were British citizens but who had received letters from the Home Office telling them they were not able to obtain permanent residency because they had not made the correct contributions and had not taken out private health insurance. These women had never before been told they needed to do this and had always assumed that being a mother or carer was an acceptable position to be in, as indeed it should be. Now they felt cornered and thought they would have to leave the UK and separate from their husbands and children. This was a cruel thing to do to them and it was absolutely unnecessary. Many people's mental health was damaged by this experience. They had nowhere to go; small wonder they felt paranoid and persecuted. It was incredibly hurtful to hear the then Prime Minister Theresa May declare that we were 'citizens of nowhere'. We were actually citizens of Europe and only became citizens of nowhere because of the draconian changes in the UK in which we had no say. Many people felt they no longer had a rightful and peaceful place of abode. It was as if we were being told we were unwelcome and unwanted.

My own story in this saga was comparatively easy, as I was eventually successful in obtaining British citizenship. Others fared much worse. Some people became locked in despair, hiding away at home, not daring to mix with British people any longer, after experiencing bullying and violence against them and losing all hope. EU citizens were sometimes spat at on public transport if they spoke in their own language. Some found it hard to get a mortgage or rent a property. Such experiences of what amounted to unfair discrimination and apartheid had been unthinkable for EU citizens in Britain just a few years earlier.

Simone de Beauvoir, reflecting on the fascism of the 1930s and 1940s, wrote in her roman à clef *The Mandarins*:

> You can't draw a straight line in a curved space. You can't lead a proper life in a society which isn't proper. Whichever way you turn, you are always caught. (1954/2005, p.625)

It sums up exactly how the five million were feeling. It was as if there was no solution.

In limbo

The pain of the five million was documented very well by the In Limbo group, who brought out several books with testimonies from EU citizens in the UK (Remigi & Martin, 2017; Remigi et al., 2020) and from UK citizens in the EU (Remigi et al., 2018). In his foreword to the latter, philosopher A.C. Grayling wrote:

> Of all the many wrongs that constitute Brexit, one of the worst is the betrayal of those who have come to Britain from our partner countries in the EU, and those British who have gone to our partner countries in the EU, to make their lives… The Brexit referendum has ripped away their security, overturned their worlds, treated them with utter disrespect even to the point of publicly and explicitly describing them as 'pawns' in a negotiation. I am ashamed of my country that this has happened. I am anguished at the thought of the uncertainty, anxiety, misery and grief this causes so many fellow European citizens. (Grayling, 2018, p.vii)

Grayling is right. It was a secret scandal that so many people were allowed to suffer in silence and that nobody did anything about it. Some of these people were not touched by the situation as they were either not aware of it or not bothered by it for their own reasons, but the large majority felt that their situation became so changed that they lost their sense of balance and safety.

The first In Limbo book (Remigi & Martin, 2017), edited by Elena Remigi from Italy and Véronique Martin from France, collected responses from EU citizens to the situation. It was titled *In Limbo: Brexit testimonies from EU citizens in the UK* and was re-edited and published in 2020 (Remigi et al., 2020). It is a shocking record of the reactions of a wide array of people, demonstrating the depth and breadth of the impact of the referendum result. Here are some quotes from it.

I, citizen of Europe, my wings clipped, my dreams shattered, my freedom chained, the result of a mad referendum in which I wasn't allowed a voice. I feel rather lost, I no longer belong. (M.P., from Spain)

I'm of Danish nationality but grew up in Brussels. I've been living in the UK for 18 of the last 20 years. Studying at university with years of working in between… I do not qualify for permanent residency. This came as a shock to me as I initially thought the application would be a formality… The UK is home to me and my family is here… Everyone keeps saying 'You'll be fine!' and I really hope that they are right. However, I feel unwanted here now, like a second-class citizen and so insecure and anxious about the future. I'm a European at heart and the Brexit vote broke my heart. (C.B., from Denmark)

There are many such stories in the books. Some people, like Professor Bruno G. Pollet from France, a long-term resident in the UK, immediately decided the situation was intolerable and unacceptable, found another job in the EU and moved to Norway with his family. He was refused permanent residency in the UK because he had spent a couple of years teaching in South Africa as part of his academic job. That gap in his residence record in the UK prevented him from getting the necessary certificate. He said:

Needless to say, I feel betrayed by the UK government. I am disappointed, hurt, angry, sad, but at the same time happy that my son will have a great opportunity to be a 'citizen of the world', able to master three languages. Lastly, the past nine months have been emotionally and physically draining and I look forward to being in a positive and healthy environment. I came to this country because of its tolerance, its diversity of ethnicity and cuisine, its great music and art, its thriving science and technology and its vibrant multiculturalism. I made the UK my home. I am now a foreigner, a migrant, an immigrant amongst British people. My home has been taken away. The time has come, it is now time to leave.

Elena Gualtieri, born in Italy, said:

When I was little, I used to lie awake at night thinking where I would hide when the Gestapo came. It was ridiculous and historically inaccurate – the war had ended 30 years earlier. But my ears had been filled with stories of my parents' wartime childhood of bullets whizzing past, of partisans hiding in a cupboard, of hunger and cold. I read Anne Frank's *Diary* before going to sleep and asked myself how long I could lie still if they came looking for me. Recently I had a dream that took me right back to those years. Except that this time it is not the Gestapo but men with tattooed arms and very short haircuts who break into my home, throw my clothes on the street and tell me never to come back.

Elena is part of a multinational family. She is half Italian, half Greek, married to a Dutch husband and has a daughter who is British. They have tried to think of somewhere else to live, but Britain is the only place where they all feel they belong and are at home.

Writing soon after the 2016 referendum, she said:

Until June we had plans; now everything is on hold. We bought a house earlier this year, which I don't dare furnish in case we have to leave. I have stopped unpacking the boxes… I look at my daughter sleeping and wonder if our family will be split up, how I'd cope with being a Skype mummy, how would we explain it to her? She is a citizen of the country that might want to expel her parents, of a country that refuses her parents' right to stay.

Helen de Cruz, a Belgian philosopher who worked in Oxford for many years, conducted several large surveys of the mood of EU citizens in the UK after the referendum. Figure 2.1 shows one of her word clouds that illustrates the words nearly 3,000 people in one of her surveys used to describe their state of mind in reply to the question, 'How do you feel since the referendum?'

Figure 2.1: 'How do you feel since the referendum?'

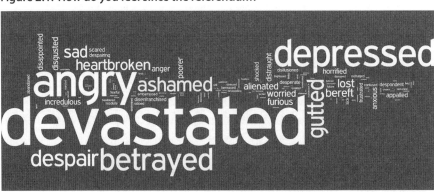

© Helen de Cruz/In Limbo (reproduced here with kind permission)

The words speak loudly for themselves. Devastation was the sense that we all shared. The feeling of betrayal was always in the back of our minds. It is a scandal that people were made to go through this hell. A Lithuanian woman, who didn't feel there was any hope for her to obtain the right to remain in the UK, hung herself. The press reported:

> Migle Faulkner, 31, battled mental health issues for a number of years, an inquest heard. She was found hanging at her Botley home on July 26, 2019.
>
> Her husband Stephen, who found the body, said his wife felt 'she wasn't wanted' by the British population and she was worried about the future. He also described a traumatic event in her childhood, as well as other anxieties she had. (Hatherley, 2019)

Anyone who had previous mental or emotional problems and was confronted with this denial of their safety and identity reacted very strongly. People understandably relapsed. But there were many who had never known such problems previously and found themselves suddenly in a state of depression and anxiety. There was just too much pain and too much sorrow to process. The EU citizens living in the UK were forced to wait in terrible uncertainty for far too long.

Here is Alexandra's story. I met her online and she gave me permission to quote her in full. She speaks for many EU people in the UK who shared her bewilderment, despair, anger and disillusion:

> Where do I even start? I'm a Romanian European citizen with a complex traumatic past, a lesbian sexuality, and no hope of being allowed to exist as my full identity in my birth country and hiding is not something I was interested in doing anymore. So, I moved to London when I was 19, for these exact reasons and to pursue an education in psychology and learn how to help others.
>
> The mere fact that the Brexit referendum was taking place shook my worldview and sense of stability that I was so carefully trying to create for the first time. It was retraumatising but in a different way. I could not do anything this time. I could not have a voice; I could not vote in something that affected me. In fact, similarly with my trauma, the only thing I could do was plastered on the news and walls and people's discourses: 'LEAVE'. Again.
>
> I was too exhausted to do that again. Can't go home because I'm queer; can't go anywhere without English as main language as I've chosen

a profession where it's crucial you understand what people say. I was stuck. Anxiety begins. When I heard the vote result, I was with my queer friends in Soho Square, on the grass. It was so sunny but felt so grey. We couldn't even speak, we were so disheartened. For the following three years I have been so preoccupied with keeping up to date with the news, trying to make sense of it all. A lot of my friends had no clue about any of this, as it wouldn't affect them at all. I felt alone, isolated, and with extreme uncertainty hanging above my head at all times. Could I still go see my family and friends? Could I continue to pursue a career here? Was there even any point in pursuing it here, besides to avoid loss of so much effort in moving and living here in the first place?

I finished university and got a job in psychiatric intensive care in NHS quickly after. I received an incredible and shocking amount of verbal abuse from my patients that was Brexit related. They used to shout, 'Go back to your own country you Polish _____ (insert your abusive word of choice)'; 'We don't want you here, f___ off! You come here to steal jobs and rape.' I've heard so many I had to forget some of them. I'm not Polish – not that there's anything wrong with being Polish, but it just shows that just my accent was enough. Throughout the next years, I've applied for tens of jobs as an assistant psychologist. I had so much experience, knowledge, drive. I knew the competition was crazy, but it felt like there was more going on. With time I've started to see the statistics about EU citizens not being offered jobs, mortgages etc. And it hit me. They really don't want me and people like me here. What am I doing here then?

A lot of people around me, throughout the years, including my manager at work, used to ask why I worry so much, nothing's gonna happen, also that they don't wanna hear about politics anymore, and so forth. All of them were people who were not EU27 citizens and not affected by Brexit in any way (they thought). I felt crazy, like I was being gaslighted. I felt like I was losing my mind. For me, it was so real and scary, but look, for all these people it's nothing; how come my reality is so different? No one seemed to know what they voted for and what it meant. I have argued numerous times with people and, whatever anyone says, I still don't think they had a clue. It was all really hurtful xenophobic lies and scapegoating for issues created by their own government. But they seemed to not be interested in thinking too long about this. As if they have been numbed to politics for decades by the media owners.

I felt hopeless. I feel hopeless. I feel scared. I cry when I see more news and more developments. I cried when I was telling my family members that I don't want to apply for settled status. It makes me feel like a doormat, having to apply for a right I had that was then taken from me and I was given no say. I cried when I read the suggestion that we will be deported without settled status. I cried remembering history and the Nazi period where everyone thought nothing bad was going to happen at the beginning; most stayed passive and allowed them to come into power. I felt like the same is happening here and no one can see it. I found some EU groups on Facebook and, honestly, without them, I have no idea how I would have managed. I feel like an intruder, an outcast, an unwanted bacterium that keeps persisting. I feel like everything I thought was beautiful and tolerant about the UK and what drew me to it has all been a mirage, an illusion.

Why home matters

The place we live in is a sacred place; it is where we feel at ease and able to relax and gather ourselves again. Home is the centre of our universe, from where we strike out into the world to make a living and contribute to society, and whither we return with a sense of relief and retrieval of safety. The right to a safe abode is enshrined in Article 8 of the European Convention on Human Rights, which states: 'Everyone has the right to respect for his private and family life, his home and his correspondence.'

In her book *The Faraway Nearby*, Rebecca Solnit (2013) puts it very poetically and poignantly:

I talked about places, about the ways that we often talk about love of place, by which we mean our love for places, but seldom of how the places love us back, of what they give us. They give us continuity, something to return to, and offer a familiarity that allows some portion of our own lives to remain connected and coherent. They give us an expansive scale in which our troubles are set into context, in which the largeness of the world is a balm to loss, trouble, and ugliness. (Solnit, 2013, p.30)

This capacity of a familiar place to become imbued with safety is even more important when we are migrants who have had to put down roots a second or third time in our lives. The homes we create in the new country are homes that are vital and matter greatly. They have to be shaped into safe spaces where we feel welcome and secure. When all around us we face the challenges of being the stranger, our homes truly become our sanctuary, our sanctum. To find ourselves no longer secure in them because our right to reside is in question is far more terrifying than anyone can imagine who takes their rights and home country for granted.

Migrants have one great advantage over those who have never left: they know that they can travel and survive their relocation (Madison, 2009); they live with awareness of their own adaptability. But the other side of that coin is that they often come to dread having to change and adapt again. Another aspect of a migrant's life is that their mobility has given them a greater map of the world. It's not the map of the tourist, who collects knowledge of many different countries and places in the world, but only as a visitor. With the migrant's knowledge of all the many possibilities the world offers also comes an awareness of the limitations. We cannot fantasise about moving again; for us, that prospect is imbued with dread. We know the upheaval that this represents and to hear others suggesting, lightly, that we should just pick up sticks and move 'back to where we came from' is incredibly offensive and upsetting. We do not want to imagine different places as possible homes, least of all places we have left. We want to feel secure and to burrow into that security; we want to know that no one has the right to question our home, the potential loss of which is equivalent to our annihilation.

Greg Madison, in his book *The End of Belonging*, summarises it astutely as the need for coherence between our inner and outer worlds:

> Feeling at home is the experience of this interaction of the inner and
> outer matching in idiosyncratic ways. (Madison, 2009, p.70)

I saw many EU citizens plunged into despair because the world they had created in the UK had suddenly been punctured and they felt as if a huge gulf, an abyss, had opened up before them, into which they dared not descend but which they could not bridge for themselves. They tried to hold onto something that was vanishing in front of their eyes, as their safety of abode literally slipped into the hole. Solnit captures this very well again:

> Despair compresses you into a small space, and a depression is literally a
> hollow in the ground. To dig deeper into the self, to go underground, is
> sometimes necessary, but so is the other route of getting out of yourself,
> into the large world, into the openness in which you need not clutch your
> story and your troubles so tightly to your chest. Being able to travel both
> ways matters. (Solnit, 2013, p.30)

In the next two chapters I will explore in more detail what happened to two of the people who looked for help when they were plunged into their own particular existential crises. I will consider first the experience of Joan Pons Laplana, a male nurse from Spain, and then that of Lucie Dun, a Czech musician who had a mental and emotional breakdown because of the situation she found herself in. I will describe what happened to them in some detail so that we can understand better how they both found a way to rise from their crises to transform their lives.

3

Joan's breakdown

In October 2019, *The Guardian* published a long article about Joan Pons Laplana, a male Spanish nurse, who had been actively campaigning to stop Brexit but who eventually found it all too much and had to deal with his own breakdown.

Having campaigned alongside Joan, I was concerned but also intrigued to see someone so strong and confident being crushed under the burden of his notoriety and his commitment to safeguarding the position of EU citizens in Britain. Joan agreed to write about his experience in some detail for this book, and I later conducted an interview with him, also published here, when we drilled down into some of the issues in more depth.

Joan was in his 40s at the time of the Brexit referendum. He was born and raised in Spain, trained as a nurse, and came to the UK to work in the NHS in 2000. He won the *British Journal of Nursing* Nurse of the Year award in 2018. He married a British woman, and he has three children. Here is his story as he told it in his own words in 2019.

Joan's story

My name is Joan and according to some politicians I am a queue jumper, a citizen of nowhere.

I studied nursing in Spain and, after graduating from university, I spent three years trying to find a stable job as a nurse but ended up delivering pizzas to earn a living. I was fed up and demoralised, so I looked abroad. During the summer of 2000, I saw an advert in my local paper offering a fantastic opportunity for nurses in Great Britain.

I grew up in Barcelona admiring British culture, its openness and its fashion. My favourite television programmes were *The Young Ones* and *Blackadder*. I grew up listening to UB40, David Bowie, Blur, Oasis and Radiohead. And, when the opportunity to come to this country arose, I did not hesitate.

I left my family and friends behind and jumped on a plane, excited for my future ahead. I landed in Luton on bonfire night with just £50 in my pocket and a suitcase full of hope. I found a job in the National Health Service and have worked hard for the NHS ever since. The NHS is one of the most multicultural organisations in the world. More than 200 nationalities work alongside each other. Diversity is what makes the NHS the best health system in the world. I fitted right in.

For 17 years, I never felt a foreigner in the UK. I chose to commit myself to this country and the UK adopted me in turn. All that changed on 23 June 2016, when the public voted to leave the European Union. It immediately made me feel I no longer belonged. The toxic narratives were too much. I felt betrayed; I felt that the 17 years of love were finished. I did not recognise my country anymore.

What happened

Like me, some five million EU citizens made this country their home. But after years of living in harmony, we were betrayed by the UK government, treated as foreigners and told to go back to where we came from.

Since then, I did not feel welcome anymore and started to feel like a second-class citizen just because of my accent. I have been attacked on social media and what makes me even angrier is that my kids are being affected.

In 2016, my 14-year-old son asked me if I was going to be forced to go back to Spain if Brexit went ahead, and since then we have been in limbo. My daughter, who was aged 11 then, came home crying from school and told me that another child had said that I would be thrown out very soon. My daughter was heartbroken and asked me if that was true. I could not in all honesty say no!

Suddenly the penny dropped. Brexit had turned our lives upside down and I had two options: to sit down and wait for my fate to be delivered to me or fight for my rights and my beliefs. I chose to stand up for my rights.

What I did about it

During the last three years, I have been up and down the country campaigning and putting pressure on the government to guarantee our citizens' rights. I have worked with several Remain groups and I have highlighted the dangers of Brexit for our NHS at numerous rallies. Before Brexit, I was barely interested in politics and had never spoken in public, but I could not look into my children's eyes and tell them that I did nothing to stop this madness.

When I heard the result of the referendum, I felt in shock and betrayed. I sat on the sofa and I couldn't move. It took a while to sink in. However, I wasn't hugely surprised, as the Leave campaign was based on two lies: 1) that migrants were to blame for everything, and 2) the famous lie on the side of a bus that £350 million a week would go to the NHS [if the UK left the EU]. I knew both these things to be wrong, but people weren't listening to me anymore.

In recent years I have been accused of stealing British jobs. A British job for British people, says the government! Yet [the UK] struggles to produce our own home-grown nurses. We have currently more than 43,000 nursing vacancies [in the NHS] and for the first time in history more nurses are leaving than entering the profession. It is getting more and more difficult to provide safe care. Unless something dramatic changes, we are courting a humanitarian crisis.

I have also been accused of bringing wages down, but it is not the European workforce that has cut public sector pay year after year, but the government. I have been accused also of being unpatriotic. I have been told, 'If you really love Britain you should apply for a British passport,' but that has never been true. My passport might be Spanish, but my heart is also British now.

All of us EU citizens [in the UK] have been accused of being the cause of the lack of housing and school places and for putting a strain on public services, when actually we are essential to those services. Without us, the NHS would not have survived. One in four doctors is a migrant and one in seven nurses is from overseas.

How it has affected me

My very identity and freedom have been put into question and, like with any loss, I have been through four of the five stages of grief and loss: 1. denial; 2. anger; 3. bargaining; 4. depression.

Initially, I was in shock and in complete denial about Brexit. I thought my life was going to continue as before, but all that changed when my daughter came home from school crying and asking me if it was true that I was going to be forced to go back to Spain. Alarms bells rang inside my head. Suddenly I was overcome with uncertainty about everything, and I became angry.

Keep in mind, all people grieve differently. Some people will wear their emotions on their sleeve and be outwardly emotional. Others will experience grief more internally and may not cry. The pressure builds up inside of us.

I decided to deal with my feelings by taking a more active role, to take charge of my destiny and fight for what I think is right for all EU citizens. I also felt I had to stand up for the NHS. As a nurse, I had no other option but to fight back. I decided to transform my grief into action and use my Latin passion to fight against the injustices that were being thrown at me.

On my journey, I found lots of people who felt the same as me and also fantastic organisations like *the3million*, Best for Britain, People's Vote and the New Europeans, to name but a few.

One thing I have going for me is that I am a good storyteller and my message got the attention of a lot of people, and by accident I found myself at the forefront of a movement. My story and face have been splashed all over the media and I have been able to have an impact all over the world. But this sudden jump into the spotlight also took a toll on my mental health.

In 2019, I suddenly had a panic attack at work and my GP diagnosed me with anxiety and depression. My anxiety had not appeared suddenly. It was an accumulation of three years of stress, anger and uncertainty. The politics were just so oppressive and this, together with pressure at work, triggered my anxiety attack when everything just felt too much.

Why the fate of the NHS matters to me

Hearing that the NHS is at a breaking point and being aware from my daily work that the crisis in the NHS is deepening every day is deeply upsetting. Nurses are leaving in droves and the working conditions that nurses are suffering on a daily basis are getting worse and worse.

The NHS is in dire straits as a consequence of the chronic under-funding over the last seven years, while demand is increasing by four per cent annually. Every year, the gap between funding and demand is widening, making it more and more difficult for staff to deliver safe care.

But what is more worrying is that overall more than 86,000 NHS posts are currently vacant while more nurses are leaving than joining the [UK national nursing] register.

As a nurse, I have a duty of care, and this government is making my job impossible. As a lead nurse, my job is to continue to deliver gold-standard care to my patients, but every year I have fewer staff and less money. I can no longer guarantee the safety on my ward. I am not a magician.

So, my mental breakdown was not sudden. I had a crisis a few months before, in December 2018. At that point I had access to therapy, thanks to the ESSE therapy programme at the Existential Academy. It helped me to reduce my stress and anxiety and gain a much-needed balance. But I kept my mental problem hidden; in a way, I pushed it aside and I didn't listen to my body. I had no time to rest and then I became an MEP candidate [in the 2019 European Parliament elections], travelling all around the country, canvassing, debating, being followed by TV crews and talking to lots of people.

The breakdown

The campaign trail was mentally, physically and emotionally draining. I was expecting a backlash from the Brexiteers – but I wasn't ready for the harsh words from the Labour and Lib Dem supporters. Let's not forget that I am not a politician and that I was still doing my full-time job as a nurse, also juggling my master's at Leeds University and my family life. It was very hard being 24/7 in the public eye.

I started to have problems at work in July, but symptoms were present before. I had horrible mood swings and terrible problems to remember anything. I struggled at work to read important documents, which made me more anxious. My confidence dropped and I became convinced that I was doing a bad job. I felt paralysed and I found myself very anxious during my journey to work.

But I still kept everything to myself. I convinced myself that I was okay and that I could continue as normal. Reality soon caught up with me. One day at lunchtime I felt dizzy and I went outside. I started to hyperventilate and sweat profusely. My heart was going really fast. I went home. I called in sick the day after but decided to return to work the next day. During the 20 years of my nursing career, I can count on two hands the number of days I have been off sick. But on the day of my return to work, the same thing happened. I went to see my GP the following day and was diagnosed with work-related stress and anxiety.

The attacks became more frequent and everything felt too much. I spent nearly a week on the sofa looking into empty space. My mood swings got worse and I was having rows with my wife on a daily basis. After I'd been two weeks off sick, my wife asked me to go back to my GP and start on medication while I was waiting to start cognitive behaviour therapy. Initially, I didn't want to start medication, but the possibility of losing my wife was scarier. The following day we went together to see my GP. I have been on antidepressants ever since then. They have helped me to control my panic attacks and I have had no more mood swings since then. Initially I felt like a failure, I felt ashamed that I had a nervous breakdown. I thought that only happened to weak people and I did not tell anyone about it.

Getting back on top of things

In September I started my CBT face to face. Slowly but surely, I have gained my balance again and I have realised that having a mental breakdown is nothing to be ashamed of. It makes me human. It has been a consequence of the situation I have found myself in.

Follow-up interview

Joan's story is very interesting, as it shows that he was struggling in all four dimensions of his life. He was physically exhausted; he was feeling socially unsafe and in the firing line; he was feeling like a personal failure, and, spiritually, he felt as if the world was no longer functioning in a moral and acceptable manner. I recognised many of the factors that we noticed in other EU citizens who came to ESSE for help, but I could also see that Joan was determined to get his life sorted out and to find a better and stronger position in relation to his existential crisis. I wanted to get to the bottom of his experience and find out more about how he was responding to his difficulties in practice. We spent several hours talking all this through in much more detail and I've summarised the interview below.

Blaming the body

When we meet, towards the end of 2019, Joan looks strong and self-assured, and he is immediately ready to start talking. He is going to be speaking at a conference that afternoon and he seems full of energy and confidence.

We spend a little time reminding ourselves of what he wrote in the story and he explains a few things in more detail. I point out to him that, in his 2000 words, he goes through a whole range of emotions, from anger to shame to depression to doubt, and that he also describes clearly his own awareness of these mood swings. He can see how far this journey has taken him and we agree to reflect a bit more on how he got into all of this and how he is moving on from it, to rise from the crisis. We decide to start talking about his emotional crisis.

He says that the first moment that he knew something was wrong was when he thought he had Alzheimer's. He couldn't remember meetings and was convinced he was losing his memory. He was blaming it on himself, finding fault with himself. Only months later did he realise that his brain just couldn't cope with all the stress, although there was never really anything wrong with it physically. He was in a supermarket and couldn't remember what he was doing there. He phoned his wife and asked her for a list. She said, 'Just buy what you buy every week,' and he could not remember what that was. He felt terrible. He couldn't absorb any more information. He would be sitting watching telly and his wife would say, 'Put on a film.' He would put on a film and his wife would say: 'Jo, we watched this last week.' He had no recollection of any of it. He had information overload and found he was dissociating when watching the TV or reading books. He just could not connect to it or remember it.

He also had severe tiredness. Previously, he used to go to sleep like a log. But now, at 2 or 3 o'clock in the morning, he was still awake. Or he would wake up several times in the night. His sleeping pattern was all over the place. He became exhausted from lack of sleep. With hindsight, he realises that this led in turn to him becoming addicted to caffeine in order to try to stay awake and function at work. He used to drink a two-litre bottle of coke each day on top, in order to rehydrate and get some energy. He was aware that this was not just making it harder to slow down in the evening; it also had an impact at night, as caffeine stimulates the bladder, so he had to get up at night to pee. Now he has deliberately reduced his coke intake to a can a day at lunchtime, and he tries not to drink any caffeine after 2 o'clock in the afternoon.

Strangely, initially he was convinced that his problems must have a purely physical explanation. He went to his GP several times because he wondered whether he had prostate cancer, because of his increased frequency of urinating and his extreme tiredness. He was desperate to find a physical reason for it all and it never crossed his mind at the beginning that he was having a mental health problem. The GP did all the tests, including a rectal examination, and found nothing wrong with his prostate. That was around September 2018, just before he had his first crisis. The signs were there but he was still pretending he was mentally okay. He thought what was happening to him was related to him hitting his 40s.

Overwhelming emotions

Joan describes how all this was soon beginning to bring on terrible mood swings. He was angry. He still remembers having daily fights with his wife and with his other loved ones occasionally. He was very irritable and would get cross about small things. Many tiny aspects of everyday life would trigger him. It was ridiculous, he says. He became quite paranoid at work as well. Brexit was taking up a big part of his brain. He classified people as Remainers or Leavers all the time. He realised he was very quick to judge people and was more and more aware of it and ashamed of that. He was labelling people. Goodies and baddies. It is a bad way to live, he says. He was feeling people were against him. His antennae were on the alert 24 hours a day. He would constantly think: 'Are they going to attack me?' He was on guard all the time.

He was also overeating. When he is anxious, he eats, he says; it's a cultural thing. He put on two stone really fast. Now he has lost one stone. He had to, as he was becoming obese and it was having an impact on his physical health. He was out of breath a lot of the time. He was also beginning to hate his self-image. It wasn't that he was totally self-loathing; he just felt a sense of disapproval of himself, ill at ease with what he was becoming. He couldn't stop eating. It was his sole pleasure, it seemed. He had so very few pleasures left and felt so beleaguered by life. Therefore, he told himself it was okay and continued doing it for a long time. He couldn't read or go to the cinema; he just didn't have the peace of mind for it. Eating was immediate gratification. It soothed him. His favourite foods were connected to a safe place – his parents' home; he ate olives, ham, all his favourite Spanish foods. But, of course, they were also fattening. This in turn also caused him to wake several times in the night, needing to urinate. It was very tiring.

And every night he was waking his wife up, too. Although he always tried to be careful, he couldn't stop her waking as, when he opened the door, the cats would come in. The whole world would suddenly wake up because of his sleeplessness and people would get angry with him. This too impacted on him negatively. He could see how the whole chain of negativity was happening and setting off this catastrophic feeling of crisis, where nothing was safe anymore and everything was falling apart.

Coping

Joan says he was still very strong, despite all this. He never used to be sick, but when he had the breakdown, he did have to take time off. During his first breakdown, he didn't take any time off at all. He is a coper; he is courageous; he didn't want to give in. This was happening at the time that Boris Johnson was going to become prime minister. It felt like the final straw and he just couldn't take it anymore. Someone he regarded as a careless, racist, misogynistic person was going to take over the country he loved so much, and it seemed so wrong and so dangerous. It was the first time he thought Brexit was actually going to happen and that he would have to give up. As long as he had been able to fight against it, there was hope, but now he closed himself like a clam. He could feel himself cutting off. He stopped talking to people, didn't want to go out anymore. He was quiet, would only say 'yes' or 'no'. He is not sure why his wife put up with it and is still married to him. In July, she said something had changed and, although she still loved him, she couldn't go on. It was too hard and too difficult. That is why he went to see his GP. His manager sent him off home too. He had conflicts at work. The manager, wisely, said, 'You can't come back until the GP gives you permission to return.' He then started therapy.

He spent time at home, going from bed to sofa and watching *Judge Judy* on TV all day long. He got gratification seeing other people's misery and seeing someone setting it to rights. Yes, this mattered enormously, for there was no one setting the real world to rights. It gave him a little bit of hope that there was still something good to believe in and some justice in the world. *Judge Judy* gave him some hope. He had lost hope in humanity. He had become desperate. He withdrew and desperately wanted someone to straighten things out again.

At that point he still had daily fights with his wife, sitting on the sofa. His wife was also getting desperate and she would start crying. He went back to the doctor when he realised things had become so dire that he had a choice: that if he didn't do something to improve himself, he would lose his wife. The GP put him on tablets, antidepressants, Citalopram. He is still on them. He'd never thought he would take this kind of medication. He is firmly anti tablets, normally. The secondary effects of the drugs, being sedating, were actually good for him. They helped him to switch off. He took the meds at night, so that he would sleep and wake up refreshed. He started feeling less tired and doing things with his wife, who gave him a list of things to do every day to help him get going. He would get out of the house and go for a walk around the town, to the parks. He started having coffee with friends but still didn't talk to anyone about what was happening. He told them he was between jobs. They didn't have an inkling what he was struggling with.

Learning through crisis

Then National Mental Health Week came, and Joan was asked to go to Manchester to speak about the impact of Brexit on the past three years of his life. He was also given therapy. CBT for six weeks. One of the things CBT helped him with was not to be ashamed. He used to be very ashamed. In Spain, you have to be tough as a man; you don't give in to mental health problems. His dad and granddad had the motto, 'Just get on with it.' So, having a problem was a sign of weakness for him. To tell people he wasn't coping was a mark of his failure as a man, so it was as if his whole image was crumbling. With the CBT, he realised that he was human; that it was okay to have such problems, as long as you were willing to learn from them. It was actually more than okay, because it allowed him to become more human and to learn from his own experience how people get oppressed and depressed and how we can become paralysed.

When I ask him what more he learnt from going through all this, he says that the most important learning was that mental health is as important as physical health. 'You have to allow your feelings and learn to share,' he says. He had to learn to get his feelings out by writing them down, then sending the piece of writing to his wife, so that they could have a conversation about it together. It was still uncomfortable to talk about feelings, but he learnt to write about it. He discovered that, if people knew he was not okay, they would react better than he thought. He thought they would judge him and condemn him. He realised that their reaction was rather different, and this surprised him. Many people seemed to embrace his mental illness much better than he thought they would.

When he had to speak at the conference in Manchester, he didn't prepare a talk. He just sat there and said what he thought, talking about his breakdown. There were a lot of journalists. They wanted to publish his story. He decided to go public. That was a big deal for him. This was also because he had not mentioned his mental health problems on the occupational health questionnaire in his job application, because he was still working when he filled it in and had not had the breakdown yet. He became afraid that speaking about his breakdown now might adversely affect his job application.

But, in reality, everyone thanked him and said to him that they were feeling the same thing. He discovered that absolutely everyone was feeling this bad, not just the EU citizens. He would not have known this had he not spoken out. So, he now knows that we should all speak about it. Everyone is feeling bad and suffering. We need to figure out why this is. It is something about the whole situation in the country. There is just too much pressure, too much stress, too many contradictions, too much conflict. It even affects British people, not just the EU citizens, who are suffering the most.

Deriving strength and courage

Joan says he feels that all this allowed him to find new strength. He has changed now. He is a lot more active and is not eating so much. His wife bought him a treadmill. He does five kilometres every day. He tried meditation but his brain is still too busy for that. It doesn't work for him. The physical exercise works well, as then he can think about things and recognise the conflicts and the feelings and name them. This has helped him to stop blaming himself for them. He does many things differently. He has stopped going on social media so much. When he does go on social media, he tries to find something positive in all the noise. He tries to transform negatives into positives. He picks what he likes and passes on the more constructive messages.

In July 2019, he was quite destructive, but now he feels much more constructive. He realises there is no good or bad. Everyone feels things strongly. He is beginning to understand the Leavers. He can see that they wanted Brexit for a reason. Sometimes for the same reasons that he did not want it. Sometimes we have shared values but go about achieving them in different ways, he says. He has learnt that everyone wanted the same thing: everyone wanted what they thought was better for the UK. It just depended on what information you had been given, whether you thought it was better for the UK to leave or to remain. So, he has been able to reconcile himself to a lot of people's views and he is not so angry anymore.

This makes things better. He has come to terms with the idea that there is only a very small percentage of bad people. He used to try to engage the very angry people and they used to swear at him and tell him to go home. Now he doesn't pursue them anymore as he has given up believing he can change their minds. He knows these people don't want to talk to him anyway. That's fine. If they are polite, he will listen and talk to them, as then he can learn something. If not, he will leave them be. He has now connected with a lot of Leavers and realises they have a lot more in common with him than he thought.

And the way he goes about other things in his life is also more positive. Before, he used to be quite negative. Now, he sets the difficulties of the day aside and finds something positive in it that he can be proud of.

The future

I ask whether he thinks about where he is going in his life, what matters to him and what he wants to magnify.

He looks thoughtful and reflects carefully on the question. Then a smile slowly creeps up from the corners of his mouth as he realises that he has learnt to ponder on things much more. He asks himself more explicit questions about the future and about what, ultimately, he wants to do. He realises that this is not an easy question, as he has learnt that the future is hard to predict. You never know what will happen in life. He takes the view that we have two options: we can either fight for something or against something. He has come to the conclusion that you should fight for what you believe in, but not fight against other people. This has taken a lot of the anger out of his life. He was angry with everyone for a while, even with those he loved. He was angry all the time with his wife. She has a business. She used to refuse to come with him in his campaigning, because she felt she could not be seen to be pro- or anti-Brexit in her job. He used to think that if you are silent you are colluding with the oppressors. He felt she wasn't loyal and not really on his side, because she was neutral. She was actually supporting him, but she wasn't visibly doing so, and he felt let down by that. He nursed a growing resentment against her. He resented her refusal to stand up for him. It made him doubt. He felt unsupported. He looks upset about this. He knows that it wasn't right and it wasn't helping either.

I ask him if he felt that way about his children too, but he says he never did. They have dual nationality, so they are okay. They will be fine whatever happens. Not him. He had refused to get dual nationality up to now. Why should he have to be anything other than Spanish, when it was fine before to be Spanish in the UK? He knows he may have to let go of this particular stance; that he has to have security first. He must safeguard his long-term future, his pension. It is too hard to be insecure all the time. He didn't want to give up his values. Now he knows that sometimes we have to let go and be realistic.

Values

When he was growing up, Joan saw England as an open country with a great and rich culture and he saw that the NHS was fantastic, staffed by and also serving people from all over the world. It felt so good to be part of that. Then things changed all of a sudden. He was singled out. He didn't belong anymore.

He was not wanted in the UK any longer. He was targeted as if he was doing something wrong; that EU citizens had been wrong for coming here and taking up jobs. He felt very bitter about the way people began to speak to him. He had worked for the NHS for so long, and somebody asked him, why didn't he go home? He was providing a service for Britain; why would people suddenly be so nasty to him? They even began asking him why he had married a British woman, as if he had stolen her away from a British man, dragging her into his lair by the hair, like a prehistoric man with a club. He didn't understand how they could see it like that. It was clear to him that you fall in love with a *person*, not because of their nationality. People accused him of not liking Spanish women. He didn't recognise the country anymore. It didn't seem to be like that before the referendum.

Changes

I ask, did he think people had changed? He says he doesn't think British people are more racist than before. There is a minority that was always racist. But it was not socially acceptable to speak in those terms before. Nigel Farage[1] and Boris Johnson and Theresa May and other people like that made it acceptable. Not everyone thinks like that or acts like that. A lot of people have been silenced by the right wing. He now wants to wake up these silent people. The Britain he fell in love with is still here, but it has fallen silent. People have gone underground. He wants to wake them up again. He wants to help bring the good values back. He can't accept people just sitting down and doing nothing about it. People let themselves be suppressed. We have been shut up. As long as he kept talking to this negative minority and feeling oppressed by them, it was bad for his mental health. Now he is choosing deliberately to be more with the people who are truly British and who hold those good values. This is how our society will be able to build things back up. He has accepted, however, that the minority is also a part of society. He says thoughtfully: 'I shouldn't see them as an enemy but see them as they are. [Nigel] Farage[1] says he wants to represent both groups. In this he is right. We should all listen to each other.' The system should be able to represent the whole society so that nobody is forgotten. But at the moment this is not the case.

'How do you manage your relationships with other people, now?' I ask. He says he is much more selective. He has told all the people he loves about his breakdown and difficulties. But he has not told others. He has, however, now

---

1. Nigel Farage was leader of the UK Independence Party (UKIP), which was set up on an anti-EU platform, from 2006 to 2009 and 2010 to 2016, and leader of the Brexit Party from 2019 to 2021. He served as Member of the European Parliament (MEP) for South East England from 1999 until the UK left the EU in 2020.

told his parents. That was a big challenge. He told them what had happened to him, but they haven't talked about it. They just listened. They asked him if he was okay now, so that was something. Yet, he didn't feel he could tell them his story. But then, when he was in the newspaper, he sent them a copy, so they now know that he is in therapy. He went to Barcelona in the summer, and they saw him take his pills but didn't ask him what they were for. He sounds upset about this, so I ask him how this affected him. He felt initially that they weren't interested in him, but as we talk about it further, he says he now realises this is not true. They gave him a space to talk to them. They are kind of letting him be. It's up to him to use that space, or not, as he chooses. They gave him the opportunity, but he is not ready. Maybe at Christmas. He realises they do care about him but are treating him like a grown up. They don't have to bail him out. So that's actually pretty good. They trust him. He was too angry with them before. He can see that now. He is mellowing so much and becoming so much more empathetic of other people and, as he does, he feels better about himself as well.

Before, he used to push all the bad feelings out towards others, but that wasn't helpful. It wasn't helpful to them and not to him either. He directed his anger at the wrong people and that made it worse, because he pushed away the people who loved him. We talk a bit about the destructive power of anger, but also about the power of our own rebellion and the need to stand up against injustice. He is aware he needs to use his anger in a different way. He wants to be more effective, more contained. He does physical exercises for 40 minutes each day now and this calms him down. It helps him to transform his anger into power. When he is finished, he has a nice meal with his wife. He is getting much better at relating to her. He is fairer and more open, but there are still problems. He is not going to pretend it is all okay suddenly now, as it isn't. He is learning a new routine. He knows he cannot expect never to have other mental health problems in the future, but he knows that there is a lot he can do to maintain his emotional wellbeing. He thought he had to be superman. He was just trying to grin and bear it. He had a lot of resilience, but at some point, when the pressure is too great, all of us crack. It is impossible to go all your life without a breakdown if you live in a challenging way. He has come to the conclusion that mental health is very much like physical health. Every day you need to take care of it. If you don't, it goes wrong. Next time he will know when to seek help. He has learnt that it's okay not to be okay.

He says, sometimes you have pain in your head or in your leg and you need to figure out how that came about and do something about it. Sometimes you have pain in your heart or your mind as well, and you need to also figure out how that happened. We learn to do physical exercises to improve our physical fitness. In the same way, we have to do mental and emotional exercises to make our mental health better. He uses an app on his mobile phone, called Wyse. It's a penguin talking to him and asking him questions. It's free for everybody. He uses it every day now and it really helps him. The question at the beginning of a session is always the same: 'How are you?' It gets him thinking and talking. It's strange, he says, that he can speak so easily to a penguin on his phone when he finds it much harder to speak to people. The app will also tell you to go to your GP if it looks like there is a bigger problem. It helps him, alongside his therapy, to have this daily reminder of the need to look after his mental health.

He still has one session left of CBT therapy but that is not enough. CBT did help him a lot to get through the crisis, he says, but he was a bit frightened that he would go downhill without it, afterwards. But it is good with the app. He laughs a bit about finding it easier to talk to a penguin than to his wife. Then he tells me that the app was made by a mental health nurse who used to work for an NHS child and adolescent mental health service, who decided to share his skills for free with the wider public. It is obvious that this brings the app very close to him. It makes him trust it, because it is based on the same values as he holds. It somehow confirms that those values were right to begin with. They are of course also the values of the NHS, which has been his backbone for so many years. He feels so much better for having his friend, the penguin, with him. It really feels like somebody is looking after him; just the fact that the penguin asks him every day, 'How are you?' makes him more aware of how he feels. It's okay to tell the penguin he is not okay. He doesn't have to pretend to be tougher than he is. If you score low, the penguin recommends you get extra help. It's good. He found this app for himself and has a feeling of ownership of it.

Being careful and self-observant

Joan does know his limitations. He notices that at 3pm each afternoon his brain still hurts. He has learnt to take care of himself and has all his meetings in the morning. He still gets information overload. He is much more aware of his brain's limits than he was before. He tries to have quiet times in the afternoon. He has become much more self-aware and more capable of managing his life and his mental health. He works flexitime. His manager tells him to clock out when he needs me-time. Joan says he is very lucky with his job and his manager. He is a good manager; he understands that his employees are more useful when they work when they are not tired. That too comes out of Joan's own new discoveries. Joan himself manages a good team of five. They are supportive. All are British, but several are married to Europeans. He is learning to go home when he is tired. He will do the work another time when he is less tired. He always makes the time up and is much more efficient this way. He thanks his manager for this; the manager taught him not to force things when he is not mentally well. Joan looks at me with a broad grin on his face and says he doesn't need to punish himself anymore.

His new job is helping digitalise NHS records. He feels his job is important in delivering joined-up care, making the NHS paperless. He wants to connect the GPs with the hospital and also with social care. He is trying to empower patients. I can hear how he is reconnecting to his career and bringing his idealism and practical know-how into the sphere where he can make a real difference. He has realised that all patients need to discover how to take charge of their own health and mental health. He was talking to someone from the City Council about connecting the systems. It is important for them to know what kind of housing a person lives in, or if they are socially isolated, for instance. Often, they do not have this information. But if they know, they can put something in place and prevent further breakdowns later on. But, most of all, Joan wants people to take back their own power in health, mental health and social care and figure out for themselves what is available and then access it. This is now a kind of new mission, to enable people to take responsibility and show them how they can take their power back.

New meaning

Joan is finding new meaning in his work. With Brexit, he was also fighting for the NHS, but in a different, desperate manner. Now he is fighting for a better society, not just for a renewed NHS. He can see that Brexit happened because things were cut off and things were going badly. If we reconnect things, they will get better. Health is not designed by the NHS. It is about how you live, what you do, what you eat. Nurses and doctors used to try to be heroes, saving people. We need fewer heroes and to shift the power back to the communities and the people, he says. He has become much more realistic and pragmatic.

I observe that he has taken his politics back into his work and that he has re-enfranchised himself after feeling disenfranchised both in his life and in the NHS. He has used his own difficulties to start understanding things better. Now he is applying his new problem-solving skills and insights to the NHS. He has not just discovered he has an important contribution to make; he has found a new purpose. He nods eagerly and says he agrees wholeheartedly. He smiles very fully as he jokes that, in a way, Brexit has educated him. He never thought he would say 'Thank you' to Brexit. But Brexit has put the broken society in the forefront. It has brought the fractures out in the open, when they were previously hidden. It has taken him three years to see this. He can see now that the Brexit mentality could be good for this country if we do the right thing with it and look beyond it. We have the challenge to take our country back now, not by leaving the EU but by facing our problems and our challenges and making things better.

Six months ago, he could never have seen it could bring some good. He thought the only good was to meet people like me, but now he can see that it has also brought a lot of problems out into the open that were invisible before and that we can now start to try to solve them.

Then he briefly speculates that maybe what this country needs is for Brexit to go ahead so that the proverbial hits the fan and people will realise for themselves that the Brexit promises were a lie. Maybe it's the only way for the people from the Far Right to discover that these things can't work. It needs to break down completely to reveal it. It needs to break open. If you keep suppressing it, you never get it out of the system. Revocation is not good, he feels. There needs to be a complete debate in the country about how we can face the facts and come to grips with reality. Unfortunately, this may take much longer. We may not be out of the woods yet for a while.

Expressing these thoughts and saying the unsayable emboldens him further. When I ask him what has changed that he can say this and look completely at ease with the situation, he says he has stopped being afraid of Brexit. If it happens, this may still lead to a better solution going ahead. He has a more balanced view. He can see a way forward, whether it happens or not. We have to face reality one way or the other. People have to take responsibility. They can't just have it easy, he says. People like you and me are ready for a new society, but a lot of Brexit people aren't ready yet. They still have to learn those lessons. People will be disappointed. They won't get what they wanted. People like us won't be worse off; it has hit us already. These people may need to experience that breakdown as well. It's the only way to figure out what a good life looks like.

Now he understands this not just for himself but for the wider society as well. He has revolutionised and altered his world. He has found inner peace in his turmoil. He realises everyone needs to have a breakdown sometimes to transform their lives. I suggest that the breakdown is required for the breakthrough. He concurs and remarks that sooner or later you are going to have some problems and how you embrace and celebrate them will make all the difference. It is important to make people aware they need both to work and to have me-time. You can't do everything or be everything to everyone all the time, for then you destroy yourself.

I say to him that it seems to me that he has faced his breakdown and has understood what it has revealed about himself, about the world and about the role he can play in it. It isn't easy to retrieve one's emotional wellbeing after a crash like this and it takes a long time to get mentally healthy again, and even more to get mentally robust. His mentality is really changing and becoming much more constructive and vigorous. He couldn't agree more. He used to be a really angry person, he says. He is a lot more open now. He was hiding many of his problems then. Now he accepts he is what he is, no more and no less. Things will go up and down and that's life. You cannot fight it. Well, you can, but you will never win that fight. If we fight with life, we lose, for life is always the stronger party. We have to learn to work with life instead and make the most of our talents.

Your physical health and your job are important, but when you fear that people will push you out if you are not fine, you cannot really be yourself, he tells me. He can now empathise a lot more with people as they see him as human now, and he sees them as human too. He knows they have ups and downs. He used to pretend he was managing. Now he is more real and he watches his own ups and downs with interest and fascination. He used to try to have all the answers. Now he allows himself to be in doubt. He is honest. This also means he can respect himself again.

He says he often finds himself puzzled or stumped by questions. He spends time searching for the answer but doesn't feel obliged anymore to give an answer straight away. Even as a team leader, he doesn't have to pretend he knows the answers. I speak about the importance of learning to problematise things – in other words, to recognise what the actual problems are that we are struggling to deal with, instead of pretending that we know everything. This is how we learn new things. We put the puzzle together slowly. It's not either/or; there are many different pieces to the puzzle and they all have a right place where they fit. We can allow ourselves to take time to start seeing the problems as they are before we try to solve them.

The same is true with Brexit, he says. It is clear we are now thinking and drawing conclusions together. People used to catastrophise what will happen with Brexit. It won't be like that, he says; it will be a slow process that will teach us about reality. One way or the other, society as we know it is breaking down and we are going to have to deal with it. Hopefully, in 10 years' time, we can build a better society because we will have managed to acknowledge all these problems and all these feelings people have when they fall foul of our broken society, and we will have learned how to deal with it in reality rather than in fantasy. We are becoming more self-aware and more world-aware. We can see that we all have the same problems and that, deep down, we share the same values and beliefs: we all want a better life, justice, equality, health, peace and prosperity.

He says he has learnt to stop and ask himself what other people might be feeling. He asks them: 'Why do you feel like that? Can I help you?' He now feels very dissatisfied with the narrative about there being a civil war in Britain. He thinks that was imposed on us and it is ridiculous. We are all on the same side. We are human and we want the same things. We just need to know there is a future again, with hope, resources and safety. We should stop believing that the solution is somewhere else. The problem we have is that we don't listen to each other's feelings. It's not just about facts; we don't have the truth. We must look for it harder, to find it together. What is healthy is to face up to the good and bad in ourselves, the strength and weakness in ourselves and also in other people. At the end of the day, this is what will bring us understanding.

Follow-up during the Covid-19 pandemic

It was obvious that Joan learnt many new things about himself, other people, society and life in general, by going through this existential crisis. He also secured his status in the country. In many ways the things he discovered are always important when rising from crisis. But not everyone has his stamina, his confidence and his determination to get it right. I followed up with him six months after our conversation, after the Covid-19 pandemic hit the UK, to see how he was coping with it, and I was not surprised by what I found.

The pandemic was a real test for Joan, as it was an opportunity to show the learning he derived from his Brexistential crisis. This is what he had to say.

Despite the new coronavirus pandemic, my mental health has been OK. One of the positive things that has come out of Brexit is that I have learnt how to protect my mental health. Brexit has given me the necessary tools to cope with uncertainty. I am more open about how I feel and I also I have learned to identify my triggers. A few good tips I learned during the Brexit crisis are:

1. I avoid watching, reading or listening to the news as much as possible, because I know that it can trigger my anxiety.
2. I have reduced the amount of time that I spend on social media.
3. I have made plans to protect myself and my loved ones in case that the worse happens and someone in our household gets infected.
4. I have made sure that I focus more on the positive things.

I feel more in control and aware of my mental health. I no longer feel ashamed of expressing my fears and anxiety. Taking care of my mental health is paramount especially in these times of uncertainty.

Joan had volunteered to be part of the trials for the Covid-19 Astra Zeneca vaccine, and showed his mettle in doing his bit for humanity, once again.

There is no doubt that Joan distilled strength and courage from the existential crisis he had gone through. His commitment was now firmly to contribute something of value to society in any way he could. We often see this kind of humanitarian action on the part of those who surmount difficulties.

4

Lucie's despair

In this chapter, we look at a second person's experience in the face of her suddenly changed status in the UK. Lucie Dun is a musician and teacher and came to the UK from her birth country, the Czech Republic, in 2000. She is married to a British poet.

Lucie's experience was one of initial despair, having fallen into a state of despondency and desolation when she believed that there was no longer any future for her in the UK, followed by a long trajectory of gradual emergence from her existential crisis. Here is her story in her own words.

Lucie's story

I decided to come to England at the age of 23, in the year 2000. I had originally planned to stay here for just one year, to learn English and get a taste of British culture. The plan was to live with an English-speaking family as an au pair and be a part-time English student, but I soon realised within a matter of weeks that this country and its culture had become my second home.

Soon after arriving here, I was leading a culturally rich life and making friends with all sorts of intriguing characters from the artistic and academic fields. I frequently attended lectures, exhibitions, book launches and poetry readings, during one of which I met and fell in love with a poet, who became my husband.

I also fulfilled my dream of playing in a band as a keyboard player. I started gigging frequently and took part in many recording sessions. I got a busking licence and played all over the London Underground. It was there that I met the legendary singer Arthur Brown, joined his band, and toured with him all around the UK and Europe.

During this time, I was also deeply immersed in my English studies, and as soon as I got my English Proficiency Certificate, I started working on my qualifications for teaching English as a foreign language. I became a qualified teacher in 2004. It was an especially happy year for me, because in May 2004 the Czech Republic joined the European Union, which meant I was now free to live and work in the UK. It was the end of the nerve-wracking visa scrutiny at the UK border control every time I travelled.

Naturalisation attempt

Shortly after my wedding in 2012, I went to the Czech Embassy in London to get my Czech passport renewed. The passport officer suggested that it might be a good idea to get dual citizenship, especially as I wouldn't have to renounce my Czech citizenship. I liked the idea, and I was glad that I would finally be able to vote in the UK general elections. The very same day I started preparing for the 'Life in the UK' test – the compulsory test before applying for British citizenship. I actually really enjoyed preparing for the test and passed with a 100% score.

With the 'Life in the UK' test certificate in my hands, I set off to apply for British citizenship.

I booked a Nationality Checking Service appointment at Islington Town Hall in London, where I lived. The appointment cost £50, but I knew it was worth it because, unlike with the online application, this service would send my application to the Home Office directly and all the supporting documents would be checked by them. I was looking forward to going there, because it was the same place where I would – hopefully soon – have my citizenship ceremony.

But my appointment quickly turned into disappointment. After carefully looking through my application form and supporting documents, my advisor told me that at present I didn't qualify for British citizenship. He noticed my expression of disbelief and informed me that, in order to become a 'qualified person', I would have to be a worker, a jobseeker, a self-employed person, a self-sufficient person or a student.

I insisted that I had been all of that, and much more. I showed him several documents representing each category. He said I would need to produce far more evidence to back it all up and started with my status as student. It appeared that, although I had been studying for more than five years in total, I was apparently supposed to have been covered by something called Comprehensive Sickness Insurance (CSI) for the whole period.

'But I have always had access to the NHS and no doctor has ever required this!' I said with certainty. 'From the point of view of the Home Office, that is your problem,' replied the advisor. Only later did I learn that the requirement of CSI for permanent residence was only introduced in 2011, which made the whole issue even more confusing, if not absurd: I was required to already have something 11 years before it was actually a requirement.

I asked about all my years of work as a teacher. He said I would need to provide more evidence in the form of pay slips, tax return records for five consecutive years or bank statements showing regular income from all these jobs that matched the amounts on the payslips – all without a single gap. I realised that, as a teacher travelling from one summer school to another and working for a number of colleges, often for just a few weeks at a time and frequently switching from employment to self-employment, I couldn't hope to provide what was required, despite the fact that I had been teaching for much longer than five years in total.

That was, I must say, the most frustrating thing about it all – knowing that I did fully qualify for British citizenship but could not document it because I was in my 20s and carefree and had not bothered keeping any payslips, P60s and so on. As I often moved about, I had naturally tried to keep as little paperwork as possible and no longer had my past contracts and payslips. Some of the colleges I had worked for had closed down and I couldn't get letters of confirmation from many of my past employers.

Another thing that took me by surprise was that I apparently didn't have the right documentation to prove that my English language skills were at the required level.

My Certificate of English Proficiency and my TESOL Trinity language teaching qualifications were deemed insufficient. I was told that the Home Office required a specific language test, apparently much easier than any of the certificates and qualifications I did have. That amused and infuriated me at the same time.

By the end of this £50 defeat, I felt pretty low and didn't bother any more to disguise it from the official. He looked quite sympathetic and said that the best thing for me to do, rather than trying to patch up all those gaps in my missing paper evidence, would be to simply wait for a further five years and then apply again. He pointed to the fact that earlier that year (2013), I had, as so often before, just restarted my self-employment, and this meant that in 2018 I could reapply for citizenship.

I tried to rise above my disappointment. After all, all I had to do was wait and work for five years, and I was sure I had more than enough great things to do and experience in the meantime. Little did I know what was to come.

Applying for permanent residency

Three years later, in early 2016, the UK was preparing for a referendum concerning our membership of the EU. Although opinion polls of voters showed roughly equal proportions in favour of remaining and leaving, I was convinced that the majority would vote to remain.

I also kept hearing from a number of EU citizens that it was a good idea to have some proof of residency in the UK – as a safety measure, just in case the unimaginable should happen. I therefore applied for a document certifying permanent residence, although I was convinced that I already had an automatic right to stay here anyway. After all, I had been living and working here for years, and I was married to a British citizen; all that would surely grant me permanent residency. In my naïvety, I didn't have a clue that the requirements of evidence for this document would be exactly the same as those for the British citizenship that I had failed to qualify for three years previously!

And then came Thursday 23 June 2016. It's hard to forget that rainy day. My husband and I stayed up till at least 3am, following the voting. First results were very encouraging – more than 90% in favour of remaining in the EU. But no wonder, when they came from Gibraltar. As the time passed, the results started to even up, which became rather nerve-wracking, so I eventually gave in to a shallow, restless sleep. A few hours later, I woke up and saw my husband sitting at his desk. His expression revealed that he had been thinking hard how best to tell me, that by only four per cent difference, the UK had voted to leave the EU.

It took me weeks to gradually absorb the shock. I felt a sense of vertigo when trying to picture the impact this political event would have on the future of Europe. It was a notion of something fatal, slow and sinister approaching; a sense of irreversible doom, with the country about to be hurled into a black hole of perdition. I was often in tears throughout the day, overcome by waves of emotion such as deep sadness, bitterness and anger, refusing to accept the new reality. At night, I would have recurrent apocalyptic dreams about Europe being cut from the UK and sent floating away into the infinity of a dark, hostile ocean.

'You may be required to leave your home'

By November 2016, life seemed to have got back to normal, at least on the surface. The tremors of the major earthquake had subsided, with only the silent ticking of the time-bomb in the background.

One evening my husband surprised me with a lovely treat: he took me to the West End to see 'Sunny Afternoon', a musical about the 1960s British band The Kinks. The remarkable performance, filled with their classic songs, got the audience into an elated state and people kept singing and dancing even after the show ended, outside the theatre and in the streets of Soho. The air was full of carefree joy. As many times before, I felt a warm wave of affection for this country, which had now been my home for more than 16 years. I was in one of those sentimental moods that, if I passed a tourist souvenir shop, I would end up coming home with a bag full of mugs depicting every single member of the Royal Family, and possibly a few 'Keep Calm and Carry On' ones as well.

The following morning, I received a letter headed 'Home Office, UK Visas and Immigration, Permanent Migration'. What great timing, I thought; the document confirming my residency has just arrived and now I will have complete peace of mind regarding the future. I ceremoniously opened the envelope, removed the single sheet of paper and scanned through it, looking for the relevant sentence confirming my permanent residency. Instead, my eyes fixed on the following phrase:

> Your application has been refused for the reasons set out in the enclosed notices. The notices inform you of whether there is a right of appeal, and, if so, how this should be exercised. The notices also explain whether and when you are required to leave the United Kingdom.

It felt like a cannonball hitting my stomach. My arms and legs flared up in a sudden surge of heat and felt as heavy as if made of lead. It was as if someone had pulled the rug out from under my feet and left the foundations of my existence deeply shaken. A wave of fear engulfed me. In a state of shock, with constricted breath, I read those few sentences again in the childlike hope that I had not properly woken up after that happy night illuminated with Waterloo sunsets and sunny afternoons.

I noticed that the word 'notices' was used three times in the fateful paragraph. It seemed my life was now in the hands of these notices – a compassionless entity with supreme powers. Filled with apprehension, I sat down to read their final verdict. It started with a paragraph listing the reason for the refusal:

> You have applied for Permanent Residence on the basis that you are an EEA [European Economic Area] national who has resided in the UK in accordance with the Immigration Regulations 2006 for a continuous period of five years. However, you have not provided evidence that you have resided in the United Kingdom in accordance with those Regulations for a continuous period of five years.

The dreaded 'continuous period of five years' had caught up with me again, three years after my first attempt to apply for British citizenship. But back then I saw the act simply as one of declaring this country my home – the very opposite of an act driven by necessity, let alone by fear of deportation.

In 2013, if anyone mentioned that the UK might leave the EU one day, I would disregard it as a highly improbable hypothesis. And a threat of deportation?! A most absurd thought. In our day and age, deportations were surely reserved for mass-murderers or terrorists. But now the word was becoming saturated with disconcertingly relevant shades of personal threat. The question of 'whether and when I was required to leave the United Kingdom' was naturally the very next thing I began to search for anxiously, and a certain degree of relief passed through me when I read the final notice of immigration decision:

> As an EEA national you are not required to leave the UK.

However, almost immediately, a red alert flashed inside my mind: 'This letter refers to *current* laws. The fact I am an EEA national won't matter a thing to the Home Office after Brexit!' Without certification of permanent residency, I could potentially be deported in the future. And this could happen even though I was married to a British citizen! The immigration laws have the power to separate married couples, and this could include us as well. That our marriage through the Church of England was considered a sacrament, known as 'Holy Matrimony', would be completely disregarded and dismissed.

I began to cry, succumbing to all sorts of dark visions. My mind was spinning with torturous thoughts. When, after a while, the blurry filter of my tears receded, thanks to the pragmatic approach of my husband who immediately started thinking of ways to deal with this, I noticed a sentence at the end of the decision:

> You have 14 calendar days from the date this decision was sent to appeal.

Immigration advice

The following two weeks could easily be considered as the tensest time of my life. I was under enormous pressure to put together a convincing challenge to the decision of the Home Office and send it to them in time.

I went to a firm of solicitors who were offering free immigration advice. To be seen in person regarding an immigration issue, free of charge, was already a little miracle, because soon after the referendum a lot of other advice centres had been either hopelessly overbooked or ceased offering immigration advice completely.

My advisor took plenty of time to go through all my files and gave me lots of useful advice in terms of the most relevant material that I should gather and what periods of time throughout my time in the UK looked most promising in terms of evidence. The lawyer also confirmed my concern that there were no special rights afforded to EU citizens who were married to UK spouses, and marriage to a British citizen would not guarantee an automatic right to residence in the UK, however long it had lasted. We also discussed the meaning of being 'self-sufficient', which was one of the five requirements for being a 'qualified person' in the language of the Immigration Regulations for the EEA. Apparently, even partners fully supported by their British spouses would not be deemed to be 'self-sufficient' unless they had Comprehensive Sickness Insurance (CSI). I was startled by this because, from my Nationality Checking Service interview in 2013, I understood that the insurance requirement only concerned students, not individuals supported by their spouses. I couldn't bear the thought of what this must mean for stay-at-home parents, who had not been informed about this previously. It was hard to accept that parents who chose to care for their children instead of building a career would not have any right to remain in the UK just because they did not have CSI.

I was also very worried that, despite years of work, I could still be considered to be 'an economically inactive EU citizen', because my yearly earnings often didn't reach the required threshold. Or, if they did in the past, I couldn't prove it. I had already paid numerous visits to all the banks I had ever had an account with, asking them for my back-dated statements, but none of them was legally allowed to keep my records for more than seven years.

By this time, I was seriously worried I wouldn't have any convincing reason to challenge the Home Office's decision. The lawyer advised me that, due to my current lack of supporting documents, my only chance for appeal should be based on Article 8 of the European Convention on Human Rights – the right to family and/or private life in the UK. But he also told me to be wary of the fact that, although Human Rights law recognises people's right to a family and private life, it also recognises that the state has the right to exercise immigration control. Article 8 is thus not absolute, and under certain circumstances this right can be lawfully breached – not just if someone is a criminal, but also (even) if one doesn't meet the rules on minimum income.

Once again, I could feel a sting of fear inside me. I knew that, without sufficient evidence that I had been 'exercising Treaty rights for the continuous period of five years', my chance to win the appeal were small, and that the only way to succeed was to gather enough evidence of my status as at least one of the five categories (ie. a worker, jobseeker, self-employed person, self-sufficient person, or a student).

I had less than two weeks to send my appeal, but fortunately I didn't have to send all the supporting documents with it. This was crucial to my potential success, because I had a mammoth task ahead of me in trying to gather enough evidence, and there was no way I could have achieved that in under two weeks.

Preparing for the court

I felt I had the most chance with the category 'worker', so I needed to gather as much related material as I could, with no gaps in any given five-year period, which was tough. As most of the time I was self-employed and had short-term contracts with different companies, there were always some gaps. But there were also periods when several jobs would overlap, and I really needed to find documentation associated with those jobs.

As the banks could not issue me with statements older than seven years, I used the ones I had, which was still a mountain of paper. I spent more than six hours in an internet cafe, copying every multiple-page bank statement, which amounted to several hundreds of pages. And each copy had to be done twice for the purposes of the court. It was the most expensive photocopying session of my life. I would often sit on the floor of our living room till 3 or 4 in the morning, surrounded by piles of paperwork.

But I still needed more evidence from the earlier years to document my past employments. This included a very unpleasant process of getting in touch with people from my past in order to ask them for letters of support, or even just a confirmation that they knew me or that I had worked for them. A particularly painful experience for me was contacting a family that I had worked for as an au pair for several months in 2001, and who I had been deeply fond of. When I emailed the lady, who used to behave very sweetly with me, she wrote back saying she did not remember me. I reminded her about all the things we used to do together, and even emailed her some photographs of the whole family with me. She replied again, this time saying she *vaguely* remembered me, but could not confirm any dates I worked for her and thus could not help me any further. It was a very cold, abrupt email.

I cried with bitter, painful disillusion. It felt as if she had taken a huge eraser and wiped out all my warm memories of the family I had felt a part of.

Doubts

I was going through a low phase psychologically, experiencing a range of emotions like sadness, depression, resentment, anxiety and fear, helplessness, and occasionally even humiliation, which was the worst emotion for me, because it drastically lowered my self-esteem.

Resentment manifested in turning my back on activities connected with British culture that I would previously actively look out for, being so fond of British history and traditions. For instance, I remember that in January 2016 I had booked a number of tickets for the 'Ceremony of the Keys', the gate-locking tradition that takes place at the Tower of London every evening at 10 o'clock since 1340. Because of its popularity, the waiting time often takes more than several months, so our turn was in January 2017, in a year's time. I had been looking forward to it very much and had invited a group of friends to join us well in advance.

But when the eagerly expected day came, something shut down in me and I just couldn't go. Because of all the dramatic events that happened during the previous year, including the letter with the words 'whether and when you are required to leave the United Kingdom', it felt far too painful to attend the ceremony. I didn't want to see the gate locked up, as it would have symbolised what I was so afraid of.

I also felt almost ashamed of my previous enthusiasm about becoming a British citizen and cringed at the memory of how I was romanticising the vision of my citizenship ceremony. I remembered that, in 2013, just before I was told I didn't qualify, I had even found a bagpipe player to play at my ceremony. The memory hurt deeply.

I started doubting myself and negating my nice memories. Everything I had ever done, including being a musician, English teacher and a volunteer in the social care field seemed like a mistake that had actually led me into this situation. I could hear a voice in my head informing me with worrying frequency, 'You have failed to confirm that you are a qualified person as claimed,' and my mind would keep replaying that sentence on a loop, day and night.

My brain was constantly in high gear, thinking over and over again how to obtain all the required evidence, which in my specific case seemed an impossible task. I was just not able to stop thinking about this, even when I was supposed to relax. When we went to a social gathering, I was trying not to bother anyone with my existential problems, but I now found it hard to interact with people spontaneously without telling them what was torturing me. I thought alcohol would numb my pain, but it usually did the opposite, and I would often end up crying in a corner, either alone or with someone willing to listen to my saga. Most of the people I told about my fears reacted with sympathy but usually said that it would be unprecedented and scandalous for the government to try to deport EU citizens and that I would be all right. However much I appreciated their optimism, it did not change the fact that I had to go to court.

I would often look with a sense of defeatism at my 'Life in the UK' test certificate, which I used to be so proud of. Now, it felt as if the 'Life in the UK' test had changed to a 'My Life in the UK' test – a test during which I had to painstakingly inspect 17 years of my life through the lens of immigration rules.

Gathering strength and taking action

I could see clearly that, in my state of omnipresent fear, it would be easy to go down psychologically and physically. I could see that even I, a health-conscious person with an optimistic nature, could become extremely vulnerable and susceptible to depressive states and that I was resorting to alcohol with alarmingly increasing frequency.

Yet I still had enough clarity of mind to realise the importance of being in good enough form to have a successful court hearing, on which relied my whole future. I gradually became able to discern those subconscious, dark whisperings of 'You are not welcome here' as self-sabotaging and harmful and started to watch out for those kinds of destructive thoughts more vigilantly, realising the importance of staying present.

One of the most important sources of moral support and inspiration for taking more action was finding out that an increasing number of Europeans living in the UK were actively fighting for the rights of EU citizens. Monique Hawkins and Professor Emmy van Deurzen were among those who brought me great hope when I read their articles and interviews with them.

Coming out of my isolation was a ground-breaking step. On 13 March 2017, I joined a rally in Parliament Square, named 'Defend EU Migrants' Right to Remain'. It was the first time that I was surrounded by hundreds of people in a similar situation, which for me was far more therapeutic than attending a local council-run drop-in session on emotional control. And the fact I was at the rally as one of their volunteers – a steward – was even more empowering. We were holding placards that read 'People are not bargaining chips' and 'No to May, we are here to stay'. It was truly liberating to see that we were finally beginning to have our voices heard on a large scale.

At the rally, I also met Roger Casale, the founder of New Europeans, a campaigning group promoting unilateral rights for all EU citizens in the UK, which I joined immediately. Two weeks later, I met with New Europeans for the 'Unite for Europe' march in London, and to my pleasant surprise I saw Emmy van Deurzen among them. Roger and Emmy delivered powerful speeches at Parliament Square and I was delighted to be standing with them on the podium, representing hundreds of thousands of EU citizens in the UK who, unable to vote on their own future, had ended up in a state of profound uncertainty.

I attended every march and rally I could after this. One of the most amazing ones was the People's March for Europe in September 2017, which Emmy van Deurzen was leading. To see her followed by tens of thousands of people filled me with hope that the country's fate could turn for the better after all. I still remember one of the banners, referring to the EU referendum result, which read: '17 million out of 65 million is not an "overwhelming majority"'.

Making more connections also helped me find out about more organisations providing free advice on matters relating to EU free movement, rights of residence and citizenship, such as the EU Rights Clinic and the Aire Centre, and other campaigning groups, such as *the3million* led by Nicolas Hatton. I was now able to offer advice to other fellow EU citizens who didn't know where to turn for help. Being surrounded by people who were so passionately involved in protecting the rights of EU citizens and also the right of UK citizens in Europe (such as British in Europe, led by Jane Golding) was so psychologically strengthening that I ceased to see myself as an isolated case or as a victim of a combination of bad luck and my personal wrongdoings.

The need to resort to alcohol every time I felt the grip of fear tightening around me had stopped. I started to recall all the nice things that convinced me I *was* wanted here – for example, the words of one of my Italian students: 'You have made me feel at home, I am no longer scared to speak English.'

I now had much more strength to take further action beyond addressing what I originally saw as just my problem. Once I realised that the insecure residency problem was affecting tens of thousands of people, if not hundreds of thousands, I started a huge email campaign, turning to everyone I knew to sign petitions for securing our rights by, for example, asking for the removal of the need for CSI in order to qualify for permanent residence.

Court hearing

9 March 2018 – the dreaded day of my court hearing had finally come. My state of mind on this big day was in notable contrast to the day of receiving the refusal letter. Now I knew how much incredible work had been done by all the campaigners to safeguard our rights and make the issue known to the public through the media, so I stepped into the day with calmness and confidence, rather than panic and fear. I was determined to win this appeal to stay in the country I considered my home.

I am glad to say I won my hearing, and in October 2018, almost exactly two years after receiving the letter containing the phrase 'whether and when you are supposed to leave the United Kingdom', I received an invitation letter to my Citizenship Ceremony. I had three dates to choose from, and to my amusement one of the dates was 5th November – Guy Fawkes' night. Of course, I chose that one!

It is not easy to keep one's head high after experiencing injustice and discrimination, being disenfranchised in the EU referendum, being treated as a second-class citizen, becoming nothing but negotiating capital in the endless Brexit squabble, in many cases being denied a vote in EU Parliamentary elections and generally living in long-term insecurity and anxiety.

However, I believe that the best way forward is to keep making sure our voices are heard and to hold onto a strong vision that a future based on real democratic values is still possible. My deepest wish is for these years of anguish and uncertainty to soon become just another dark phase in our history, calling us to learn from past mistakes, and to be replaced by times where human rights are of the highest priority and EU citizens in the UK as well as UK citizens in Europe will be able to continue living their lives as before.

Follow-up conversation

A few weeks after I edited Lucie's account of herself and she had approved it, in late 2019, we met to have a long and in-depth conversation about her experience. What follows are my impressions of this occasion, edited by Lucie.

Lucie and I sit in comfortable armchairs in my consulting room, in front of a woodburning stove, which symbolises the need for us to re-create a homely and comfortable feeling after all these years of agony. I remind her of the purpose of our meeting, which is to go more deeply into her experience and see what we might learn from it. She says she often doesn't really want to think about it all, because it was such a terrible experience. She is still trying to understand it better. She will only revisit it because it is such an important issue. She does feel it is all in the past for her now. The bad feelings stopped soon after she got her UK citizenship. She is determined not to plunge back into the fear and doubt she felt all the years before that.

Leftover feelings

Lucie tells me she is still preoccupied a bit by the attitude of some of the people who did not want to support her battle for residency. Her good memories have been soiled, particularly in relation to the families she stayed with as an au pair who had refused her any help or support. It is clear that Lucie finds this hard to come to terms with. She recoils into herself as she tells me how she contacted three people she thought she had been close to but they all let her down. She has been thinking about this so much and has come to the conclusion that she had become a threat to them. Her difficulties alarmed them. She thinks they were scared of the system. They didn't want to be compromised with the Home Office. It is the only explanation that makes sense to her.

These relationships were her first in the UK and had meant a lot to her. Now she has had to conclude that knowing her didn't mean as much to them as she had previously believed. It changed everything; it meant that the affection she had thought they had for her was not actually real. They did not want to stand with her in her plight and they would not fight alongside her.

Her sadness and hurt are tangible. She says it changed her self-image and also her sense of other human beings – that people would let you down like this, when you were most in need. She had found it much less upsetting to deal with the faceless bureaucracy of the Home Office officials who rejected her. She knew they were just doing their job. She had had no illusions about them. And she hated having become this needy person whom nobody wanted to know any longer. This was not her normal way of being. It was humiliating and she felt that this humiliation had been one of the worst states a person could be plunged into. She had previously been told by these people that she was special, or liked, or loved; she had even been told she was a shining light for people. And now she had become a problem to them instead. This affected the way she saw herself a lot. She had felt diminished, tarnished and annihilated by it.

Self-blame

Lucie tells me that the original reason she wanted British citizenship was out of her love for this country, because she felt such a sense of belonging (which came partially from all these people treating her as if she were part of their lives and families). She was so enthusiastic about Britain that she wanted to belong here fully and to be able to vote. It was the last step to becoming fully integrated and it was a huge blow when she wasn't able to achieve this straight away. That first refusal was already hard and changed things. By the time she re-applied in 2016, she was no longer enthusiastic but felt like a supplicant instead.

She looks deeply miserable again, as if the tragedy has become part of her. She knows she has been completely transformed by the experience of going through this existential crisis. It came out in all kinds of unexpected ways. At first, she started losing enthusiasm about the British things she had been involved with. She stopped such activities as volunteering to work for charities. All the things she used to love doing before, enjoying the British way of life, suddenly didn't seem the same anymore. She no longer felt part of that world because she had been denied access to it. She could not pretend to be part of British society anymore because being part of it had made her weaker.

She blamed it on herself initially. She thought she had been too carefree, giving so freely of herself and her time and not thinking about the consequences in the future. She thought it was her fault for having been naïve and gullible, thinking she was part of it all and that she was accepted, liked and loved. Even though she had begun trying to obtain British citizenship long before the referendum, she felt still that she had been lacking in care and had overlooked the things that were necessary to safeguard herself. She had thought herself safe when she clearly wasn't.

I can't help but notice this continued self-blaming, which was such a characteristic aspect of all our clients in the ESSE clinic. I came to think of it as a hidden and twisted attempt at claiming back some control. When we experience something so demeaning, it is better to think we are responsible for what has ruined us than to feel completely at the mercy of outside forces or fate. It makes us feel we would not make the same mistake again and would be safer next time.

Lucie says she is amazed by how much her experiences changed her self-image. Before, she had been confident, optimistic and cheerful. She began to see herself as someone who was in the wrong; someone who was perceived as just bothering other people all the time instead of someone who contributed a lot. She had felt so ashamed. For the first time in her life, she had felt like a nuisance, and she just wanted to disappear. For several months after the refusal letter, she didn't see anyone. She was so scared that she would just keep talking to everyone about her troubles. She couldn't stop herself asking people for help. But it was too upsetting to keep asking for help and being refused, so she avoided people so as not to be tempted to ask. Being with people and asking for help or showing her fear and her terrible plight just made it worse.

Steps towards freedom

Lucie was only able to overcome this lowest time by deciding she had to do it on her own, then applying herself to the task and concentrating on it. She had to put all her effort into planning out how she was going to get her permanent residency and then her UK citizenship. She knew she had to do it and she made herself do it, even when it was hard. Where did the strength come from? It came from the suffering. She told herself this was the way things were and she had to deal with it. The only way was to work hard, stop complaining about it and release the bitterness. She had to let go of her resentment and she had to forgive people.

This idea of forgiveness came naturally to her from her background, and she knew she had to teach herself how to do this. She read a lot of Eckhart Tolle, which helped her ground herself in the present. This was the solution for her: to focus on the present situation as it actually was. She made herself relinquish the regret. But forgiving other people was hard to do. She is still working at that, still doing it, person by person. When she is tired, she gets overcome by involuntary thinking and then she catches herself still feeling that same old pain, at a cellular, unconscious level, about the people who let her down. This is by far the most difficult lesson to learn.

When she catches a thought or a feeling or resentment or disappointment like that, she notes it is happening and then she tries to disidentify from it. She is getting better at this. She knows she is not that bitter, resentful, disappointed person who feels so let down by everyone. She is in touch with the person she really is, and this person is observing these bad thoughts; they are nothing but temporary visitors. She can retrieve herself and her strength in this way. She is learning to be her own coach and getting better at it. This builds her self-esteem back up again as well.

Regaining strength after illness

Lucie has so much more strength now than she did in the worst period. Around the time of the 2016 referendum and the refusal letter, she frequently became ill. Her immune system was compromised and very weakened. She had blocked this out and it only comes back to her because I specifically ask her about her bodily experiences. She realises with a shock that she left this out when she wrote her story. In fact, the physical trauma was the worst part of it. She had frequent chest infections at first, very heavy ones, and she had felt as if she was returning to her childhood asthma. It felt so familiar and made her aware of her fragility. Yet it was different too. As a child, she used to like her illness, because it gave her an opportunity not to go to school and to go to a sanatorium in the mountains instead. They focused on her spine and made her do lots of exercise. She became good at sports. This happened in her puberty and she developed real strength in this way. The weakness was turned into strength by practising.

But in 2016, it didn't feel like that. The illness stopped her earning her living. She lost her willpower completely. She was ill and not working and she was isolating herself from other people. All this, predictably, led to her starting to have panic attacks. Soon after the referendum, even before the refusal letter, her anxiety just kept building up and she couldn't sleep much. She was drinking coffee to keep herself going, which made her more anxious and exacerbated her nervousness. After a while, she became irritable with people too. Her life was now one of chronic, permanent worry; the insecurity was constant.

When I ask her what image came to mind of this period, she describes an image of being thrown off a plane. She felt she was hurtling down a black hole. She was drinking coffee all day and then alcohol at night, to stop the fear and stop the anxiety. She was drinking *becherovka*, a Czech herbal liqueur, which gave her a sense of familiarity and was sugary and comforting, bringing her a sense of warmth and relaxation. Only recently could she let this go and, of course, that improved her confidence in herself straight away.

Her sleeping patterns also went haywire. She used to wake up at 3am with a strong image of being pulled away by the sea into infinity from an island that was being cut in half. She would drift between nightmare and reality and feel a sense of loneliness and despair. She would try to lie still and breathe deeply, as she didn't want to wake up her husband. She was only too acutely aware that he was doing as much as he possibly could. Although he never reproached her, she was afraid that her state of mind and her difficulties would change something in their marriage. She tried very hard to avoid that happening.

All the strength came from her parents' example, she tells me. Her dad had been through something very similar when he had been prevented from doing his job as a priest for 17 years during the Soviet occupation of Czechoslovakia. He had been interrogated regularly by the secret police and she remembered all this very well. Her father tried to protect the family from witnessing this state interference, which included house searches at 5am and having their house watched by the secret police, who were sitting in cars parked outside their front door. She realised fully now why her parents had frequently taken her and her sister to their grandmother's house in the countryside, while they returned to the city to face all that by themselves.

It touches her deeply to understand how they tried to protect her. She admired her father's strength. She was very aware that he never let himself become a victim. When she felt low, it made her feel twice as bad about herself to remember how valiantly her father had coped with an even worse situation. But it also gave her courage to recognise now that her father had also felt bad and had got through it, nevertheless.

Solidarity

The fall of the Iron Curtain in 1989 was such a liberation for them, Lucie says. With Brexit, she had felt she was caught in something similar, but the wall was being built back up again. She could see the similarities: how external forces and politicians make life impossible for people who disagree with them. In her dad's case, it was clearly the fault of the government. In her own case, at first, she felt she had brought it upon herself by moving to a different country. She felt she should have been more careful and that the whole battle was purely about her own survival. But, as she met more people in the same situation, she began to see that this wasn't the case; that she too was in a situation where she had been wronged by a government, and this made it easier to fight it.

She was able to start freeing herself from the inner guilt as soon as she began joining in with these other EU citizens in different organisations, like *the3million* and New Europeans. Rallying with others gave her new hope that something could be done. And she could see that she didn't have to be a victim any longer: she could push back. She shared her problems and saw that it was a universal problem, not just her own. This freed her from the fear of rejection.

She also realised she couldn't trust people anymore; that they would always become indifferent to her if she became a nuisance to them. So, she had to become more independent and stronger in herself, and she did that.

Now she says she is more detached, more self-reliant and tougher. She thinks she has become more realistic about humanity too. She doesn't idealise people anymore. She can see that nobody is perfect, that people have limitations and that they can change their attitude towards you overnight if your situation changes. But that should not taint the good memories of times spent with them. She refuses to be negative. She has been trying to retrieve some of the good things that happened in the past, instead of feeling it was all worthless, as she did when she was at her worst and lowest moments. She won't let her good memories become so crushed that she loses them.

The importance of self-care

Lucie says she has also learned to start looking after herself. She has changed the way she deals with food and drink. She has started learning about her energy flow and how to look after it. She has tried bringing herself into better balance. She has got into new routines, exercising and eating better. She used the tapping method to improve her clarity of thinking, and this really helped her. She realised she had to become more grounded and started walking barefoot on grass whenever she could. She and her husband then decided to move out of central London, where they had lived in the middle of so much smoke and noise. They moved to the Surrey countryside, and this has made a huge difference. She had been yearning for ages to be closer to nature and had been feeling trapped in the city, where she was always on stony ground.

Now it became possible to start paying more attention to her emotions as well, and she started to see she could regulate them. She had become quite extreme in her emotions for a while, and had even started cutting herself. The first time she did it in anger, when she was denied her rights. But then she began to do it every time she felt rejected; even small things could trigger it after a while, like missing a bus or arriving late for a course. She was far too stressed and could not cope with any more bad news. She would sit in her kitchen, on her own, and take a knife and cut herself in order to feel the physical pain releasing the emotional pain. It was a way to make her plight and her suffering real to herself. It was something tangible. But sometimes she became far too angry with herself and even aggressive. She knew this wasn't right. She is much kinder with herself since she has started working with her body and looking after herself. Forgiving other people also meant she had to forgive herself for her breakdown.

The anger was the worst thing. It had seemed alien to her at first, as it wasn't at all like her. She learned to see that she was self-sabotaging and, by reading self-help books, she was able to teach herself how to stop this. She started by accepting her extreme states of mind and then began to be able to regulate them. It then became possible to join in with others again, once she had stopped condemning herself for feeling so extreme. And once she forgave herself and started regulating her emotions, she regained her self-respect.

The learning from her experience

I ask what Lucie would say to other people in a similar predicament. She says, 'Take your pain seriously. You have to find your own way of getting back in touch with yourself. Nobody else can do it for you.' You might try meditating, or simply breathing deeply, grounding yourself in the moment, pulling back from all the stress and letting go. She says, with a big smile on her face, 'It is vital to find calm and peace in yourself again.' We agree she can now do this.

One of the things that helped her in doing so was to go out into nature and reconnect with the roots of her existence, walking in woods and on grass, not allowing virtual reality to take over and not getting overwhelmed by her online existence all the time. She has learnt that trees and fields will look after you if you go to them. 'Also,' she says, 'you need to pay attention to your food and drink. You must learn to eat and drink things that build you up instead of things that will only just break you down.'

She says she discovered how important it is not to isolate yourself, not to retreat and become a hermit, absorbed by your own grief. You need that input and connection with other people. But she has also learnt that some people are toxic, while others are genuinely caring and understanding. You need to find them.

'Most of all,' Lucie says, 'you have to keep believing that it is possible to change your situation and to see a result of the project you devote yourself to in order to get out of your difficult situation. If you can imagine that and work patiently towards it, then everything will start to improve.'

Lucie also tells me how much it mattered that she felt loved by her husband throughout her trials and tribulations. She discovered that it mattered greatly to be true to that love and to keep trusting the other person and keep talking. But, she says, don't expect a particular reaction from them; don't set standards they cannot meet; be content with the love that's there, instead of wanting it to be different. She learnt how vital it was to have the love of the people around her, or just to know that they were there and willing to listen. That was a true blessing – one she learnt to appreciate, preserve and take care of.

She was also now beginning to feel that it was possible to listen to other people's distress as well and contribute something to help them. She could see how important it was to do something positive and to make a contribution. She had even begun to realise that it was important to make her peace with people who voted to leave the EU. She was beginning to see that they just had a different worldview; for them, the EU was an enemy and an empire that was dangerous to them. They had been fed this dream of British independence. She could see that some of them regarded the EU as she used to see the Soviet Union – a large power that had taken over their country. But they had so many wrong ideas about immigration and the objectives of the EU; she wished she could help them see it wasn't like this and that it wasn't true. She feels more patient with them about this now. We don't have to be so divided or fight each other, she says; we have to mend those divides.

She has learnt to see that every person deserves to be taken as they are. She is more modest in her expectations of others now and knows she is much stronger than she had thought. She has a much clearer idea about politics too, and realises you can never take anything for granted; anything can happen to alter the situation at any time. You should never rest on your laurels because everything could be put into question and you could be left with nothing.

On the bright side, her difficult times have taught her to appreciate the good times, especially the times of peace, and she has learnt to make the most of those, instead of just taking them for granted. It is still a bit too painful to keep up with politics. She can stand a bit of it, but not for too long; she makes herself do it in order not to fall back into an isolated or naïve perspective. She feels a strange emptiness inside when she reads too much about the political process, because it all feels so wrong. It continues to upset her that bad people took control of a country she loves so much and that they were able to do so much harm to so many people.

She feels grave concern for other people who haven't yet been able to sort out their own situation. She wonders whether she could be a coach to others, although she knows she is quite susceptible to emotions and that it is important to be vigilant and keep her life in balance. She has gained a sense of collective responsibility for the consciousness around her. She senses that her emotions and those of other people are connected and, while politicians may have been able to harm her, she will now take responsibility for affecting others positively whenever she can.

It is clearly a very genuine, hard-learned lesson that she will remember for the rest of her life. She feels she is stronger for having survived this tough and hellish experience, but she is very glad she has been able to move beyond it.

The Covid-19 pandemic

When we met, we were just entering the Covid-19 pandemic. I asked Lucie how she was coping, and she told me this:

For the past few weeks of the current crisis, I have felt remarkably calm, present and grounded. I think that the unpleasant events of 2016, governed by my deep existential uncertainty, have provided me with a sort of emotional vaccination. I have learned not to take anything for granted, especially when it comes to man-made structures, both material and abstract. I am aware of the fragility of the human body and I have accepted the fact that, sooner or later, I will lose a number of people I love. I savour every moment spent with my husband. The awareness of impermanence is with me every day. I feel deep gratitude for my life, and if I was destined to die tomorrow, I would consider the 42 years of my life complete and utterly meaningful.

I feel this way especially because of the amount and many forms of love I have experienced throughout my life. I believe that every instance of suffering in my past has contributed to my current sense of inner peace. At times of sadness or upset, I find that, unlike in the past, I don't tend to blame external circumstances for my momentary unhappiness, but instead try to go deeper inside myself to become more centred again. I am blessed to know of specific tools for maintaining my physical and emotional health, like the basics of energy medicine (working with meridians, chakras, the aura and other energetic systems), emotional freedom techniques (EFT, also known as tapping), meditation, and the teachings of Eckhart Tolle. I have gained all this knowledge thanks to my own personal crisis caused by the events of 2016, so I can say that the Brexit saga has actually helped me cope with the current situation by forcing me to become more emotionally resilient and prompting me to set myself on the path of personal and spiritual growth.

There is so much learning in both Joan's and Lucie's stories. In the next chapters I will draw on some theory about crisis and resilience to see whether these lessons can be applied more generally.

5

Making sense of life and loss

As we have seen in the previous two chapters, one of the crucial tasks of overcoming crisis is to make sense of the challenge it poses for us. As long as the situation looks overwhelming and does not connect with our usual framework of reference, we cannot move on, or even begin to tackle it. One thing that has made it possible for me to face crises, not just in my own life but also with my clients, is that I learnt early on to allow myself to feel deeply into the experience, instead of denying, avoiding or diminishing it. To feel deeply into the experience is to welcome it into your life and find a place for it. It is to own it and make it your business to make sense of it. It is to allow yourself to soak it up, trusting that you will find a way to accommodate it, and this in turn leads to the start of the easing of your anxiety. Instead of fighting against your misfortune, you embrace it and ask yourself what you need in order for you to take in and absorb the situation. We learn to feel our anxiety as a necessary rise of energy required to deal with the difficulties, and we welcome that energy instead of trying to squash it. We go towards the greatest point of pain, instead of running away from it. The pain is the path towards meaning-making.

We have already seen how both Joan and Lucie had to experiment with different coping strategies before they found a way to live with their challenges and this new burst of anxious energy. Eventually each of them had to accept that the situation was really dire and difficult and that it was up to them, and nobody else, to accommodate that hardship somehow. Only then could they allow themselves to feel the extent of their upset and sadness and give in to their need for a period of grief and despondency – a time when they could regroup and lick their wounds. In the peace of that sadness, they began to create effective coping strategies.

Facing the situation

It is all too easy to shy away from really feeling what it means to face catastrophe. It is always tempting to try to erase it from our consciousness in an attempt to deny what is happening. Escapism and sticking your head in the sand can work for a short period, but we can only overcome difficult situations if we are willing to acknowledge and process their full and awful reality. In order to survive and thrive, we have to allow ourselves to be fully present in the experience so that we can oversee the situation and gain mastery over it. Only if we come to terms with it, explore it and understand it will we be able to handle it effectively, learn from it and eventually find a way to go beyond it and transcend it.

Initially, it is often a good thing to safeguard ourselves by putting up protections, defences and shields to keep the very knowledge of what is happening out of our perception. Before long, however, we find that such barriers between ourselves and the experience only postpone and therefore often worsen the impact. The less effective we are in dealing with it, the more damage it can do to us. We saw this very clearly in Joan's situation, when he was initially trying to tough it out and not give in to his sense that things were overwhelming and calamitous. It was only when he allowed himself to fall apart that he could take proper time out to feel into his experience and realise what he needed to do about it. We cannot battle with an enemy we are not getting the measure of. We cannot absorb new information until we are willing to let it into our consciousness (Tedeschi et al., 2018; van der Veer, 1998; Vos, 2017).

The same was true with Lucie, who initially tried to cope with her situation by appealing to friends and past employers. Only when she began to discover that this was counterproductive, because people did not want to know about her difficulties, did she give up trying to find others to rescue her and staunchly faced her shattering experience by herself. Of course, both Joan and Lucie had the support of partners and friends, and they also had the mental capacity to work out patiently what would be best for them, instead of falling apart in a blind panic. Nevertheless, both went through a cataclysmic moment of despair, when they had to give up and give in temporarily. This opened the door to the full realisation of the situation they found themselves in.

Sooner or later, we have to respond vigorously to our misfortune. Viktor Frankl (1978, 1984, 1986) pointed out that this was the moment of truth. Before we are able to stand strong in our moment of truth, we often feel we want to give up, but we then fall headlong into hell, overwhelmed by the enormity of our plight. It is at that moment, when we are willing to take charge of our position and assume it as our own, that we begin to rise again. We stop trying to pretend all will be well and we accept that things will never be the same again and that a major intervention is required on our part. We face the fate that has befallen us, and we begin to wonder what is required of us in order to deal with it. This is when we take responsibility for what will happen next. This is when we own our fate and take charge of our destiny.

This doesn't mean that we accept that the situation is our fault. The situation may have been caused by the state, by people close to us, by strangers, by circumstances, or we may have caused it ourselves. The cause stops mattering when we accept that the situation is what it is and that it is entirely up to us to tackle our predicament, to turn things around or find a way out. Frankl spoke about life's challenges and misfortunes as questions that life is posing us. If we deflect the questions or avoid searching for answers, then we are not rising to our crisis; instead, we are denying our reality and plunging ourselves more deeply into hopelessness and helplessness. It is only when we slow down and allow the pain and truth of our situation to fully unfold in front of us and inside us that we are touched by reality and get this sudden shock of the full horror, which leads to an automatic influx of anxiety and, thus, energy. This is what drives our quest for resolution of the problem we have been confronted with. This is when we begin to experiment with our own capacity for courage in formulating new actions, new attitudes and new responses.

From reactivity to activity

As long as we allow ourselves to act blindly, trying to remain in denial or handling things with a sense of wishful thinking or temporary dampening of bad feelings, we remain simply reactive. This means that we respond in a shallow, immediate and often emotional and impulsive fashion. This is an instinctive response, which is based on habits and reflexes. It usually means we regress towards a lesser or lower level of operating than we are capable of. Frequently, it means that we grab someone's hand, or want to strike someone, as we try to stem the tide of despair by silencing the voices of reality. We may be angry or annoyed or upset, but we are unlikely to use the best of ourselves, because we do not make sense of our emotions yet. We are not fully functional when we feel out of our depth. We are more like the toddler, rebelling. We feel the world and our fate are unfair. We want to throw ourselves on the floor and kick and scream, or hide under a table or chair.

Of course, we are right about that: the situation is maddening, and we feel out of our depth. Nevertheless, the task in facing crisis is to become calm and capable again, enough to be able to retrieve our full presence in ourselves. It is there that we can access the quiet, calm and mature thought and introspection with which we will formulate a sound and creative plan. In effect, we have to learn to facilitate and mediate our own revolution in our inner world as we adapt to the changes on the outside.

Reactivity and reflex actions should never be questioned in the midst of acute and active physical danger, however. Our bodies are wiser than us on those occasions. They know the right way to react when we are under immediate threat. When we are in an accident or are suddenly under attack, our bodies become protective and react with a shot of adrenaline, which lessens pain, fires our muscles for action and starts the programme of necessary repairs immediately, without us having to think about it in any way.

It also means that we have the option to fight, flee or freeze. My coma, following my childhood accident, was a good example of freezing and fleeing. My body just put all my conscious actions on hold. I no longer carried any responsibility, temporarily, while my body protected me, truly marvellously, and let other people take over. I remember a couple of other times in my life when I was under physical or emotional attack and I had to either suddenly fight back without a thought or flee rapidly. I remember a time when I was standing outside a shop on Kilburn High Street in London and saw the reflection in the shop window of two men coming up behind me, reaching for my handbag. I didn't think about it for even a fraction of a second; I just swivelled around with my fist flying. As it happened, I hit one of my attackers rather hard on the chin, with such impact that my hand was badly bruised afterwards. They shouted something nasty at me but fled, cursing me, as other people came to my rescue.

I was so completely nonplussed about the incident that I didn't even report it. People asked me if I was okay, if I wanted the police, and I waved them away, but half a minute later I realised my legs were numb and I could hardly walk because paralysis had taken hold of my body. It still amazes me that the body is that clever and has this self-protective reflex of going into shock. Sometimes it's a bit counterproductive: if I'm a passenger in a car and the driver is not totally careful, I immediately feel that shot of adrenaline coursing through my arteries and, afterwards, a little bit of the paralysis even, before my body is able to absorb the surplus and redress the balance. When I am the driver, this does not happen. Bodies and brains are astute, and it is important to stay in harmony with them. Trusting that organic response is almost always a good thing. It makes us combative, fearful or phlegmatic in our response, depending on the situation we find ourselves in. Each of these can be excellent strategies in the emergency of the moment.

But if we stick with these responses beyond the initial threat, they lead to us becoming compulsively volatile and reactive. For those who stick with the fight impulse, this will manifest as them coming across as temperamental or even aggressive; those who stick with the flight impulse will become irritable, frustrated and avoidant; those who stick with the freeze response will become passive and inactive, listless and impassive. After a while, most of us begin to realise that we can do better than that. We realise that we can approach any situation in a much more active, interactive, flexible, engaged and considered fashion. We can learn to be observant and reflective, making sense of all the information we can gather. We can teach ourselves not to be quite so immediate and intense in our reactions, but to interpose some thoughtful understanding, mediating our response and adapting to what is most effective. 'Pause to look and listen carefully to what is happening' is a good mantra to help us achieve that.

Problem-solving

This is really about learning to trust the human capacity for solving problems, using a whole range of resources and personal ingenuity to find creative solutions. It is exhilarating to discover that we are much more resourceful than we initially thought we were. We find that we are capable of engaging our whole self and our entire brain in dealing with threatening and difficult situations. We remember we are in charge and can cope with whatever is thrown at us. We saw how Joan and Lucie did it. It took them some time, but both of them, eventually, looked deep within themselves and found new resources to use to get through their crisis. They rediscovered that they were filled with human ingenuity and imagination and could avail themselves not just of everything they had learnt in the past but also of what other people could contribute to their capacity to rise again.

As we begin to re-engage our curiosity, we find a new perspective on the situation, observing what is really going on and where, and how we have come to be in this predicament. We re-engage our discerning mind instead of allowing ourselves to feel crushed and victimised. Switching off, as we have seen over and over again, is a good first response, but it will not do in the long run: we must stand strong and face up to and elucidate what is going on. This is exactly what I had to learn to do on that hospital bed, on my own: to give up panicking or feeling upset and forlorn, drowning in sorrow about my losses. After the first few days of miserable withdrawal, I had to start scrutinising my environment and the different opportunities it presented to me. Similarly, Joan had to give up for a bit and allow himself to fully understand the fix he found himself in; then he could figure out what methods would best help him look after himself more carefully. Lucie had to give in to her despair momentarily before reconnecting with the world and focusing on the task ahead to gather her strength, do battle with the Home Office and win.

The same was true for me when I was first faced with the rejection of my own UK citizenship application. I had to let myself drop into dejection and self-protection for a few days before I could begin to figure out what was truly happening. When you find yourself in a fix and are slithering down that slippery slope of crisis and catastrophe, you have to allow yourself to hit the rock bottom of your life in order to find solid ground. Sometimes you have to just stay in that low, helpless place for a few days, or even a few weeks, to recuperate. Then you can build from there, not just learning to withstand the strong emotions with equanimity but also cobbling together the resilience and endurance to climb back up the hillside of life and not stay dumped in the gutter.

We cannot afford to stay at the bottom of that deep well of despair. We owe it to ourselves to rebuild our stamina and start the climb, slowly but surely, step by step, until we find a solution to our problems. At first this will seem impossible, but I have watched people gain incredible momentum by working through the worst of human experiences, and I have seen them becoming formidable and brave in that process.

Learning to see in the dark

When you are going through your tragedy, you will, inevitably, have dark nights of the soul where you will feel all alone and forlorn, forsaken by the rest of humanity. Whether you are by yourself or with others will make very little difference. It is in those dark nights that your courage will start to grow. Plants need to be buried deep in the ground in order to start creating new shoots, pushing towards the light. Courage is a fabulous strength that grows at night, as you allow yourself to hold strong and persist with your deepest doubts and torments. Crisis happens, despite our best efforts to avoid it. When it does strike, it's a fact of life and has become inevitable. When you have been there once and have learnt to scramble back up that slope of life without giving in or going under, you will recognise that same experience the next time. And, if you have dealt with it, you will also notice that your crisis has toughened you up and provided you with new stamina for the next one. It is rather like running: you learn that you have to hit the wall of your exhaustion in order to get your second wind.

However much trouble fate throws at you, you have to remember that, unless you are prepared to take it on the chin, nothing will settle or get any better. You have to be able to stand in the breach of your own pain and problems. It is never helpful in the long run to attribute blame or shame to other people, or even to yourself, in such a situation. Others may have caused your troubles, but this is now the situation you are in. It will almost always feel unfair and wrong and undeserved, but that doesn't exempt you from still having to step up to the plate and find an affirmative way to respond. Your reaction to the fix you are in will define what will happen to you and how you will emerge from this phase in your life. Stop doing special pleading. Nobody is going to let you off the hook.

If you are largely responsible for the crisis yourself (as was the case with my accident), it is an important step forward to forgive yourself so that you can stop paralysing yourself with regrets and recriminations – although, of course, you have to learn the lessons (I had to learn that being a bit of a dreamer is not compatible with road safety on a bicycle).

The same is true when other people are at fault. It is better to deal with the situation first and sort out attributions of guilt later. What you have to do is to focus on the mess you are in and clear it up as best you can. This is well summarised by the old saying, 'There is no point crying over spilt milk.' You have to mop up the spillage and either get some more milk or make do with water. There will be time later to figure out how the milk was spilled and draw conclusions. And yes, it is better to forgive than to remain in resentment. Don't sit around waiting for the people who hurt you to show contrition and remorse. Avoid them, if you can, until they are willing to work things out with you, but don't expect them to make everything right. They never do, as they will have a different perspective and point of view. The most important thing is that you learn what life is teaching you and get better at protecting yourself next time. You can only do this if you are honest with yourself and are willing to look at the situation with clarity.

One of the best things about learning such lessons is that you may feel more compassion for others in future and you may want to help them when they find themselves in similar predicaments. What matters in the first instance, however, is for you to find your backbone, your second wind, your reserve energy. This is a good opportunity to build character and expand your capacity for responding with calm and determination in difficult situations. When the worst happens and your life is in question in so many ways, the best way forward is to match your strength to the situation and let yourself be stretched. You will discover that there is a vigour at your core that will build itself up and become greater. You will find that you can gain the kind of stamina and confidence that you would never have thought possible. Instead of giving up, you will learn to find ways of sorting things out. Instead of expecting immediate results, you will discover that it is a long-term process and that you will need to be patient and enterprising and willing to learn by trial and error. You will also discover that joining with others who are in a similar situation can be reassuring and helpful. Mutual support and inspiration are necessary for success.

When I lay supine and docile on my hospital bed at the age of 10, and when I found myself in a new country with no real credentials, connections or fluency in the new language, I soon figured out that it was my responsibility to find the capacity to meet the challenges. When I lost my company, my college, my networks, income and colleagues, the only response that would both get me through the immediate catastrophe without going under and allow me to re-establish myself, survive and eventually thrive was to recreate a new company and a new college, building new networks that were even better than the ones I had lost. But I could never have done it without the many kind and supportive people around me. Knowing there is fairness and goodness in the world, despite the nastiness that brings one down, is particularly crucial.

This was hugely important for the five million disenfranchised EU citizens in the UK, as Lucie's experience demonstrates. She was shamed by her feelings of betrayal when those she called on for help refused her; what strengthened her was joining forces with others in the same plight and fighting for justice. It was similarly important in the Covid-19 pandemic: many people stepped forward to support others in their community; many went the extra mile to improve the wellbeing of the communities it was their job to serve. We must remember that it is often in times of trouble that we discover and appreciate this human capacity for generosity, survival, cooperation and ingenuity. Crisis takes us beyond the normal and therefore can bring out the worst and the best in human beings (de Wind, 1947/2020; Eger, 2017; Frank, 2007; Frankl, 2019; Woodhouse, 2009). We have to learn to ensure that it is the latter.

What to do in a crisis?

As I have shown in previous chapters, doing practical things like making your physical situation more tolerable and bearable is always the first step after encountering a situation that undermines personal safety or may be life-threatening. Creating a sanctuary in the chaos should always be a priority, because once we feel we have a safe haven, we can cope much better with hardship. We need to have somewhere to retreat to, where we can lick and heal our wounds. We need to feel that essential sense of trust and protection and have sufficient medical care, food and drink and pain relief to relax and be able to rest. We also need a clean, warm and pleasant environment to be able to find solace and start healing. We can establish relative safety in even the worst conditions. Mandela described this very well in his autobiography *The Long Walk to Freedom*, about his many years of incarceration (Mandela, 1995). Eddy de Wind, whose book about surviving in Auschwitz (de Wind, 1947/2020), is perhaps the most sober of reflections on this topic, wrote:

> In concentration camps people experience many happy hours every day. The lights are turned off for them, the electric current is shut down and the wire is cut. The soul can free itself from the exhausted and tormented body. (de Wind, 1947/2020, p.28)

Looking after our body is always first and foremost, and sleep is crucial. Getting the necessary human support and establishing alliances is the next step in dealing with disaster. Rebuilding damaged networks and knowing we are not isolated in our plight are also urgent. After that, it becomes a matter of patient and diligent progress, working things out and solving difficulties one by one, until a better future can be imagined and crafted. For this we need to use our creativity and find inspiration, as well as learn new skills and hone existing ones. If people are not available to teach you, you can turn to books and other sources of information. Finding out new things about your predicament and learning from other people's experiences are the means to your salvation. Hiding away is only the fallback position and should never be pursued as the overall single strategy. Much as we crave safety and need to cocoon and cradle ourselves for a bit occasionally, we also need to apply ourselves to improving the world and fixing the problems, be they practical, relational, personal or ideological. Once we have learnt to help ourselves and can start helping others in similar situations, we are definitely on the road to mastering the human condition, rising to our challenges and building our courage.

Courage is energy

I had to learn all these lessons, over and over again, the hard way, and I continue to do so, especially after periods of relative ease and happiness. Good times can make us complacent and self-indulgent. They weaken our alertness to danger. In the process of moving forward in life, I have learnt more from the troublesome catastrophes and crises than I have in times of relative ease and comfort, although the latter have been havens of peace and welcome periods to take stock and relish the sheer enjoyment of being temporarily off the hook. When things went pear-shaped, I was always keen to seek cover and hide for a while, to have a good cry over the inevitable losses. Then the time would come to clear out the dross and clean and dress my wounds.

I am good at rolling up in a ball and hugging my agony closely, weeping or sleeping until I am ready to think a bit more bravely about my situation. I learnt over the years that others react differently. I have never used medication, alcohol or food to get through difficulties, as my stomach knots up and rejects interference of all sorts. I turn to self-deprivation and stoical endurance and find solace in taking time to restore my inner composure. I have observed that those who do turn to alcohol, food or drugs are often more able to cope initially but less able to cope in the longer term. Crying and sleeping bring you to a natural ending: you exhaust yourself with the crying and you wake up refreshed after sleeping. Comfort eating and drinking or taking drugs can easily become addictive and escalate into not really dealing with the issues.

I still find temporary sanctuary in films and books; it is a way to reconnect with a different narrative. But there is an art to escapology: you have to choose carefully what you watch and read, lest it throw you into further chaos instead of providing order and safety. I know it is crucial for me to start talking to people as soon as possible, not to get succour and compassion or have a shoulder to cry on but in order to start formulating the troubles that are so deeply affecting me. It is important to have a sounding board and a witness to your misery. Affection from someone who understands and loves me is by far the most healing thing; it helps me find the pluck to get going and start working on solutions once the initial shock has subsided. I need to see the best of myself reflected in loving eyes, so I can make that side of myself prosper. Then I need to be in solitude for a while, as I formulate and sketch a plan for repair and renewal.

I know how important it is to take time for a little self-indulgence in this process. When hardships happen, we do not just need to seek out the kindness of our loved ones, but also the kindness of strangers. What is most needed is a feeling of goodness and generosity, so if it is not on offer to us, we must create it. Doing something helpful to another person can really get you back into the right frame of mind to want to sort things out for yourself again. Never get mean with yourself; never get nasty or self-damning; always stay gentle. Take it easy, step by step. Take yourself by the hand and go more slowly than you think is expected of you. Take your time. Do things carefully, in the right way. Find your own pace. Healing is a slow process. Stick with it and be patient, consistent and diligent.

I learnt the hard way that courage is not the same as long-suffering martyrdom and is also a far cry from recklessness. Courage is not the opposite of cowardice. Existential courage is the capacity to stand strong when you are frightened and confronted with a threat to your safety, or a true disaster (Tillich, 1952). To be brave is to act with valour and resoluteness when in a tight spot. It is to build fortitude, not to pretend you have already got it. You learn to endure and find your stamina. You find new ways of survival that help you go beyond the obstacles as well as beyond your previous capacity.

So many of us are inclined to seek ways to renege on our responsibility to life when things get difficult. We are all like this, initially, as our instinct is to run. It is a good instinct, as long as it helps us find safety. But it becomes damaging when we seek to make things easy instead of making them right again. If we apply ourselves to staying alert in the situation and finding new paths towards the improvement we are craving, then we will build grit and we will become resilient. If we notice that we are distracting ourselves, taking it easy and just seeking to soothe the pain by pleasure-seeking or numbing ourselves, then the time has come to find our nerve again and call ourselves to attention.

Curiosity and investigation

I have found that a good way forward is to follow my curiosity about what has gone wrong, exploring every aspect of the situation. It is best not to be in a rush with this. We need to give ourselves proper time to re-orientate. When you can do this, you will find that the crisis becomes a moment for reflection that exposes what was wrong with your life previously and gives you a chance to make a new start (remember again the meaning of that Chinese word for crisis – *weiji* – danger *and* turning point). This is exactly what I was talking about in previous chapters: the misfortune of my accident became the catalyst for my greater understanding of what had gone wrong with my life in a way that I would never have been able to formulate had the accident not happened. Crisis gives you perspective. Once you have confronted a death threat and have faced it down, life will never be the same again (Schneider, 1999; Solomon et al., 2015; van Deurzen, 2015a).

Similarly, Joan and Lucie came out of their predicaments renewed in strength and with a much better understanding of some of their previous errors. This is the bonus of going through crisis: when everything is shattered, you can reorganise your life and start afresh. Many people who are crushed by fate later realise that they were blind to their own narrow-mindedness. It is actually very hard to review your situation without a catastrophic *force majeure*. As long as we live in a self-protective manner, maintaining our usual routines, hoping that difficulties can be averted, we are not in the mood for big reviews of our *modus vivendi*. As soon as something goes really haywire, it becomes possible to consider looking at things differently, because we have to. When the disaster has fractured your world, there is no alternative: you must use your imagination to try to make sense of your new situation. When we do so, we stand a chance of creating something of value not just from what remains but from whatever else is also available to us. We often gain more than we have lost.

Resources

Most people who have been through existential crisis have built up a store of wisdom. Many of us have learnt to turn to literature as well as to the many accounts of human knowledge and wisdom that can be found in psychology, philosophy, education and religion. These external sources will significantly complement our own experience and expand our horizons. I read so many books throughout my adolescence in an attempt to make sense of what was happening to me. I read books on philosophy, psychology, anthropology, politics and sociology, voraciously seeking to throw light on a situation that had been revealed to me when my life was in the balance. It helped guide me in new directions and set me on a lifelong journey of discovery of what I was capable of and what human existence was made of.

I always sought out books that I felt personally connected with, be they non-fiction or fiction, and I took it all very much to heart. Rather than distracting myself with my reading, I always felt as if I was greedily adding to my supply of inner strength and understanding. Every novel that I valued became part of my life, not just a story. I ate and drank in the stories and absorbed what was good in them, making them an integral part of my existence. They were like portholes to the outside world. Good authors became like favourite friends. But I also came to realise that not all stories can be trusted. Some novels are toxic and undermine our inner strength and trust in the world, whereas others are nutritious and build our intimate understanding of ourselves and our power. My task was to find those I could make friends with and that I could trust to give me guidance.

There were also some authors that I was initially scared of because they broke all the rules. Some of these turned out to be misleading, but others were just perfect in times of hardship. Ironically, it was the existential novels that initially upset and disturbed me as a teenager, especially the novels by the French existentialists – Sartre, de Beauvoir and Camus. Novels by Tolstoy and Dostoevsky seemed more substantial and they spurred me on to seek to understand the unfairness of society better as they drew me into a completely different experience of the world. American authors like Hemingway, Faulkner and Steinbeck made me feel small and weak but also woke me to the challenges that lay ahead for me, as they also gave me a taste for adventure.

I rarely felt again as deeply touched by a novel that spoke about my own troubles as I had been by the Kästner book. The novel *Rosie's Eyes* (*De Ogen van Roosje*) by Dutch writer Clare Lennart (1957) was one of these touchpoints, because it captured my struggles with my sibling to perfection. The novels *Waiting for the Sun* (*Wachten op de Zon*) (1963) and *Leaping into the Net* (*De Sprong in het Net*) (1965), by Dutch author Steven Membrecht, were startlingly spot-on in their descriptions of my own loneliness and despair. When I started reading Shakespeare and Dickens in English class, Verlaine and Stendhal in French, Goethe and Hesse in German, Cicero, Tacitus and Virgil in Latin, and Homer, Herodotus and Plato in Greek, I became quite dizzy with the pain and beauty of the world. But it also gave me perspective and a sense of historicity. It was no longer just about me and my life, but about the whole of humanity. I relished the images of mythology and religion that captured the human struggle.

For me, these were always embedded in art, with which I was deeply familiar from a very young age, because I had been taken to museums all around Europe by my parents (my father was for many years the director of the antiques auction house in The Hague). I had absorbed images that were also reflected in the best novels, poetry and movies. There was also a strong resonance with music, because my parents had always played piano, violin and mandolin when I was a small child and I had been an enthusiastic singer in my folk music school and had learned the recorder and music composition too. I taught myself to play the guitar and sing my own songs as a teenager. In the 2020/21 Covid-19 lockdowns, I finally taught myself to play the piano.

The process of making the arts my own and daring to write my own stories, paint my own pictures and create my own songs, melodies and poems were what gave me a sense of the creative source of life within. It was about playful discovery, never about proving I was an expert. I was interested in other things like history, geography, politics and biology as well and was in many ways fascinated by the regularity of maths, algebra, physics and chemistry, but I never felt as called or deeply moved by those disciplines as I did by the human arts and sciences. I did have a huge thirst for knowledge and understanding, but I needed creativity more, in order to create a framework of meaning in my life. I learnt that I preferred to work things out on my own and this definitely built my strength and confidence in myself, but I also learnt that I needed others. There is no doubt that this was a direct consequence of having to cope with my solitary existential crisis in hospital, which showed both the need to be able to withstand isolation and my need for other people. I can see the same process all around me: people who go through existential crises go through a period of self-isolation but learn to turn to creativity and community, communication and collaboration to regain their sense of safety. Such times are often the nodal points of our transformations. We need to learn to appreciate them at their true value. We can all see how some of the most moving stories in literature are narratives about such experiences.

Literary heroes' journeys

Shakespeare's Hamlet or King Lear, Hesse's Steppenwolf or Sophocles' (and Anouilh's) Antigone are all struggling to make sense of a senseless society in which they face overwhelming turmoil on their own. Their cathartic transformation is always a search for the hidden depth of morality in an attempt to find or found a new world in which meaningful acts can redeem us. Life can sometimes be very much like Greek tragedy or a Shakespeare play. We can either try to deny this or grab a firm hold of the challenges and contradictions we face. Persistence and tenacity are important qualities when we deal with obstinate troubles. This is all the more important as, in some cases, surmounting a crisis can take a lifetime. That extraordinary book *The Lord of the Rings* (Tolkien, 1968/2005), with its multiple challenges and never-ending fights and adventures, illustrates particularly well this need for unending stamina and perseverance in dealing with adversity. It was my favourite book around the time I left the Netherlands to live and study in France. Such epic stories are heroes' journeys. They include Homer's *Odyssey* and *The Epic of Gilgamesh*. They teach us about living and dying and show that existential courage is the only true remedy for human tragedy.

There are many such classics, but also newer, cinematic ones, like *Lawrence of Arabia*, *Gone with the Wind*, *Dr Zhivago* and *Star Wars*. Each provides great insight into the way human beings meet adversity. As in Tolstoy's *War and Peace*, crises are shown to come in cumulative and repetitive sequences. These wide-ranging sagas, where there seems to be no end to people's suffering and adversity, teach us about the importance of resilience and stamina. Sometimes the focus is more on specific personalities, illustrating the flaws but also the strengths and possibilities of human character, as in Dostoevsky's *The Idiot*, Tolstoy's *Anna Karenina*, Balzac's *Father Goriot*, Dickens' *David Copperfield* and Eliot's *Middlemarch*.

Such stories are always set within their own social and political background, and the interaction between the characters and their cultural problems gives them particular poignancy. This is how it feels with existential crisis too. When we begin to face up to the pickle we are in, we begin to set our life in its historical perspective, and we gain depth and breadth not only in our own character but also in our awareness of the human foibles of our era. We are aware that what happens to us is often determined more by the times we live in than by us. Most of the classics find a way to intersperse political and personal events in equal measure. In all of them, human beings are dealing with fatal existential crises that are usually not purely of their own making, and they all portray aspects of the human struggle that each of us is bound to encounter, both in our inner world and in the world around us. Those characters that accept the heroic nature of their plight generally do well. Those who remain lost in egocentric resentment tend to go under.

One of my favourite examples in contemporary literature is *Watership Down* (Adams, 1972/2018), with its vivid and apt descriptions of the trials and tribulations of a rabbit warren on the move. If ever there was a story showing the pain of forced migration, this is it. It describes the journey of life both as an admirable adventure that teaches the highest values and as a continuous challenge to show our pluck, loyalty, curiosity, persistence, love and solidarity. Another example in this genre, teaching us about stamina and resilience in the face of adversity, is Pagnol's wonderful two-part saga *Jean de Florette &* *Manon of the Springs* (1988), which focuses sharply on human tragedy and our difficulties in overcoming adversity in order to redress injustice. It was made into a memorable and mind-blowing two-part movie by Claude Berri, which has been watched gratefully by many a person going through crisis.

Such books and films have often given me succour and relief when I have been alone in my plight, and I know that, when clients are going through troubles, they often seek a narrative that can inspire them. Initially, people tend to find it impossible to take time to read or think. But once they are determined to slow down and begin to confront their situation, they find it helpful to have such a map to orientate themselves. I have written about these aspects of life elsewhere and won't go into the details here (van Deurzen 2009, 2010, 2012, 2015a); suffice to say that it is vital to start seeing ourselves objectively, instead of drowning in subjectivity and suffering. When we begin to crave inspiration, we are ready to stop our desperation and aspire to climbing to a higher place, from where we may find perspective and a sense of direction. This is precisely why reading about other people's battles can be so helpful. As soon as we can see the drama of life as an epic experience, instead of as our personal tragedy, we can also begin to start looking after others. Armed with the bigger map of human existence, we will be better able to find a way through our own trials and tribulations by reconnecting again.

6

Existential explorations

This is what existential therapy is about: enabling people to explore their lives and the crises they have been through in order to learn the lessons and understand human existence better. As they face their plight, they learn how to live their lives with more freedom and with an open mind. Existential explorations in therapy draw on all the resources we have discussed already: philosophy, psychology, psychotherapy, literature and personal experience (van Deurzen, 2010; van Deurzen & Adams, 2016; van Deurzen & Arnold-Baker, 2005, 2018; van Deurzen & Kenward, 2005; van Deurzen et al., 2019). I will explain briefly how this framework can help us make sense of the world when we are under duress and in critical circumstances.

One of the basic starting points is the observation that life is a play of paradoxes and tensions that underpin all human existence (van Deurzen, 2015a). We are constantly being pushed and pulled by polar opposites. During relatively good times, we do not allow ourselves to be aware of this struggle as we try to stay on the sunny side of the street. We are inclined to deny that we will all suffer pain and losses and that we all must die (Barrett, 1962/1990; Barnett, 2009; Becker, 2011; Jaspers, 1951, 1969). It is important that we can take life for granted during good times, at least to some extent, and this is how we learn not to notice the dangers and risks that we run on a daily basis. We simply cannot afford to be too aware, lest we end up living in fear all the time. I discovered this after my accident, when I could see every danger all too clearly and acutely and had to unlearn this acute sensitivity in order to lean back into the natural (although often erroneous) assumption of safety.

Life becomes too much of an effort when we are constantly conscious of all the things that can go wrong. It becomes joyless and frightening. It's a strange balance we have to strike: to be vigilant and on the lookout for danger, yet at the same time take safety and wellbeing for granted so we can enjoy the good things while we have them. We need to be prepared for all eventualities and not put our heads in the sand, but we also have to be able to forget our worries and concerns and live in the moment, at least occasionally. Knowing how to strike the balance is one of the secrets of good living (van Deurzen, 2015a). It means living with the lessons of the past, being in the present and preparing for the future, all at the same time. We exhaust ourselves if we are on the alert continuously, but it is not right to force ourselves to chase happiness either (van Deurzen, 2009). It is a very counterproductive reality of our consumerist societies that we are made to feel that we should aspire to having it all and should constantly show off our blissful good fortune, displaying a bright smile and denying and hiding the darker aspects of our lives. Our first confrontation with death and loss is usually a very important moment that changes our perception of the world and makes us more aware of the fragility of life, starting our journey into realism and suppleness.

Children often get too little guidance with this and are sometimes reproached for showing their upset when they need support to absorb their worries and disappointments. Aged five, I saw my classmate knocked down by a car. I was totally thrown when I saw her lying in the gutter, but I never really got a chance to tell anyone about it. Nobody asked me how I felt about it or enquired into what precisely I had seen. I remember feeling guilty for having witnessed this near-death event, and I knew that the grown-ups wanted to believe I had not really seen anything much or had not taken it in. That was far from the truth. It is true that I found it hard to make sense of what I saw, though, and initially thought it was a doll that had been torn apart and was lying in the street. But this led to me seeing my own body as a fragile thing that could be broken, like that of a doll. I lost my innocent pleasure in simply being alive. It would have been better if I had been able to talk about this to an adult who wasn't anxious to stop me crying.

Having survived my own accident at 10, I found myself thinking a lot about my friend's near-death experience and also about my parents' traumatic experiences in the war. It was as if my reservoir of traumatic and fatal challenges had been opened wide and I had to deal with all those memories at once. I had to become brave and strong, but I acquired as well a sense both of my own fragility and of the temporal nature of life. In doing so, I ultimately gained a deep confidence in the human capacity for survival, healing and surpassing and I also became sensitive to the reality of wounding and scarring. That capacity to see the many sides of the human condition is the foundation of existential thinking.

Existential ideas

Existential ideas are ideas about human existence that are derived from centuries of careful thinking about the human struggle. There is a long line of philosophers on all continents who have described the human predicament. Wherever culture has thrived, people have tried to make sense of all the tumultuous and messy experiences that human beings can and will encounter. Existential authors have, over the centuries and in these different cultures, thought and written about exactly the same kinds of problems. They have had different views and solutions in relation to the human confrontation with disaster and the loss of certainty. Nevertheless, all these descriptions of the human condition have a lot in common, as they are all based on the same raw realities.

Existential authors like Plato, Aristotle, Zeno, Pascal, Spinoza, Heidegger, Kierkegaard, Nietzsche, Sartre, Camus and de Beauvoir have much in common with Buddhist, Taoist, Confucian, Hindu, Islamic and, indeed, Christian religious writers on life. They have each tried to put their finger on the things that really matter to humankind. They have sought to gather and transmit wisdom about physical, social, mental and spiritual survival.

Existential philosophy is the theory that underpins existential therapy. This kind of therapy deals with difficulties at the real-world level and aims to understand the plight people are in, in terms of their situation and circumstances. It doesn't look at problems as generated in people's minds or due to their childhood experiences; it looks at them in the round, considering what the person is making of the problems they have encountered so far. The objective is always to help them re-establish their own balance, their personal perspective, their understanding and their creativity. It is about rendering freedom to a person where this has been lost. It is also about enabling a person to see their plight in relation to their social, political and cultural background. It means to see a person as a historical character, struggling with complex circumstances and the other people around them. It is always about learning to rediscover our own talents, capacities, habits, skills, values and potential.

Ultimately, existential therapy seeks to help a person find meaning and purpose in life in order to be able to create a dynamic, confident and enjoyable movement towards a spirited, inspirational and productive future. While it will look at a person's internal, intimate relationship with themselves, it won't reduce them to intrapsychic structures or relational realities. Existential theories are theories that enable us to recognise that human beings have to deal with many predictable and also unpredictable problems, situations and issues that do not necessarily stem from their own genetic disposition or their childhood experiences; they are simply part and parcel of being a person (Adams, 2018; van Deurzen, 2015a; van Deurzen & Adams, 2016).

Existential ideas can be found in the writings of human beings across history and all around the world, because these are the ideas human beings generate about their actual day-to-day existence (Boss, 1979; Frankl, 1985; May et al., 1958; van Deurzen & Arnold-Baker, 2018; van Deurzen & Kenward, 2005; Yalom, 1980). As soon as we start living our life, we are immediately engaged in making sense of that life. We will also, inevitably, be confronted with situations that floor us. People make sense of their troubles in lots of different ways, depending on the culture they are part of, but there are some universal aspects of life that are predictable and ontologically unavoidable and inexorable (Brown, 2017; Heidegger, 1927/1962, 1961, 1969; Hoffman et al., 2009; Sartre, 1943/1956, 1960/1982).

People can make sense of their lives through many media: by drawing pictures, telling stories about their experiences, and by creating habits and customs that establish predictable patterns of relating and communicating to each other in certain ways (de Board, 2014; Denham, 2008; van Deurzen & Iacovou, 2013). They also try to make sense of the wider parameters of their world experience by establishing belief systems and religions that make them feel hopeful and protected. Storytelling is an important part of working out what went wrong and how we can make things go more right for ourselves and others. Religions always tell stories about the start and end of the world. They have a myth of creation and genesis; a cosmology (a view of how everything that exists fits together); an ontology (a theory of being and where human beings fit into everything); an ethical system (a prescribed way for people to act and abstain from certain acts and actions), and an eschatology (a theory of how things will end and what happens after death). These stories are about revelation, rather than fact-finding, and they provide people with a mythology that regulates their lives. They are always dogmatic – that is, prescriptive in terms of how people should think and act – and they set out a wide range of punishments for those who disobey.

When people find themselves in crisis, they have a need to make sense of their lives and they begin to think about such matters. Existential work will enable them to do so without imposing a particular orientation, belief system, dogma or direction of travel. It is never prescriptive and does not dictate any view; instead, it encourages people to make their own observations about their lives and draw their own conclusions. If people value their religious views because they make sense to them, then these views will be respected. If they wish to challenge their beliefs, they can do so. We follow the existential structures of life that are a given for everyone. This is what the existential philosophers wrote so much about: the invisible structures that underpin human society and human existence. There is a wide variety of ideas among them. Some base their thinking in spiritual notions and may even posit the existence of a god (Jaspers, 1969; Kierkegaard, 1940, 1954, 1980, 2000; Marcel, 1965, 2001; Tillich, 1951–63, 1954); others are firmly atheistic (Nietzsche, 1883–85/1997, 1886/2010, 1889/2012; Sartre, 1938/1962, 1939/1962, 1943/1956, 1952/1963, 1960/1982).

Charles Taylor's views (2018a, 2018b) on the relationship between secular and religious societies are very interesting in this respect, as his writing shows that people need to have a spiritual allegiance to be able to feel authentic. This has been borne out by the experiences of many of my clients who greatly value their belief systems, even though they may no longer actively practise their religions. It is hard for human beings to take full responsibility for everything, and many find it a consolation to turn to a supportive god or higher principle to give them trust in life and in themselves when they are in a dire situation (van Deurzen, 2009, 2010, 2015a). Religions remain attractive to many people because they provide coherent structures of meaning and storytelling in times of trouble, when their own existence is under fire and at risk of crumbling completely.

Religions are also good at providing physical and social support and can provide a supportive community for their adherents. We should never underestimate how much this means to people in times of trouble. Having an ultimate source of succour is a very hard thing to abandon. Existential therapist Irvin Yalom speaks about this in terms of people hanging onto the idea of an ultimate rescuer (Yalom, 1980, 1989, 1992, 1996, 2001) in order to give themselves peace of mind. Yalom thought that this was an obvious denial of a person's personal responsibility for their lives. I am not so sure of this, having seen how many are helped to get through crises by their religious allegiances and communities.

Although religions help people, especially in terms of their commitment to daily rituals and religious practice, which provide calm and structure in times of trouble (Peterson & Seligman, 2004), they can also become the source of new problems. If the religious system becomes too fixed and prescriptive, it can lead to self-recrimination and obsessive behaviour. The religion may provide a framework by which people explain to themselves and each other what is happening to them, but it can also harm and hamper their freedom to understand fully what is being asked of them personally. The problem with religious explanations and theories is that they invariably become static, as the ideas become doctrinaire and frozen in time. Any system that becomes closed to fresh ideas and questioning and claims (divine) authority, instead of moving forward through open inquiry, research, questioning and investigation, will ultimately create stasis. Usually, religions claim this very place of stagnation and inertia as further proof of their divinity, which they define as fixed and eternal. By contrast, existential thinking is highly variable, flexible and changing. It has no set rules that must be obeyed and feared. Some people practise their religions in an existential manner.

Facts and fictions

It is evident to most people that the scientific developments of the past few centuries have in some ways taken humanity beyond the stories of religions. Physical sciences have corrected some of the cosmic theories and myths of genesis, for instance. They have shown not only that some religious beliefs are demonstrably false but that some of them are based in fear and fantasy. However, scientific theories of reality are never sufficient in themselves to guide people. Science is an ongoing search for knowledge, but it is not a moral support system. Science constantly moves from one set of findings to the next and this can be confusing to some people. Science is specific and mundane and cannot provide the universal and eternal stability or support that people need when they are going through crisis.

The other way in which scientific theory will never close the gap with religion is that it does not deal with the depth of human feelings, relationships and emotional experiences. It does not reach people's need for meaning, value and purpose. Scientific theories are always focused and narrow and do not provide a wider framework to make sense of our personal quandaries. The search for a theory of everything in science will not solve that problem either, for it will not address the longings of the human heart. The songs, the stories, the meetings, the meditations, the images and rituals that make religion attractive to people are in a different domain altogether. Science doesn't even come close to binding people together through art and imagination. When visionary scientists provide theories of everything, they practise existential philosophy, not science. David Bohm is a good example of this search for existential wisdom based in science, when he reminds us: 'Ultimately, we are intertwined with the cosmic order: the implicate order of the universe' (Bohm, 1980/2002).

To deal with existential issues, we need to cut a path that steers clear of the Scylla of science and the Charybidis of religion. It is a hard path to find and there are remarkably few people who do so. Bernardo Kastrup's rational spirituality (Kastrup, 2009), Mary Midgley's writing on myths (Midgley, 2004) and Thomas Nagel's thoughtful explorations in *Mind and Cosmos* (Nagel, 2012) are honourable exceptions. Michel Henry's work is invaluable in helping us think about all this in detail (Henry, 1993, 2008, 2012; Davidson & Seyler, 2019).

Existential philosophy is a branch of philosophy that is not highly valued in academic circles because it is so concrete and pragmatic. It is seen as lacking in scientific rigour and philosophical method and clarity. But that is precisely its value. It takes account of many different possible descriptions of reality and is not beholden to any authority in exploring meanings and experiences that make human life valuable. Diversity and rigour of investigation in this area of human ideology are every bit as important as they are rare.

Turning to psychology

Psychology also has a lot to offer in dealing with existential crisis. The psychology of religion, for instance, is a separate branch that carefully studies the impact of belief systems on human beings. Positive psychology is a relatively recent addition to the study of what makes human beings most able to find happiness and wellbeing (Linley & Joseph, 2004; Peterson & Seligman, 2004; Peterson et al., 1995; Snyder & Lopez, 2005). It has shown, for instance, how people's values and beliefs both help and hinder them in finding a sense of wellbeing (Heim et al., 2019) across cultures when they are in difficulties.

Cross-cultural psychology is also a rich resource because it explores many different systems of thought. The recent movement of indigenous psychology, which places value on the importance of the different ideologies and value systems found in different regions of the world, rather than measuring each by the standards of the West (Sundararajan, 2014; Wong, 2012; Wong & Wong, 2006) is particularly noteworthy. These are all new theories of meaning-making and they help us to understand much better what happens when meanings are interrupted or fractured. What the discipline of existential phenomenology has to offer is a more intimate and deeply experienced exploration of such human realities (Moran, 2000; Stolorow, 2015, 2016; van Deurzen, 2014, 2015b; Wertz, 2016).

My own contributions in the fields of philosophy, psychology and psychotherapy have often been focused on creating meaningful narratives and actions in dealing with the challenges of life (van Deurzen 2009, 2015a). A world-wide movement of existential therapy has been generated over the past decades, allowing for a lot of interesting cross-fertilisation (Cooper, 2015, 2017; Hoffman et al., 2009, 2020; van Deurzen & Arnold-Baker, 2018; van Deurzen et al., 2019). This is always focused directly on people's actual experiences in the real world, rather than on theorising or controlled experimentation. It exposes the limitations and possibilities of the human condition. It is non-prescriptive and open-minded and favours diversity instead of seeking to press people into a particular mould of being.

This approach, particularly when connected with psychotherapy, is based in phenomenology (Husserl, 1927/1971, 1983; Moran, 2000), and therefore has a solid methodology to rest on. The method of existential therapy that this book is based on has developed slowly and gradually over a century and has been shown to be effective in many situations, especially those involving life crises, trauma, change and transformation (Cooper, 2008; Norcross, 1987; Vos, 2019; Vos et al., 2015).

One of the characteristics of this approach is that it is based in meaning and sees the loss of meaning as an important factor in therapy (van Deurzen et al., 2019; Frankl, 1978, 1984). This is very well captured by Frankl's existential work, which was a direct consequence of his experience of internment in several concentration camps during the Second World War. He observed the way in which he and his inmates lost their sense of meaning and purpose and how they could regain this, even if initially it was only about avoiding dying and having some soup to look forward to in the evening. His books were also an attempt to fill the vacuum of meaning that he observed occurring in post-war society (Frankl, 1978, 1984, 1985), and this same objective was also to be found in American humanist approaches in the 1960s and 1970s. These include the work of Erich Fromm (1941/2001, 1956/1995, 1993) and Abraham Maslow (1970, 1973), and also particularly that of Rollo May (1967, 1969a, 1969b, 1977, 1983, 1999).

The approach was initially laid out most carefully and fully by May and his colleagues in the classic book *Existence* (May et al., 1958), which introduced the work of continental existential philosophers and therapists to an American audience, showing how it could be applied to psychotherapy directly (May & Yalom, 2013). Out of these early seedlings has grown a large forest of existential applications that has turned into a worldwide movement that is now ready to tackle the problems generated by today's global moral crisis. Let me share with you some of the maps of life that can help us navigate around the obstacles we bump into when our life hits disaster.

Life maps

As I have said, people are as much shaped by their society and culture as by their biology, family and early experiences. We are in many ways defined by the connections we have created between ourselves and the world. Some of these connections are foisted upon us; others may be chosen or gradually formed through small changes we make in our lives. As we have seen above, in existential crisis, some, or most of these connections are severed. It is important to understand the landscape of our connections so that we can think about how to repair them when they are damaged.

In existential therapy, we work with the circles of power and influence that surround the individual and that determine the space in which they can move around freely. We soon discover the many ways in which people can be held in place by these structures and how they derive their identity from them. But their connections can also become tight and suffocating and can deprive them of the oxygen to breathe or the room to move in.

Figure 6.1: Circles of power and influence

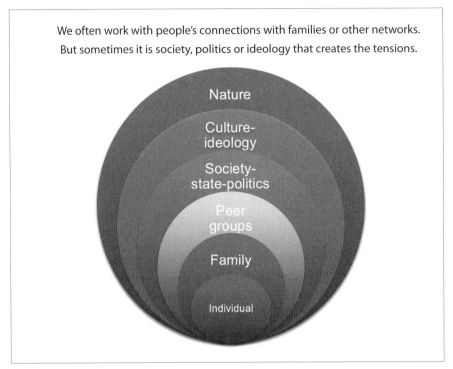

We often work with people's connections with families or other networks. But sometimes it is society, politics or ideology that creates the tensions.

© Emmy van Deurzen, 2021

Figure 6.1 shows some of the many ways in which the individual is inserted within the circles of influence that surround us. We are part of our family, our peer groups and the society and state we live in, and we are also held in place by our culture and the natural environment around us. In existential therapy, we often work with people's connections with families or other networks. But sometimes it is society, politics and ideology that create the tensions. So, these too have to be scrutinised. In the case of the Covid-19 pandemic, it is the natural world that challenges us, at least in the first instance.

None of us is a blank slate. We are intertwined with the world in myriad ways from the moment of our conception. If we have many connections, we may be better able to tackle our existential crises. The worse the crisis, the greater the number of connections that are severed. It makes it easier to understand the intricacies of our personal response to crisis if we look at ourselves as living on a number of different dimensions. It is simpler to reduce these to the four dimensions of experience that most people recognise: the physical, the social, the personal and the spiritual.

These are often associated with the German words for these different worlds (van Deurzen, 2010, 2012):

- *Umwelt* – the physical world, including our body and our environment
- *Mitwelt* – the world of our relationships
- *Eigenwelt* – our personal world
- *Uberwelt* – the world above the everyday that determines what matters to us.

On each dimension, we are confronted with polar opposites and contradictions. It is as if we move through a force field where we are attracted by positives and repelled by negatives, although we have to learn to work with both. Let's take a look at these dimensions of existence and their polarities, paradoxes and dilemmas.

1. **At the physical level** – we connect to nature, to our own body, to the things in the world and to the cosmos. The opposing forces are those of life and death, health and illness, pleasure and pain, and harmony and chaos. The more we feel able to enjoy our body, the more confident we are in our sense of mastery and do not feel burdened by the threats of death, illness, pain, poverty or other forms of bodily diminishment. The Covid-19 pandemic made many of us aware of how dependent we are on there being a state of harmony, not just in our own bodies but in the physical world.

2. **At the social level** – we connect to other people around us and to the private and public worlds of our human relationships, through the ego that we create in order to relate to others. The opposing forces are those of love and hate, dominance and submission, acceptance and rejection, belonging and isolation. The more confident we grow in relation to other people, the less we fear that they will reject, exclude, despise or dominate us. In the Covid-19 pandemic we became aware of how interwoven we are with other people and how much we miss these connections when we have to self-isolate for any length of time.

3. **At the personal level** – we become aware of our inner world by self-reflection, through which we learn to recognise and develop a sense of self and identity and relate to our own most private feelings, ideas and often secret and hidden objectives. The opposing forces are about identity and freedom, perfection and imperfection, integrity and disintegration, confidence and confusion. As long as we feel sure enough about who we are and can stick with a basic level of confidence and integrity, we feel on pretty safe ground. When we have our freedom taken away from us in some way (as, for example, in the lockdowns to control the spread of the Covid-19 pandemic), we will need to find a new inner balance.

4. **At the spiritual level** – we relate to the ideas that influence us and help us understand the world around us. This is the meta-level that ties things together for us and provides us with meanings, purpose, objectives, values, beliefs and standards. The opposing forces are about good and evil, truth and untruth, meaning and futility, right and wrong. We often take our worldview and values for granted, but in an existential crisis they get challenged, as they may no longer work so well. In the Covid-19 pandemic, many people began to worry about the lack of ethics and truth in the world and began to realise that these things matter more than we sometimes think.

These layers of human experience are not lined up symmetrically on top of each other; rather, they are intertwined and interrelated, and in many ways are more like aspects of our experience that interact and are interspersed together. Table 6.1 provides a map for our experiences, our conflicts and challenges that can help us orientate ourselves.

Table 6.1: Overview of conflicts, challenges and paradoxes on four dimensions

World	Umwelt	Mitwelt	Eigenwelt	Uberwelt
Physical	Nature: Life/ Death	Things: Pleasure/ Pain	Body: Health/ Illness	Cosmos: Harmony/ Chaos
Social	Society: Love/ Hate	Others: Dominance/ Submission	Ego: Acceptance/ Rejection	Culture: Belonging/ Isolation
Personal	Person: Identity/ Freedom	Me: Perfection/ Imperfection	Self: Integrity/ Disintegration	Consciousness: Confidence/ Confusion
Spiritual	Infinite: Good/ Evil	Ideas: Truth/ Untruth	Spirit: Meaning/ Futility	Conscience: Right/ Wrong

© Emmy van Deurzen, 2019

Reclaiming meaning

In an existential crisis, we can be sure that many of these aspects of our lives are affected. The more of them are involved, the harder it will be for us to resolve our crisis, but, ironically, the more opportunities we will have to make essential changes in our lives. Joan and Lucie both felt insecure physically, because their very right to stay in their home was at stake. This affected their sleep and this in turn affected their physical health by making them weaker and more vulnerable. This then made them both keen to find physical safety, and they sought it in things that were familiar and comforting, such as food and drink. Socially, they both felt alienated by the politics of the country and the oppression they were exposed to. It made them mistrust other people in a way that was very undermining to their sense of belonging and acceptance. Personally, they each went through a process of doubting their own responses and self-questioning, and in some instances they turned to self-destructive narratives and habits, such as Lucie's self-harm and Joan's caffeine intake.

Beyond this, both were deeply troubled by their loss of faith in a world they had believed in and for which they had made significant personal sacrifices. For both of them, this was about an open, free and democratic UK in an open, free and democratic Europe. For Joan, it was also about the NHS and its multicultural and social ideals. For Lucie, it was about doing voluntary work and being part of a collaborative and creative society. Losing their connection to such values and principles was really difficult. It made them question the meaning of many things they had previously taken for granted.

We can see how they desperately wanted safety but had to learn to handle the unsafety of their situation; how they badly wanted acknowledgement of their belonging and acceptance but had to harden themselves against a sense of rejection and isolation instead. They wanted to hold onto their personal integrity but felt themselves disintegrating in the face of so much difficulty. They were troubled by the untruths people were being told and sought to transcend this by establishing right and wrong in a new way. They were at risk of losing their sense of meaning but both found ways to make their struggle matter and thus establish new, deeper meanings in the process. In doing so, they retrieved safety and integrity as well.

They both ended up feeling stronger for having overcome their difficulties. The more we tackle our challenges, the better we become at living. The more we are engaged with the world, instead of trying to avoid it, the better our interconnections become. The more we are connected, the better we feel and the more meaningful and fuller our life seems. When we become disconnected, our life flounders and we feel empty and forlorn, literally as if we have lost the source of the energy that fuels us and makes us feel vital. Some people find it hard to trust the world enough to connect to it. This is for various reasons, including biology, character, upbringing, traumatic past experiences and dislike of closeness. Although they may be content to remain fairly isolated, it will still not make them feel as if they are on top of their game. We all need a minimal set of connections to feel as if we are worthy and fully functional.

In his book *Meanings of Life* (1991), Roy Baumeister summarises how we can best create meaning in our existence. Below, I show how the four levels of meaning that he pinpoints are situated in the four worlds.

For human beings to feel a deep sense of meaning in life, they have a basic need for four different things:

1. **Efficacy** (physical) – this is the need to feel we are skilled and well-adjusted to the physical world in a way that allows us to take joy in our body's dexterity as it accomplishes all sorts of things, learns new things and creates and produces new things while enjoying the physical world.

2. **Value** (social) – this is the need to feel of value to other people, the sense that we are contributing something to society and are therefore of use and helpful to the community.

3. **Self-worth** (personal) – this is the need to be at ease with oneself and have an inner sense of respect, appreciation and compassion with ourselves that makes us feel like we are a good person.

4. **Purpose** (spiritual) – this is the need to know that we have a plan and a direction, which will enable us to affirm our values and therefore our own value more. Doing so gives us a global sense that life is meaningful and that we can increase its meaning.

It is the process of going in the general direction of these four objectives that makes for a good life in which we feel connected up with the things that matter in the world (Baumeister, 1991; van Deurzen, 2009). This is nothing to do with being happy or having a good and easy time. On the contrary, it is about leading a good life and being dedicated and engaged with the world. In existential crisis, we are temporarily prevented from doing so. Some people's lives become like a chronic crisis, because they are unable to re-establish a basic equilibrium, often because of external circumstances. We have to ask ourselves how a society allows for people to become so isolated and disconnected that this happens to them.

The role of society

Sartre, in his foreword to Franz Fanon's book *The Wretched of the Earth* (Fanon, 1963), wrote:

> When one day our humankind becomes full-grown, it will not define
> itself as the sum total of the whole world's inhabitants, but as the infinite
> unity of their mutual needs. (Sartre, 1963, p.27)

But this is precisely what people are not capable of doing yet; right now, in the world as we see it evolving, there is such competition of needs and aspirations that there is hardly any room for people to create an infinite unity of their mutual needs. More often than not, we are fighting to prioritise our own needs over those of others. Competition invariably outstrips co-operation.

Fanon himself argued that people live in a culture of dominance and submission, where those who dominate try to keep the upper hand and those who are dominated dream of that same kind of possession. He speaks of colonialism, but the same ideas apply just as much to the conundrum of those who migrate for other reasons:

> The zone where the natives live is not complementary to the zone
> inhabited by the settlers. The two zones are opposed, but not in the
> service of a higher unity. Obedient to the rules of pure Aristotelian logic,
> they both follow the principle of reciprocal exclusivity. No conciliation is
> possible, for of the two terms, one is superfluous. (Fanon, 1963, p.38)

This kind of low-grade warfare is very much part of all our human relationships: to survive in the world, we do not just have to learn to keep ourselves physically safe and sound, sheltered, fed and watered; we also need to learn to stand our ground, protecting ourselves from being pushed around and dominated by others.

In his book *Anti-Semite and Jew* (1948), Sartre elaborated on this theme, describing the way in which people establish themselves as superior to those who are newcomers, immigrants or foreigners in order to take them down to a lower level and stop them being a threat. He described how limited our freedom always is and how easily we come to fear that others will put further limits to it:

> Then it is easy to see that the exercise of freedom may be considered as
> authentic or inauthentic according to the choices made in the situation.
> Authenticity, it is almost needless to say, consists in having a true and
> lucid consciousness of the situation, in assuming the responsibilities and
> risks that it involves, in accepting it in pride or humiliation, sometimes in
> horror and hate. (Sartre, 1948, p.90)

At the end of his book, speaking more concretely about the way in which Jewish people have been oppressed and destroyed by Aryans, he comes to the conclusion that:

> What must be done is to point out to each one that the fate of the Jews is
> his fate. Not one Frenchman will be free so long as the Jews do not enjoy

the fullness of their rights. Not one Frenchman will be secure so long as a single Jew – in France or in the world at large – can fear for his life. (p.153)

It is not possible to exempt oneself. The fate of all human beings is directly related to our own fate, because we are a unity. If we keep oppressing others, we are, in a sense, oppressing ourselves. We create the kind of tyrannical world that we will encounter ourselves and that sooner or later will betray us. It is a terrible truth that many people fail to grasp. They act as if they can rise above others and put them down in order to be safer themselves. But the opposite is true: as soon as we create a two-tier world in which we seek to dominate, we become immediately caught up in the fear that we will be dominated by others, lose our advantage and be put down and suffer in turn.

This makes for a very adversarial and hostile way of living. It is the kind of world that we often encounter when we migrate from one country to another (Hoffman, 2011; Huston, 2002). Making ourselves the new kid on the block, the person who is both no longer and not yet in a position to feel truly at home and at ease, means we offer ourselves up for ransom (Handlin, 1973). We will be held hostage by the culture we join, because we will never enter it on a par with those who are established in it. We are very much the underdog in any new country or culture we join. It is a humbling experience that eventually may become a source of great frustration, as we feel homeless and lost for a while (Hayes, 2007; Madison, 2009). Of course, this also generates a sense of authentic living, in that we learn to face life without protection, simply seeking to survive. We learn to adapt to diversity (Lago & Charura, 2021) and to become intercultural and cosmopolitan (Kim, 1988, 2001, 2005; Nussbaum, 1994).

Bi-rootedness

Nancy Hakim Dowek, a colleague at the New School of Psychotherapy and Counselling, did her doctoral research on the experience of migration. She focused on people who have voluntarily moved to a new country and who have thus become 'bi-rooted': that is, they have their roots in two countries. There are also people who have roots in more than two countries and these she calls 'poly-rooted'. It is a good way of thinking about the problems faced by immigrants. I consider myself to be poly-rooted – or poly-radical. When I left the Netherlands, I had to grow a new rhizome to put down a second set of roots in France. Then, when I migrated to the UK, instead of pulling up those double roots, I shot down another, deeper root in my new home country. When I moved to Yorkshire, after living in London for 20 years, in some ways all those roots became loosened. I had long thought of myself as having air roots, allowing me to travel and easily adapt to new environments, and often reminded clients who were in a similar situation that having air roots gives one mobility and adaptability.

Having lived in different cultures and being able to speak more than one language certainly helps to make one versatile and more tolerant. What I had not fully appreciated, though, is that many of us came to identify not as poly-radical but as Europeans. Our European citizenship was the common denominator that made sense of our diversity, and it mattered a great deal, and all the more as it brought with it many rights and privileges. The European Union's principle of free movement between member states had been the key to our identity and our lives. It had defined us. To be so free and mobile made it very easy to live a poly-radical existence. We felt like world citizens, and it was only when the UK government began treating us like 'citizens of nowhere' that we woke up with a shock to the realisation that having air roots was far from safe.

Hakim Dowek's research (2019; 2020) illustrates very well why this might be, as it concerns people who, like her, created multiple (poly-) root systems. She was born in one country in the Middle East, grew up in a different Middle Eastern country, and thus speaks two languages. As an adult, she settled in London, where she made her home, speaking English, while married to a Belgian husband. Her research aimed at making sense of this bi-rooted or poly-rooted existential identity through interviews with people in similar situations.

She observes that:

> Relocating to a new country is a complicated psychological process with considerable effects on personal identity. It may start with a sense of loss (Akhtar, 1999; Grinberg & Grinberg, 1989) or a sense of liberation (Madison, 2009) but usually evolves into a much more complex position. (Hakim Dowek, 2019, p.9)

All her participants had relocated to the UK from non-English-speaking countries, either inside or outside Europe, and the themes that emerged from the interviews were very pertinent to this book. She found that roots become seen by those who migrate as relative to where they currently are. People become more adaptable. On the one hand, this leads to a certain kind of existential fragility and a sense of being different, but, on the other, it leads to a feeling of flexibility.

The people she spoke with expressed a strong experience of ambiguity, as they were no longer defined solely and solidly by their social environment.

This is very similar to what we see happening in anyone who goes through an existential crisis. They become less attached to their previous situation and more able to adapt to new situations, but also less secure and less confident about their identity. Having multiple homes forces us to open ourselves to multiple values. Having more than one language adds further to that sense of diversity of perspective. People who have been exposed to the realignment and relocation of migration often get a better overview of themselves and humanity. Seeing yourself and others adjusting in different ways to new circumstances is an eye-opener. Migrants learn to be more modest and less bold in defining themselves.

Hakim Dowek found that such intimate changes can lead to a sense of brittleness. People in this situation need to learn to accept a new feeling of fragility and vulnerability, as they are having to start from scratch and make significant efforts to resettle themselves. This is typical of the post-existential crisis experience as well. Perhaps we can say that, in a sense, an existential crisis is a move from one home to another. When crisis destroys our usual habits and bearings, it is as if we lose our home. When everything is in flux and we have to start from the beginning again, we at first feel diminished and inclined to regress to a previous phase of life. When security is in question, it brings anxiety and challenges. The person going through this situation is immediately inclined to try to fit in and to be more submissive and humbler than they might otherwise have been.

It is notable that people who migrate often carry unnecessary but acute guilt about their situation. If we have chosen to migrate, we can't blame circumstances. But we may feel deeply bereft, lost and guilty about leaving families behind, or about not fitting in well enough with the people around us. It is as if we are aware that we have brought these changes upon ourselves and must accept what comes with them. When we are cut off from our past in our former country and are thrown into a raw, new present that is uncertain, we have to take stock of who we are and what we bring into the new situation: we become more self-conscious about any lack we display or experience, be it linguistically, culturally, personally or socially. It can be excruciating and humiliating. We become less confident, but this also means we have to learn to be less set in our ways and more flexible in terms of how we adapt to the people around us and more aware that the future is always uncertain. Being aware of multiple possibilities leads to much insecurity and anxiety. Some migrants experience this as a loss akin to death, and they have to find a way of burying the past and grieving for it before they can find any comfort in the present or begin to create a new future.

Hakim Dowek found in her research that deep roots can only be shot down into the earth if we remain where we were born. When we move about a lot and migrate, we can only ever manage to shoot down shallow roots. Not only are we therefore not so attached to things and people in our lives; we also need to find a way to connect in a more relative and malleable manner. We become more acutely aware of connectivity and we make emotional roots or pragmatic roots where cultural and linguistic roots are failing us. We might in fact become rooted in the very idea of our freedom. We may learn to prefer the feeling of following our own choices and responsibilities over the sense that we are being guided by others or dictated to by our environment. Nevertheless, most migrants are aware of the loss of the sense of belonging and certainty.

Hakim Dowek puts it like this:

> Living in the space held between two emotional and physical 'homes' and constantly moving from one to the other, as testified by the participants, combined with the lack of a support system in the country of residence, resulted amongst other things in a sense of exposure. A sense of precariousness is described as part of the experience to differing degrees; there is a sense of instability and uncertainty expressed through feelings of being exposed and living with a sense of personal vulnerability. (2019, p.239)

Her research showed that what made the difference between people who ended up feeling homesick, torn and forlorn on the one hand and people who were successfully bi- or poly-rooted and dynamic on the other was the extent to which they could find a sense of fluidity of self that could adapt and change according to new circumstances. In this respect, what the person who lives between two or more countries has to learn is something that we all have to learn in life:

> It is not about demarcating oneself in opposition to the 'Other' as much as consciously moving toward oneself and so becoming closer to a real Self; reaching a better grasp of how there is an ever-changing sense of self. An authentic experience of the fluid Self can be achieved only through that understanding. (Hakim Dowek, 2019, p.238)

One of her key findings was that these bi- or poly-rooted people had to learn to live in a state of constant relativity, unable to demand ultimate safety or belonging, always ready to change and shift position. However, she was not investigating what happens when the migrant experiences a blow to their constantly readjusting balance. What happens when their precarious sense of belonging in their new world comes suddenly under severe attack? For that is when the existential crisis really happens.

The study of what happens to people in this position, who have to create a transcultural identity for themselves, shows that they find ways to value elements of different cultures; they create a kaleidoscopic view of the world that broadens their outlook and facilitates their capacity for flexibility and adaptation (Banks & McGee Banks, 2001; Baumeister, 2005). Even as they are faced with multiple problems, in the long term they may learn from these difficult conditions and in the end may even thrive on them (Bazzano, 2013; Bonanno, 2004, 2010). Overall, the effect can be very positive as long as people are able to find the safety and security to establish a base they can rebuild on (Akhtar, 1999).

When that new base turns out to be unreliable, however, we have a problem. It is clear that the denial of a home to a person already made insecure by migration is a particularly cruel thing to impose on them. The research carried out by ESSE, the emotional support service for European citizens in the UK, bore this out completely (Vos, 2020a, 2020b). Many of these people felt betrayed by the country and the people they had trusted with their lives. They felt unable to feel safe in their homes and they struggled with their identity and their faith in humanity, in equal measure. It was as if their entire existence had been turned upside down and nothing was any longer the way it had seemed. In Hakim Dowek's terms (2019), their experience was that they suddenly found themselves to be *eccentric*: that is, standing outside of their own centre. They had to learn to make horizontal rather than vertical roots, but they also had to absorb a lot of rejection and hatred that they had never bargained for. This is perhaps why the plight of EU citizens in the UK after the referendum was so detrimental to them. It comes close to becoming a refugee, when you are told that you may no longer be safe to remain in the country you have adopted.

It is very much harder to be a refugee, who is refused a home, than to be a simple migrant. When people are forced into changes that make them traumatised and unsafe and render them stateless, we encounter a new level of intensity of distress. Those who have changed their countries for political reasons, when it became no longer possible for them to remain in their home country, suffer greatly. We shall speak in the next chapter about those who have had to escape their home country to save themselves from oppression, war or torture. These people struggle with an additional burden that is a well-known and obvious risk factor for psychological problems, because they find themselves under such intense pressure (Berry & Kim, 1988; Bhugra et al., 2010; Miller & Rasco, 2004; Morrice, 2011). There is a rich literature on how to work with people in that situation (Bemak et al., 2003; Blackwell, 2005; Boyles, 2017; Papadopoulos, 1999, 2001, 2002; Sue, 2015; Tribe, 1999).

When people have their roots ripped away from them altogether, because what used to be their safe places have ceased to be safe, they are literally fleeing for their lives. Feeling thus persecuted and facing a level of insecurity that can ravage their entire sense of identity, belonging and value, they will feel shattered and devastated. Such people need to be helped gently to refind their bearings, not just physically and socially but also from a psychotherapeutic and philosophical perspective (Corbett & Milton, 2011; du Plock, 2010; Jacobsen, 2006).

This is what we need to look at in our next chapter, which explores what happens to those who find their entire life in the balance. This will give us further insight into what makes it possible to overcome extremely serious and severe existential crises.

7

When crisis destroys meaning

In this chapter I will look at the impact of crisis when the catastrophe that has caused it is so severe that it rips apart a person's entire framework of meaning. This takes us from situations of crisis to situations of trauma, and it's important to know the difference. It helps us understand how crisis can turn into catastrophe and how to prevent this by being cautious in critical circumstances. What happens to people when they hit rock bottom and everything falls apart, so that life suddenly seems futile and hollow? What happens when all the meaningful connections in a person's life unravel or are totally severed? Why is connectivity such a central principle in human existence and how can we live beyond disconnection? How do we build our bonds and weave our lives and how can they be so suddenly unravelled and unwoven? I will explore how people falter and fail when they can no longer rely on the things that normally keep them safe. I will seek to pinpoint how we can safeguard our feelings of safety, even in the face of unsafety and uncertainty.

In order to grasp the significance of human connections and their role in providing us with fortitude, I will trace the experiences of two specific groups of people who were exposed to losses beyond what is usual for human beings to suffer: veterans who have been involved in armed conflict (Iacovou, 2015) and refugees who have had to deal with the trauma of torture and persecution before fleeing their home country (Danesh, 2019). These two groups have been through extreme crises and are likely to continue to feel unsafe for years afterwards. Moreover, the circumstances of their lives after these events may exacerbate their social dislocation. Veterans who have seen active combat often feel excluded from normal society when they return to 'civvy street' (Harmand et al., 1993; Harvey et al., 2012; Iversen et al., 2005; Jones & Wessely, 2005). Refugees frequently continue to suffer from the humiliating, long-winded and hostile process of applying for asylum in their country of refuge (Bhugra et al.,

2010; Krystal & Niederland, 1968; Papadopoulos, 2002). Building up a new life in these conditions is really difficult.

I will take a brief look at the experiences of British Navy personnel who survived the bombing of HMS Sheffield in the Falklands War, because their plight highlights what can go wrong for people if they become disconnected from their own experiences and therefore from society. Service personnel may have been brought back safely to the UK, but the violent deaths of so many of their shipmates and their confrontation with the terrible dangers they encountered left indelible marks on all of them. I will also look at the experiences of Iranian refugees who have found themselves in a state of limbo. Both these examples are inspired by the doctoral research of two colleagues at the New School of Psychotherapy and Counselling (NSPC).

Connectivity

To understand what happens to people who go through crisis, it helps to observe what goes wrong for people who aren't able to work through the crisis fully. As we saw in the previous chapter, when crisis hits, it rips to shreds part of our connective existential tissue. When the fabric of our life is severely torn, we are severed from nature, the social world, ourselves and even our beliefs and values. We literally become detached, disconnected and frequently alienated and disenfranchised. As we find ourselves without that connective existential framework to make sense of the world and our role in it, the meaning of our lives can become diminished and, in the worst-case scenario, non-existent. We have already seen how connectivity, links, bonds and attachments are the very core of what we are and of our experience as human beings. Without that connective tissue, we cease to exist in any meaningful way.

Relationships are one aspect of this and, indeed, relationships will tend to suffer. But our disconnection goes well beyond that of our relationships, and we may feel as if our presence in the world has stopped being of any consequence or value. Many of our bonds are forged at a deeper, more visceral, less explicit and less articulated level than our relationships. Our ties to our parents and family are very important, but they are no stronger than our ties to our home and our country, to our own face and body, to our habits and food preferences, to our culture, politics and belief systems. The ties to what we regard as the minimum decency, respect and understanding we can expect from other people are also vital to our sense that we matter and have dignity in the world.

Yet, we are much more aware of the relationships we have to our family than of the less tangible but equally important framework of reference of other layers of our existence. These only tend to become evident when they are put into question. Our preferences for the things that make us feel real, true to ourselves, whole or 'at home' are at the level of the substratum of consciousness, and much of the time they are invisible to us and we take them for granted. They consist of subtle smells, feelings, sounds, cultural experiences, intuitions, expectations, assumptions, standards and visions that form the very texture of our sense of selfhood and our feeling of being at home or of things being well with the world. We are so enmeshed with these familiar acts and experiences that we are not thinking about them or focusing on them. They are things that are usually subliminal to our awareness. They nevertheless define us, shore up our self-confidence and make us feel at ease, relaxed, cosy and comfortable. When they go missing from our background, we feel deeply perturbed. Suddenly the lack of these things may be called to our attention, though often people simply describe this as having a feeling of 'emptiness', 'nothingness' or 'futility'.

The tragedy is that, although sometimes such elemental experiences may be negative – that is, related to some kind of deprivation or even abuse (such as a feeling of hunger, or a sense that we are only loved or even alive when someone shouts at us or notices our mischief) – they still become a constituent part of our essential being. The tiny apartment I grew up in was a typical example of this. When my family finally moved, I could not settle in the new, bigger house, and I wanted to fly away completely. Having been deprived at a young age, I had to learn to get in touch with and assert my own desire for good-enough living conditions. It is hard to do so when you do not have a sense of entitlement. I had to learn that it was safe and fine for me to want to own a house and a garden. Initially I mistakenly assumed that I didn't care about homes and just wanted to be free, to move about and own nothing.

People who go through the mill of life often end up depriving themselves of connectivity because they believe it is harder to lose things and people than not to have them in the first place. Sometimes, when we think we have nothing left to lose, we fail to notice the many things we still take for granted. When I escaped from what felt like a small, dark and oppressive existence in the Netherlands and moved to the South of France to find space and sunshine, I had not bargained for the losses this entailed. I had not realised how I would grieve over the grave loss of my mother tongue or my fatherland, with its flat, low landscapes and the dark grey waves of the North Sea, the skating over frozen ponds, canals and rivers, ambling through the soft, silver sand of the dunes, and eating raw herring with onions, or chips in a cone, slathered with mayonnaise or Satay sauce.

These are the kind of things that are written between the lines of our lives. They are the background to our narrative. We don't even know we value them until they are stripped away. We miss them in a primitive, primaeval manner, for they form a part of what defines us. We absorb our background scenarios in a way that remains unspoken and unheeded, until we hit a crisis. When such elemental experiences are suddenly absent or become unsafe and unreliable, we find out that they truly were defining aspects of our existence. We don't have *relationships* with these things, ideas and situations: rather, we have absorbed them with our mother's milk; they are part of our innermost world and we are immersed in them and intermingled with them. We haven't made an explicit commitment to them; they are our default settings that secure us and are essential to our functioning.

These imponderables, in all their mystery and enigma, define our outlook on and orientation to the world. We never know that we are so attached to a particular landscape, climate or language until we lose it. We have not forged deliberate connections with a specific songbird, wildflower, staple food, style of clothing or TV programme; they were woven into the fabric of our being when we were growing up. To tear ourselves away from all this takes quite a lot of wrenching, shredding and unravelling. It is hard enough to do this deliberately, as we saw in the case of bi-rooted or poly-rooted people in Nancy Hakim Dowek's research (2019). But when the fabric of our lives is brutally ripped away from us, we are simply numbed by the onslaught and often unaware of the amount of reweaving and reknitting that will be necessary.

We rarely plan to ransack our world on purpose and, when it happens to us despite our best efforts to protect our reality, it is always a painful, hostile and difficult experience. We can get better at it by making ourselves more flexible, training ourselves to adapt to deliberate changes. We can get good at being adventurous and at welcoming new experiences and transformations. Many people play with this when they go travelling as tourists. I remember having to learn to adapt to this on our annual family holidays, camping throughout Europe. My parents were insistent that, post-war, we should rebuild our links with the other European countries across our common continent. On these trips, in my early childhood, I often felt homesick for the Netherlands, but after a while I got used to it and learned how to handle myself in the absence of my familiar environment. I learned how to attach to the skies and the elements, or to the car and the tent, instead of to my usual sources of safety.

I used to marvel at the British capacity for colonisation – the way in which British people create British hubs in their favourite tourist destinations – but we used to do something similar ourselves. We used to bring favourite home foods on our trips, and mine was Marmite. I also usually carried a small, secret stash of salted liquorice with me, not just as a child on holidays but on all my journeys and wherever I have lived ever since. My melancholy yearning for the Netherlands and its cones of chips with peanut sauce was easily fixed when I could relish French fries with mustard in France. When I moved to the UK, I quickly switched that allegiance to an appreciation of good quality fish and chips with tartar sauce and I consider myself a bit of an expert on the subject of chips. Learning to secure ourselves with the means at our disposal is a precious and important bit of physical and mental agility. We saw how Joan craved Spanish ham and Lucie turned to a specific Czech liqueur when seeking comfort in their despair.

Dealing with disconnection

But when we are thrown out of kilter by a catastrophe that tears through our security like a rip tide, such considerations are neither here nor there. When your entire world is in shreds, you have to start from scratch. Or perhaps you feel unable to do so and you only seek to survive for a while. Those who do have to overcome such catastrophes tend to find their bearings by the things that persist. The stars, the moon, the sun and the planets will become their allies, as will the seasons and the weather. When I have worked with people who have been through hell and back, they initially often speak of their feelings of desolation, dislocation and disenfranchisement. Then they discover they can turn to the wider, earthly coordinates that keep them feeling embedded in a wider, universal safety. They adopt the heavens, the weather, rivers, oceans, animals in nature and the seasons to provide them with company and guidance. They value turning their face to the sun, the wind and the rain. Sometimes they relish extreme conditions, like ice and snow or hurricanes. Climate, landscape, fauna and flora become safer and more reliable friends in their universality than the less enduring specifics of human, culturally and regionally determined variables. Trees and birds are often mentioned as markers of a sense of continuity and community of life, when other aspects, especially human beings, have been subtracted.

And so it was for me on my travels in life. I learnt to appreciate skies, sunrises and clouds, and trees, wherever I could find them. If I missed the silver birches from the Dutch dunes, I re-attached myself to the lush mimosas of the South of France, or the regal oaks and beeches of England. Finding a beautiful banyan tree in India or a wonderful sequoia tree in California, an elegant eucalyptus in Australia or a robust rambutan in South East Asia could immediately make me feel safe and at home. The same goes for climate and geography: walking up a road, climbing a hill or following a river can be done almost anywhere. A landscape view can generate a sense of awe and pleasure wherever you are (Harkness, 2018; Schneider, 2009). It helps us find our bearings. The smell of fresh rain can bring succour anywhere in the world. It is really about moving ourselves from specifics to elemental aspects of our connectivity. This is what allows us to be a nomad in body and spirit, to be safe and to adjust.

The same can be done mentally and socially, as we shall see. However, in some situations, we are too wounded to see such things or to connect to them. Then we may be plunged into total darkness and devastation. This strikes us much the harder if we have not been able to learn to be flexible and we derive most of our security from our more dependable environment.

Existential courage

Existential therapists would say that re-engagement with the world and with life is necessary for us to begin to take up our position in the world again. This means having the existential courage to open ourselves to feeling the loss, anxiety, despair, regret, pain and guilt, but also, soon enough, to welcome back the joy we excluded from our lives when we shut down and stopped feeling altogether. As we liberate ourselves from our confinement on our island of suffering, we start to see that we have allowed ourselves to be totally defined by the bad things that happened to us. When we realise there are new possibilities ahead, and, indeed, all around us, we can begin to explore again. Then we can start to make sense of what has happened to us, at the same time as we inventorise the resources currently at our disposal. New meanings can only be created when we are willing to make new connections, including connections with other people. It is the disconnection that gets us stuck, although it felt essential to us at some point to protect ourselves by cutting off.

Peterson, Maier and Seligman, in their book *Learned Helplessness* (1995), came up with a complementary hypothesis: that we often deal with trauma and difficulties by becoming passive or frozen, and in this process victimise ourselves. It can have a devastating effect when we see ourselves as a victim in need of other people's help and give up responsibility for and control of our lives, instead of discovering our own capabilities to cope with crisis (Peterson et al., 1995).

Whether a person responds to disconnection by blaming society, the world, specific other people or themselves for being weak or incompetent is unimportant; all of these are by-products of the experience of suffering. What matters is that our eyes are opened and we understand that these are temporary positions that we are forced into. Trauma is an existential crisis that has not yet been resolved. It is vital to understand that, at times, a person may become incapable of coping with crisis because their pain is too big to comprehend. It may take years before you are ready, but eventually you must process the impact of the crisis event. Remaining wounded is not a long-term option. If we remain disconnected for too long, it becomes much harder to re-engage. By blocking the bad stuff that has happened to us, we are also blocking the good stuff that is possible for us in the future. We may have insulated ourselves from pain, but we are also insulating ourselves from the love, the pleasure, the communication and the connectivity that bring back meaning to our existence.

It is indeed tragic to watch people who are condemned by circumstances to become reduced to living in apparent indifference but who are actually in constant fear or seething with anger. When a person has become frozen or hardened into dispassion and detachment, they become numb to the very things that matter. It is crucial to find the exit from that prison of cold nonchalance, angry defiance or constant dissonance.

There is good reason to be hopeful that this is possible. Tedeschi and Calhoun (1996, 2004) began their work on post-traumatic growth at the end of the last century. They have shown that 90% of survivors of trauma also report some specific positive as a result of their suffering. It is important for us to understand how the 10% who stay caught up in the pain can be released so they can begin to savour the natural consequences of overcoming their trauma. Many survivors report a renewed appreciation of life – the beauty of nature, their own health, other people's love. This is not just a matter of rebound after survival, or a simple recovery of what was lost, but a genuine new perspective on the world and human existence that allows survivors to thrive and come out stronger from their ordeals than they ever were.

This shows that the existential idea that we grow when we are challenged is borne out in practice. If we survive our most difficult tests and afflictions, we can indeed reap benefits. To be tested and tried occasionally is definitely good for learning to be more resilient, but we may need some help to get over the traumatic experience first.

This is all about learning to be robust yet pliant and flexible. It is also about learning to be more adaptive and creative. Those who can do this manage to move beyond their pre-traumatic level of functioning. In other words, they learn valuable lessons from their experiences and look back on the traumatic event as a point of learning.

Meichenbaum (2006), looking at the evidence from numerous studies, concluded that 75% of those who survive traumatic experiences do not need mental health interventions and spontaneously recover through their own resilience. He concluded that it is the person's self-narrative and the narratives of the group or the collective narrative around them that determine whether they will continue to suffer chronic and persistent distress and PTSD or will achieve resilience and post-traumatic growth. He speaks of creating a constructive narrative perspective on a traumatic situation to allow a person to emerge from being caught in the aftermath of the trauma and create a new viewpoint on their experience. It has been shown that the likelihood of such a resilient memory being created is strongest in the first three months, or at least throughout the first year following the traumatising experience (Meichenbaum, 2006).

Connor and Davidson (2003) have even developed a measurement of resilience: the Connor-Davidson Resilience Scale (CD-RISC). Resilience is defined by Connor (2006) in very specific ways, which can be summarised and paraphrased as follows:

1. Having an internal locus of control.
2. Having strong self-esteem and self-efficiency.
3. Having personal goals.
4. Having a sense of meaningfulness.
5. Being able to use past successes to confront current challenges.
6. Viewing stress as a challenge and a way to get stronger.
7. Using humour, patience, tolerance and optimism.
8. Being able to adapt to change.
9. Having an action-orientated approach.

Sisto and colleagues (2019) have created a transversal definition of psychological resilience, using the five macro areas often used in studies. This can be summarised and paraphrased as:

1. The person has the ability to recover.
2. The person functions in a way that is true to themselves.
3. The person has the capacity to bounce back.
4. The person realises this is a dynamic process that evolves over time.
5. The person is capable of adapting positively to new life conditions.

They concluded that psychological resilience is a very complex and multidisciplinary phenomenon and that there is no agreed understanding of the phenomenon, although they did attempt a definition: '… the ability to maintain the persistence of one's orientation towards existential purposes' (Sisto et al., 2019, p.1).

This is an important observation that takes us right back to our own discussion about the existential freedom discovered by people who have been confronted by existential crisis. How do people recover their freedom and establish a more resilient way of being? It is by becoming focused on the things that truly matter (Corbett & Milton, 2011; Joseph, 2011).

Active service and its impact on relationships

I will now turn to the two research studies I mentioned: one about war veterans and the other about political refugees. Starting with the traumatised veterans, I will report my colleague Susan Iacovou's findings about what human beings experience when they go through very extreme situations while their loved ones continue to live in a basically secure and sheltered world. It is this sense of becoming isolated in our sorrows that often makes it hard to rise from our crisis. When a breach is created between the person who suffers the crisis and the person, or people, they love, there is a risk that loving communication and understanding cease altogether. The alienation and isolation created in this situation is very much part of the problem. This is highly relevant to the experience of EU citizens in the UK who were married to UK citizens.

Susan Iacovou (2015) did her doctoral research on a topic very close to her heart – the impact of the experience of active service on the intimate relationships of military veterans. This was an existential-phenomenological study that aimed to throw light on the tremendous stresses and strains that couples in this situation have to face, following on from our joint work on existential relationship therapy (van Deurzen & Iacovou, 2013). Dr Iacovou was a therapist on the British military base in Cyprus, working with service personnel stationed there who had seen active service in Iraq and Afghanistan. But her interest in the subject was also personal: her husband had fought in the Falklands War and was on board HMS Sheffield when it was destroyed by an Exocet missile. She writes:

> At the time of the Falklands War, I was only 17 and had just been
> accepted to study psychology at the University of Edinburgh. My future
> husband, on the other hand, was 27 years old and, on the 4th of May 1982,
> was Officer of the Watch on the bridge of HMS Sheffield when he spotted
> what was later identified as an Exocet missile heading towards the ship.
> On a day when the British Navy lost its first ship since World War II, he
> lost 20 of his shipmates. (Iacovou, 2015, p.1)

In just these few lines she captures the chasm between their life experiences that she was later to research.

For her study, she conducted intensive psychotherapeutic interviews with 10 former Royal Navy personnel who had seen active service in the Falklands War in 1982. The research focused on the psychological journey and relationship issues they had faced following their active service. This was a unique study in that it drilled down into their emotional experiences and particularly examined the impact of their experiences on their relationships.

The study was conducted in 2014/2015, and the men were all aged 51 to 73 at the time of interview and had therefore had several decades to make sense of the way in which their war experiences had affected them.

The descriptions of their experiences are often matter of fact, couched in tough language, but always there are flickers of the real experience they were exposed to and how this sapped their confidence. These men were confronted with experiences that were so extreme that they felt unable to discuss them with their families. They became isolated and, although they apparently coped for many years, when other difficult experiences occurred in their lives, they suddenly found themselves breaking down. Mostly, their marriages did not survive the onslaught of this trauma.

Iacovou concluded that:

> … active service confronted the participants with the existential givens of existence, including death, freedom and finitude, and meaninglessness and absurdity. This confrontation shattered their worldviews, changing them and their priorities, and creating overwhelming emotions that they struggled to understand. (Iacovou, 2015, abstract)

While there are a number of studies on how post-traumatic growth may emerge from PTSD, especially if the veteran is in a supportive intimate relationship when they return (see, for example, the study by Tsai et al. (2015)), they are often quantitative and do not aim to deeply understand the experiences of the people involved. Rather than looking at these men's experiences in terms of post-traumatic stress, Iacovou chose to explore them in terms of how what happened to them had changed their values, the meanings of their lives, their behaviours and their relationships. She did a thorough investigation of current research on the specific symptoms of trauma and trauma-related behaviours, such as alcohol misuse/abuse and anger and violence, and their impact on relationships. But she demonstrated that none of this was sufficient to fully comprehend what these men had really been through. This required an in-depth understanding of what it means to face an existential crisis of this vital nature. She rightly believed that nobody had ever really probed that deeply and that these men deserved to be heard and understood.

It is a well-documented fact that social support is important in coping with stress in general, and with combat stress in particular (Keane, et al., 1985; Solomon et al., 1990a, 1990b). Yet, Iacovou found:

> Unable or unwilling to share their experiences, and feeling alienated from the world around them, most of the participants withdrew from

their partners and isolated themselves emotionally and physically. After struggling for many years to cope with and understand the impact of active service on their way of being in the world and on their relationships, six of the participants broke down, with five of them receiving a formal diagnosis of Post-Traumatic Stress Disorder (PTSD). (Iacovou, 2015, abstract)

I found the same thing in my work with survivors of the Holocaust in the 1970s and 1980s. One of the main problems for these people was not so much their traumatic memories as their deep sense of being different, leading to them isolating themselves from the people around them. They felt they knew things others didn't want to know and that what they had seen and experienced was unmentionable. They also felt other people would not wish to hear about their past experiences as they could not understand them and would just dismiss them.

I once worked with Jan Sebastiaans, a Dutch medical doctor, who was conducting experiments in using LSD therapy with Holocaust survivors (Ossebaard & Maalste, 1999), and who sometimes referred his England-based clients to me for psychotherapy. While he was trying to access people's buried memories with his unorthodox methods, I would see them for therapy afterwards. They were Dutch people who had come to the UK as refugees, either before the war, as part of the Kindertransport or after their return from the concentration camps. Most of them had lost every other member of their families. They frequently struggled with survivor guilt and considered themselves as falling short in how they had lived their miraculously saved lives, which they feared had been saved in vain. They would tell me that friends who had died would have lived more wisely or bravely. It made them feel their own lives were futile and wasted.

Each of them had had to find a way to bury their memories and they frequently did this by holding themselves apart from other people and not speaking about their experiences at all. This led to them having numerous other symptoms of unease, such as insomnia, nightmares, phobias or using obsessional rituals in order to try to cope. I came to the conclusion that the re-activation of their terrifying experiences was not very beneficial to them, as it made them feel even more different and unwilling (or unable) to get close to the people around them. What I found was that focusing on helping them find meaning in their plight was an essential counterweight to their attempts at remembering. They knew they were fragile, and they knew this could never be changed; they could not unsee what they had seen or unknow what they knew. They felt they carried the weight of the world on their shoulders; that the ordinary people around them did not want to be burdened by their knowledge of evil. If they could use this knowledge to help others in a similar situation, however, they were much more able to feel that their experiences had been meaningful. Working with organisations like Survivors of Torture, Jewish Care or the Samaritans was therapeutic for them in some cases because it made them reconnect and showed them that their experience had made them useful in helping others.

Iacovou's findings from her study of the Falklands War survivors reminded me very much of this observation. It also reminded me of neighbours I had known in the Netherlands, who had been tortured in Japanese war camps in the Second World War and who never quite connected to other people in the neighbourhood. They too found it immensely difficult to reinsert themselves into a society that wanted to pretend these things had never happened. They could never trust other human beings fully and were often plagued by nightmares and flashbacks, feeling dreadfully alone with these experiences.

Iacovou's literature search revealed that it was helpful to allow war survivors to explore their experiences, but only if we can find a way to transform anger or other bad feelings into something more meaningful. Iacovou cites McCormack & McKellar (2015), whose longitudinal case study with a 60-year-old man who was injured in the 2005 Bali bombings suggests 'that anger following trauma acted as a facilitator of growth and change, particularly in social relationships, empathy for others and increased personal meaning' (Iacovou, 2015, p.27). She also cites research by Park and colleagues (2008), who demonstrated a link between anger towards those who perpetrated the US 9/11 terrorist attacks and post-traumatic growth.

Anger can sometimes be a good thing, if it is focused in a determined and positive way. There are many studies showing that anger, hatred and desire for revenge are common forms of emotional release for refugees who have suffered human rights violations. We often speak of post-traumatic stress reactions when they are as extreme as this, but it is vital for people to find a more constructive use for their anger (Beck & Sloan, 2012) so that it doesn't consume them.

This is something well worth thinking about. It seems to suggest that if the person can move from victimhood to anger and from anger to meaning-making, they stand a much better chance of rising from their crisis. But, unfortunately, in former service personnel exposed to active combat, the capacity for anger often leads to violent behaviour in close relationships rather than to meaning-making, as numerous studies show (see, for example, Harmand et al., 1993; Orcutt et al., 2003).

Former service personnel also have difficulties in remembering stressful and disruptive events and they are frequently unaware and unable to account for their considerable suffering. They also have difficulties in making choices, and they frequently feel alienated, isolated, incapable of socialising, inauthentic with others and impaired in their capacity for intimacy.

As one of Iacovou's participants said:

> So, unless you've actually had that experience, to me you will never understand it. You might think you understand it. You might have a perception of what it's like. But you don't know how that individual felt about that situation. And… hence I'd fail to see the point of telling anybody, so they didn't have to think about it 'cos they couldn't really understand it. (Iacovou, 2015, p.202)

We found a similar process with the EU citizens fighting to stay in the UK who felt wronged and panicked about their future. After trying to speak to their in-laws about it and finding that they minimised the experience they were going through, they often gave up talking about it at all, to anyone. This cuts the person off from society and from their nearest and dearest, which leads to a significant loss of connectivity and therefore a loss of meaning. It also leads to a loss of the sense of reality, in that we no longer get feedback or validation from those around us about our experiences.

Russian psychologist Magomed-Eminov (1997), in his research with 200 veterans of the Soviet War in Afghanistan and the Russian Federation's war in Chechnya, also referred to Frankl's (1978) logotherapy to define PTSD from an existential perspective as a loss of meaning. Magomed-Eminov understood that what we call PTSD is essentially the outcome of a clash of meaning and values: those from before the traumatic event and those from after it simply do not match up. He lists six things that are produced by this failure to integrate these two sets of values (Magomed-Eminov, 1997, p.242):

1. Negative interpretation of one's own deeds.
2. Realisation and rejection of values based on ideological grounds.
3. Perception of the absurdity of the situation.
4. Prolonged cognitive representation of the conflict in the meaning of life.
5. Actively trying not to think about the situation.
6. Feelings of emptiness and being closed to feelings.

These six things were also present in our research with EU citizens (ESSE, 2020; Vos et al., 2020), who were similarly confronted with existential crisis and questions around meaning and purpose and felt unable to reconcile or make sense of the clash of values from before and after the event. These people were all dealing with overwhelming emotions of loss, insecurity and bereavement, with a changed identity and with their sense of exclusion and being an outsider in a world where they once thought they belonged (Brophy, 2019; Bulman & Bussy, 2019; Coates, 2018; van Deurzen, 2018c, 2019c). The belief that 'nobody else can understand this except other people who have been through this experience' led to a sense of existential isolation. Only when such people dare to go to this dark place of isolation and desolation will they find a way to emerge stronger from their experience and find meaning in it (de Jong et al., 2020).

Iacovou also reports how her participants described being confronted by what she terms 'existential givens':

> When they described their experiences of active service, the participants
> spoke about being confronted with death, having to deal with chance
> and being out of control, and being faced with the meaninglessness and
> absurdity of war. (2015, p.132)

Iacovou quotes one of them:

> When you actually watch somebody get shot. When you see somebody
> who's stood on a landmine, actually behind them, and watch them go
> up. That also is a futility, waste of life, and it's something you don't forget.
> (Iacovou, 2015, p.138)

These men were confronted with the fragility and senselessness of life, and when they returned home, they felt that everything was suddenly worthless and trivial by comparison with what they had been through. They didn't feel in charge of their experiences anymore. They had learnt that circumstances can plunge you into hell all of a sudden and so it was hard to keep a sense of having any control over their own fate. Fate was stronger than them. People in that situation stop having confidence that they can make a difference for the better. Some even lose faith in simple skills that they have long taken for granted.

Iacovou's participants talked a great deal about the loss of their home (the ship) and of course of the loss of their shipmates. They also talked about the loss of professional pride (an important part of their identity) and the loss of the good standing or reputation of the British Navy. They felt shame and guilt in relation to all of that. It was hard for them to realise they were the lucky ones, compared with their mates who had been killed in battle.

Iacovou proposes that existential therapy is the best kind of therapy to help people like these Falklands veterans make sense of their situation, because it can help them hold the paradoxes in their lives and find a way to face up to what has happened and what it means for the future:

> ... the experience of trauma, together with our responses to trauma, are underpinned by basic existential conditions that are indicative of what it means to be human. The role of existential counselling psychology is to support the individual while they are in 'existential limbo' (Harmand et al., 1993), trying to make sense of the world and the transitory nature of life. (2015, p.217)

So many people's lives can be destroyed by events beyond their control and responsibility. This is even more the case for those who have to flee from war zones, civil war and political, religious and racial persecution. It is time for us to consider the case of refugees.

The existential plight of political refugees

Armin Danesh's findings from his phenomenological research with Iranian political refugees living in the UK (2019) paint yet another poignant picture of the way in which human beings' lives can be utterly torn apart by a political situation. The political upheavals in the Middle East have created millions of refugees over the past decade – both within the region and outwards into other countries. We are more familiar with what has been happening in Syria, but there are other examples too numerous to mention. Millions of people across the world have been displaced by war, famine, genocide and persecution, and have been forced to go through the upheaval of fleeing their homes to seek sanctuary in another country. There are around 18 million asylum seekers and refugees worldwide, mostly (approximately 86%) in developing countries, and most of these are living in vast refugee camps, which have become their settled homes and communities. A tiny proportion – some two per cent – have found sanctuary in the UK – just 0.27% of the UK population (Refugee Council, 2021; UN Convention against Torture, 1984; UNHCR, 2002, 2014).

Fleeing one's home, the dangers of doing so and the long and tortuous task of applying for refugee status are a harsh and wearisome process; it requires a huge amount of determination and perseverance. Many get rejected, even by enlightened countries that one would think would not be so cruel as to refuse safety to someone who is so patently in danger (Said, 1994, 1999; Samasundaram, 2010; Taylor, 2015).

Hannah Arendt once said that refugees, 'driven from country to country, represent the vanguard of their peoples' (Arendt, 1943). And it is true that it is usually the strongest, most enterprising and often the best qualified people from a country who make it across the oceans to start a new life elsewhere. But they are rarely treated as such; instead, they are regarded as interlopers and undesirables, as burdens on the host country's resources, as false applicants for sanctuary, until, as Danesh puts it in his research, they 'rise from their ashes'. As the EU citizens in the UK found to their cost, when you do not have a country's citizenship, it is far too easy for those in power to treat you as second-class, denigrate you and disregard your human rights.

It is therefore not surprising to find that asylum seekers and refugees are more likely to experience emotional and mental distress (Bhugra et al., 2010; Sadavoy, 1997; Samasundaram, 2010). The Refugee Council (2021) states that 61% of asylum seekers experience serious mental distress and that refugees are five times more likely to have mental health needs than the UK population. These are due in part to pre-migration experiences, such as war trauma, torture and the perils of the journey, and in part to post-migration conditions, which include separation from family and community, grief for what has been lost, acute poverty, poor housing, inability to get work or have any meaningful occupation, hostile communities and (chiefly, for many) the process of the asylum application process itself.

> … the length (sometimes over 10 years) and complexity of the asylum application process in the UK creates its own hopelessness, uncertainty and acute anxiety. There are reports of suicide among asylum seekers whose applications were refused or inexplicably delayed… The host country's hostility, disbelief and style of interrogation further imperils and often destroys the asylum seeker's sense of safety. (Danesh, 2019, p.49)

Danesh is himself an Iranian political refugee and worked with other political refugees for decades in the UK before embarking on his research. He reminds us that around four million Iranians, many of whom were intellectuals and professionals, were forced to flee their homeland after the 1979 revolution (Eilk, 2012).

The Iran-Iraq war created a further two million refugees and left nearly two million people dead or wounded (Danesh, 2019, p.27; Razouk, 2015). Most refugees suffer trauma of some sort: so much so that, in many Western host countries, 'trauma' is sometimes considered synonymous with the refugee experience (Overland et al., 2014). As we have already seen, the experience of migration is synonymous with loss of safety, and especially with the loss of a safe home. According to Papadopoulos (2002, p.9): 'Loss of home is the only condition shared by all refugees: not trauma.'

As with service personnel who have seen active combat, refugees are exposed to terrible experiences that are the consequence of a political situation and are not of their own making. It is not enough to look after their physical and psychosocial wellbeing. Their entire identity and value system have been turned upside down by these unexpected and unwanted experiences. They too must reinvent themselves in order to make sense of their lives again. They too have gone through the upheaval of a total existential crisis – but for them, all their previous existence has been destroyed and they have to literally rebuild their lives anew in a completely unfamiliar, sometimes hostile place. Like the service personnel who have seen their comrades dying around them, many refugees have lost family, friends and other loved ones – often seeing them die before their very eyes. This exposes them to the rawness of human existence in a way most of us get to avoid and can close our eyes to.

It is a well-known phenomenon, described by numerous existential authors, that we like to deny the reality of death as long as we can get away with it (Becker, 1971, 2011; Jaspers, 1951; Tillich, 1952, 1954; Yalom, 1980, 1989, 2008). We are so keen to live our life without seeing its dark side that it is hard for us to acknowledge the troubles of those who find themselves suddenly exposed to so much hardship.

I found, when trying to get professional support for the EU citizens, that many psychologists and therapists in the UK were doubtful that they needed it. In the ESSE clinic, we heard many stories about people who had gone to therapists who wanted to explain their difficulties as a form of personal pathology instead of recognising the political and social pressure as the cause of their problems. Few therapists have worked with political refugees and not many people are sensitised to the plight of those who have been faced with the double whammy of war in their country of origin and lack of support in their adoptive country.

Danesh documents the importance of establishing trust with people in this situation. He also points out how important it is not to avoid political discussions. These people need to be able to freely express their political views and frustrations. Their first concern is often whether or not the therapist is their ally against the regime they have fled from (Danesh, 2019, pp.40–41). This resonates strongly with our experience in the ESSE clinic, where EU citizens often asked whether we could guarantee that the therapist they would see would not be a 'Leaver' who might not understand their pain and suffering. They fared best when they could see a therapist who was a fellow EU citizen, whom they felt they could trust implicitly. Ironically, we were criticised on several occasions by our peers in the therapy profession for providing a safe haven for these people. They accused us of political indoctrination and a lack of therapeutic neutrality. The very point is that there are times when people are so traumatised that neutrality is not appropriate and would constitute re-traumatisation. People must be able to rest assured that they will be received sympathetically and that their story, their views and their feelings will be fully and utterly respected and honoured. Would we expect women who are victims of sexual abuse to accept therapy from someone of the same gender as their abuser and who held misogynistic beliefs?

I have worked with a few Iranian refugees myself and I had to learn to adjust my practice in myriad ways. I documented this carefully in a long case study, with my colleague Claire Arnold-Baker supervising the work, describing how I had to find new humility and accept that I needed to let my client teach me about their personal circumstances, their deepest preoccupations and their values, which were very different to my own (van Deurzen & Arnold-Baker, 2019; van Deurzen, 2020). For me, the challenge was particularly about understanding the importance of strong and deeply held religious values – in this case, Islamic ones – that I had my own prejudices about and which I thought initially were the source of my client's predicament. It is easy to be liberal in one's thinking in principle; it is harder in practice to accept that some clients may hold values that are far from liberal and that create a clash between themselves and the life they have opted to live in their new country. I discovered how much inner conflict can be generated by that clash and how hard it can be to find a way through this.

My client, who had to flee from his country because of his homosexuality, had never fully accepted his sexuality and was as judgemental about himself as his country had been about him. In consequence, when it came to the crunch, he could not accept my Western permissive views and I needed to comprehend that and let him find his own way of going beyond his impasse. He did so, to a large extent because we had an open conflict that we were able to work with constructively.

Establishing trust with a person who has been through hell and back is never an easy matter. It becomes even harder if a person has been tortured, exposed to moral, emotional and economic pressures beyond what we are used to and has been harmed in body and mind, facing physical death threats or damage to their bodily or mental integrity. We also cannot assume that they will feel respected and safe with someone who is relatively privileged and secure in the culture they have just joined and who does not fully understand their lack of confidence and the enormity of the obstacles in their path.

The impact of torture is massive (Gerrity et al., 2012; van der Veer, 1998). Such experiences destroy a person's capacity for feeling safe, for feeling valid, for daring to communicate and for having any kind of trust in others. The paradox is that, the more a person has been treated in such an inhuman way, the more likely they are to carry a sense of guilt or failure. They have learnt to blame themselves as much as blame the world. This is not just about survival guilt either; it is often simply that they feel that everything is wrong and that they must therefore be in the wrong as well. They may feel it is hopeless to fight or resist or even to try to make sense of things. The only way to get beyond it is to regain the capacity to find a goal, a new purpose in terms of making things right again.

Danesh's in-depth interviews with his nine participants threw up some important new findings about what allows a person to survive and thrive in such dire conditions. He interviewed several escaped political prisoners, who variously were human rights activists, members of women's rights movements, supporters of banned political parties or members of student protest movements. Some were authors and journalists fighting for democracy. They were all people who had become targets for the regime by daring to express their opposition or by refusing to cooperate with it.

These people had been imprisoned, humiliated, silenced and threatened; some had been tortured, but eventually they all had managed to escape their country, often with great trouble and suffering. Therefore, the idea of making a new start was a very important part of their identity and of their survival.

These people had all consciously chosen to stand up for social justice, freedom and democracy in their homeland, and they had, at great cost to themselves, placed these values above their commitment to their own families. Such decisions and actions raise many issues, and it is clear that someone who flees from oppression in this manner is making a deliberate choice to opt for freedom, justice and fairness. Moral dilemmas ensue from this, as was very clear in my own case study of the Iranian refugee (van Deurzen & Arnold-Baker, 2019), who thought of himself, destructively, as a coward for having done so.

Refugees often continue to feel responsibility for the impact of their actions on their families, who may be left behind, in danger. Nevertheless, Danesh found that most of his participants felt that they had empowered themselves by their choices. They had chosen what was meaningful and important. They had had the courage of their convictions, regardless of the cost:

> All my participants suffered many losses: not only family members and friends who were executed, or loss of home and possessions, but also of their support networks, their natural and cultural environment and their identity. (2019, p.160)

He found out many interesting and important things about how his participants managed to achieve rebirth for themselves. He presented these along the lines of structural existential analysis (van Deurzen, 2014) and considered them important factors for consideration when working therapeutically with political refugees (Danesh, 2019).

In my own work on grief and loss, I use the four dimensions of existence to facilitate a person to recreate new connectivity. Making sure to address all four levels of a person's existence is necessary for them to be able to re-establish a secure framework of meaning. The more links they can make, the better they will feel about themselves, the world and the potential in the future. Figure 7.1 illustrates this.

Figure 7.1: Living with conflict and trauma

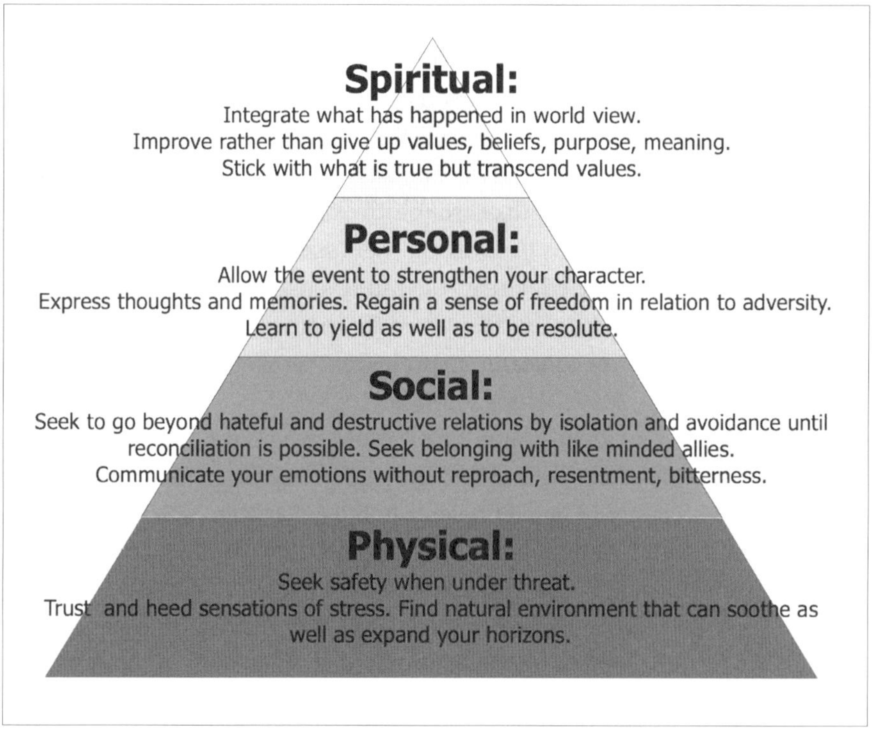

Spiritual:
Integrate what has happened in world view.
Improve rather than give up values, beliefs, purpose, meaning.
Stick with what is true but transcend values.

Personal:
Allow the event to strengthen your character.
Express thoughts and memories. Regain a sense of freedom in relation to adversity.
Learn to yield as well as to be resolute.

Social:
Seek to go beyond hateful and destructive relations by isolation and avoidance until reconciliation is possible. Seek belonging with like minded allies.
Communicate your emotions without reproach, resentment, bitterness.

Physical:
Seek safety when under threat.
Trust and heed sensations of stress. Find natural environment that can soothe as well as expand your horizons.

© Emmy van Deurzen, 2021

1. *At the physical level*, people need to seek safety and heed their pain, lick their wounds, build a sanctuary and begin to repair what has been destroyed. This requires equal amounts of self-care and courage.

2. *At the social level*, they need to avoid destructive relationships, initially by avoidance, until reconciliation, peace-making or robust disagreement

are possible. But they also need to make alliances with those who are like-minded. Learning to express emotions without reproach, blame, resentment and bitterness is an invaluable ability to acquire.

3. *At the personal level*, it is important to be prepared to question and challenge our past expectations and our own habits and character and to be flexible and free enough to change and adapt to adversity.

4. *At the spiritual level*, crisis is a time to allow the fractures of life to help us find the kernel of our values and search for greater existential understanding. This can allow us to find new and more purposeful life directions.

Adaptability is definitely a key factor. It is something Danesh also concluded from his research. His participants found the most strength when they were willing and able to tap into the inner resources that allowed them to be adaptable. If we find the inner elasticity to start imagining ourselves and our lives anew, we can adjust to many more challenges than we ever thought possible. Affirming our human rights (Freeman, 2005) is often an important step on that path (Freedom from Torture, 2017). We may even come to relish our capacity to create new paths through the chaos and figure out how the new situation might allow us to bring out new aspects in ourselves that were previously hidden or unused. Great role models like Gandhi, Martin Luther King and Nelson Mandela, who all suffered for their values and gained greater strength out of it, describe this same struggle and that same path of overcoming (Gandhi, 2001; King, 2019; Mandela, 1995).

The people who can adjust and adapt to new circumstances learn vital lessons from their experiences and they find it much easier to rise up from their crisis and move forward to greater heights in life. Invariably such people, when they surmount their troubles, tend to want to put their traumatic experiences to good use and engage with something that is of benefit to others.

In our work with EU citizens in the UK, we found exactly the same thing: people wanted to be able to understand what had happened to them so they could respond appropriately. They needed some perspective and also to feel that their experiences were validated. Then they craved some recognition for how brave or determined they were in getting themselves through the difficulties. Once they gained this sense of competency in overcoming their troubles, they were able to accept their worries and the complications of their situation much more easily. They then invariably wanted to put their experience to good use and make a valid and important contribution to those around them.

There is something in the experience of going through the fire for one's beliefs and values and realising that we can survive much more than we thought we could that makes us rise above petty resentments and reproaches and seek out situations in which we can focus on the things that matter the most. People cannot wait to make things right again, not just for themselves but also for the world around them. They wish to use their new resilience, agility and strength to help ease the world's problems.

8

Surviving a global pandemic

So much in the previous chapters has been about connectivity and its importance to our sense of safety, feeling at home and finding meaning. What happens to us, then, when that very connectivity becomes a threat to us, and even a mortal danger? This is indeed what occurred from late 2019 when the Covid-19 virus began its deadly spread across the world. In China and the Far East, where two previous viral pandemics had already occurred, they knew that the only way to contain it would be the total severing of human connections to one another. It took us far longer in Europe, and especially in the UK, to face this grim truth and impose the necessary lockdowns that might halt the killer virus until a reliable vaccine could be developed and distributed.

In the UK, we first watched in amazement and horror as the virus reached Europe, Italy locked down and Italians were filmed singing to each other from their balconies. We thought, 'We are an island; we don't have such porous borders; we will be alright.' We were sure that we weren't going to go down that same path. We felt sorry for them – and then we realised that the virus was no respecter of any borders. We could see that every country in the world was going to follow suit, sooner or later, and that lockdowns were going to become the new normal.

Psychologists realised that all this was going to have a considerable impact on human beings, especially in terms of their mental and emotional wellbeing. Joel Vos, one of my colleagues at the New School of Psychotherapy and Counselling, carried out a meta-analysis of some of the numerous studies that were being conducted (Vos, 2021). He considered the impact of the pandemic on society, including the mental health implications.

From his analysis of the 26 studies he reviewed on the psychological impact of Covid-19 (involving some 104,361 people), he found that a third of all people treated for Covid-19 and in the general population reported symptoms of anxiety, depression, stress and insomnia. Among healthcare workers, almost 60% had symptoms of acute traumatic stress, and almost one third experienced moderate to severe symptoms of depression, general distress, insomnia or anxiety (Vos, 2021, p.122).

Some groups of people were particularly at risk in terms of the emotional impact of the pandemic. Those who were on the frontline and worked in the highly stressed environment of hospitals were of course particularly affected. This was even more the case if they had poor protection from the infection, as this made them more acutely aware of the considerable risks they were taking and also put them in significant physical danger. At the start of the pandemic, the personal protection in hospitals left a lot to be desired. Many health professionals who were working on the frontline were not sufficiently protected and caught the virus, and far too many died. They were like soldiers on the frontline of a battlefield, and PTSD, anxiety and depression were evident in more than half of them (Grover, 2021).

Many health professionals reported dreading going into work, not only because of the terrible conditions on the wards, where they were working under enormous pressure, but also because they were dealing with numbers of deaths that none had encountered before. Hospitals are not meant to be places where people go to die; healthcare workers are trained to treat, cure and save, yet their patients were dying at a rate that few were prepared for. In the UK, more than 100,000 people died in the first year of the pandemic. Although the public was hugely supportive of the NHS, many other frontline public sector workers, such as bus drivers and refuse collectors, and delivery drivers and supermarket staff were frequently insulted and treated badly as people began losing their patience during the second wave (Blackall, 2021). Such public-facing workers were also those at higher risk, as well as crucial to the country continuing to operate basic services.

The pressure on those who were staffing the intensive care units treating Covid patients was extreme and intense. One nurse, writing anonymously, captured their dislocation from the rest of society:

> Many of us NHS staff are experiencing a disconnect from our friends
> and family because our experience throughout the pandemic has
> been very different. I don't always know how much to tell them about
> what I'm seeing, because in a way we're trying to protect them from it.
> (Anonymous, 2021)

This reveals a process similar to that observed with the Falklands War service personnel in the previous chapter. When we are forced to engage with a level of difficulty that is out of the ordinary, we can easily become isolated and disconnected. At one point in the thick of the pandemic, it was reported that nearly half of NHS critical care staff suffered PTSD, depression or anxiety (Vos, 2021; Grover 2021). We know how important it is for professionals under that kind of pressure to find some relief and to be able to communicate about their experiences and have them acknowledged and validated. Providing emotional support and debriefing sessions for people in this situation is crucial.

I got in touch with Joan Pons Laplana, the nurse from Chapter 3, who was happy to let me include his personal account of what happened to him during the Covid year. Here it is, in his own words.

During the first wave of the pandemic, I was redeployed to work in intensive care (ICU). Hospital intensive care wards are unlike anywhere else in the NHS. Patients are mostly sedated, their beds surrounded by towers of equipment that emit a grim chorus of continuous beeps and alarms. Banks of monitors display vital signs and heart rhythms and sound the most disconcerting alerts when they detect changes. Working on these wards as a nurse has always been tough, but the huge influx of very sick Covid-19 patients has been making the job much harder.

Essentially what happens in ICU is that we take over the running of a patient's body. We control their heart rate, their blood pressure, their breathing. The patient's life is in our hands, and it's a huge responsibility to hold. We have to monitor patients constantly because change can happen so quickly. Any fluctuation in their blood pressure or breathing could mean having to adjust their treatments or could be a sign that they are deteriorating. You have to have complete and total dedication and constant attention for each patient.

Since working in ICU with Covid patients, I have often woken at night worrying about decisions I have made during my shift. There is so much to process. You have to be alert all the time. You can't lower your guard for a moment. If you press the wrong button on a piece of equipment you are not familiar with, a patient might die. If you make a mistake, it can also cost you your own life, as you might get infected.

This is why, during Covid treatment, we have to wear full PPE protective kit, which makes the work extra difficult. It's extremely hot and you sweat a lot during a long shift. But you cannot simply lift your visor to wipe your face and have a drink of water. Instead, you have to plan your breaks so that you can take regular sips of water. You can't go to the toilet without carefully removing all your kit, and then you have to put it all back on again. So, you have to plan that too.

Also, Covid has dehumanised our care. Before the pandemic, we used to meet families and get a picture of our patients' lives. We had some idea of who they were as people, as we were able to pay attention to the little details that matter so much. But now we usually only have a few minutes to talk to a family, and the only time we see them is in the final moments of a patient's life. This dehumanises patients, and this affects us too, leaving us feeling numb.

Also, because everyone is wearing full PPE and working in bubbles, it is very difficult to have any conversations. Everyone looks the same. The only thing you can see is other people's eyes, nothing else. When you have actually managed to take a break, everyone is sitting at a distance from each other and wearing masks. I spent nearly five months in ICU, but if I met some of my colleagues outside of the hospital, I would not recognise them.

I had a real problem with disconnecting when I came home from shifts. There doesn't seem to be any space to rest. You go home, turn on the TV and the only thing you see is more news about Covid-19 – it's Covid, Covid, Covid. So, you try to use your days off to get away from it and not be so overpowered by it all, but it is very hard. During the pandemic, I had a panic attack when things were very bad in May 2020, and I returned to CBT sessions with a psychologist at that point. That helped me to manage my mental health balance, but it has been very tough. I know this is the same for most of my colleagues, too.

It is obvious how brave medical staff like Joan were during the pandemic. In the article I quoted above by an anonymous NHS frontline worker, there is a final passage that is heart-breaking and that I know would also apply to Joan and many others. It says:

I'm an EU migrant, like a vast number of people working in intensive care. Many of us were working on New Year's Eve [2020] when the law changed, and we went from being residents of this country to being guests with settled status. When all this is over, I hope there is an acknowledgement that we didn't leave this country; we didn't leave our posts, even when it felt like Britain abandoned us. (Anonymous, 2021)

Emotional and mental wellbeing

So many people have suffered emotionally and mentally during the Covid years. We shall never know how those who died alone were feeling at the end, but it cannot have been an easy death. The author Michael Rosen, who was in intensive care for months and in an induced coma for more than four weeks, described his experience of not fully knowing what had happened to him until quite some time later (Sanderson, 2020). He wrote a highly evocative book about it called *Many Different Kinds of Love* (Rosen, 2021), in which he expresses his admiration and gratitude for the people who put so much effort into keeping him alive. With his usual philosophical humour, he describes how he spent months in a state of dreaming in intensive care: a state between life and death. He was one of the lucky ones; he rejoined the living. Yet, when people congratulated him on having recovered and wished him back to his old self soon, he says:

> I look at the word 'recovered'.
> I want to change it to 'recovering'.
> I'm not sure that I will be 'recovered'.
> As for that old self,
> He's that guy I knew six months ago. (Rosen, 2021, p.178)

When we go through crisis, the person we were previously dies. What we become afterwards is different. We suffer the losses and we overcome them as best we can (Aho, 2021).

Not everyone has had the fortune of surviving the illness, however. Worldwide, many million people have died of Covid. As I write, people are still dying in thousands. Clearly, the friends and family of all these people have been profoundly affected by these sudden and violent deaths. Once their loved ones were admitted to hospital, most were unable to see them. Most of the deaths occurred after the patient was admitted to intensive care and placed, unconscious, on a ventilator. Families and friends couldn't touch the dying person, couldn't speak to them, seek to reassure them, or say goodbye. The last they saw was the person being loaded into an ambulance. The lockdown regulations meant only a very few could even attend the funeral. These are exactly the circumstances that can lead to prolonged and complex grief. Charities supporting the bereaved have reported much greater demand on their services.

As we have seen over and over again, existential crisis is bad enough if it involves our physical safety. When our social connections are also cut off and we lose a sense of inner balance, things get even more complicated. However, when it touches our values and trust in the world, it becomes very serious. When meaning is robbed from us altogether and we lose our faith in politics, in humanity, or even in life itself, we face a tricky and difficult situation. It can take months, even years, to overcome such a complex and long-term grieving process. As is always the case in crisis, the capacity to learn something of value in the process of reconnecting our lives to a wider meaningful framework of reference is what will save us.

This can be seen mirrored in work with the bereaved. Robert Neimeyer (2006, 2011a, 2015), founder and director of the Portland Institute for Loss and Transition in the US and a world-wide recognised authority, has specialised in working with people who are experiencing complex grief after a sudden bereavement. Neimeyer's (2015) approach seeks to help the bereaved person to re-story the narrative of their loss in a way that has meaning for them.

He has demonstrated in his evidence-based research how important it is for a therapist to be open and truly available to being a companion to the bereaved person on this journey of meaning-making. It is a process that he has come to see as an existential exploration, where people learn to understand and make sense of the enormity of what is happening to them. What is necessary, he believes, is to find a balance between allowing people to feel the depth and significance of their experience in telling the story and encouraging them towards new ways of understanding of what is happening to them and creating new meaning.

> Meaning-making contributes to adaptive outcomes, as longitudinal research on widowhood demonstrates that sense-making in the first six months of loss predicts higher levels of positive effect and well-being a full four years after the death of a spouse… Fostering reconstruction of a world of meaning would therefore seem to be a therapeutic priority for many bereaved clients, one that could bring benefits, not only in alleviating complicated symptoms of grief, but also in renewing a sense of hope and self-efficacy in their changed lives. (Neimeyer, 2011b)

Neimeyer's work (2006, 2011a) is itself deeply rooted in his own experience, aged 12, of finding the body of his father, who had taken his own life, and of living with the grief of his mother (and his own and that of his siblings) throughout his teenage years. He is a shining example of the way in which people can learn from their crisis to forge a capacity for overcoming, then put their experience at the disposal of others to help them grow from their personal sorrow. His work shows that if we are strong enough to own our losses and absorb our shocks, we become better human beings for it and are able to pass our new understanding on.

The impact of the Covid-19 pandemic on emotional and mental wellbeing has by no means been caused only by the deaths, bereavements and serious illness, however. There have been multiple causes. Even people who were not directly touched by the illness have been dealing with many unexpected losses, such as loss of freedom, loss of income, loss of companionship, loss of communication and loss, quite simply, of touch, tenderness and hugs. Children and young people have been no less deeply affected, and for young people just starting out in their adult life, loss of opportunity has been a major factor affecting mental wellbeing. When the Prince's Trust did its annual survey on the happiness and confidence of young people in 2021, it found the worst results in its history of doing these surveys (Hill, 2021).

And, as always, the most disadvantaged have suffered most – women, Black, Asian and ethnic minority people, elderly and disabled people and those already on marginal incomes (Children's Commissioner for Wales, 2021; NHS Digital, 2020; Royal College of Psychiatrists, 2021; Health Foundation, 2020a, 2020b).

Throughout the pandemic, there have been repeated surveys and warnings of an impending mental health crisis. In an article written at the beginning of the pandemic, one of the UK's leading psychiatrists, Dr Adrian James, President of the Royal College of Psychiatrists, warned that the coronavirus crisis posed the greatest threat to our mental health since World War Two, with the impact likely to be felt for years once the pandemic was brought under control. He predicted that as many as 10 million people, including 1.5 million children, were likely to need new or additional mental health support as a direct result (Sample, 2020). Modelling by the Centre for Mental Health similarly forecast that some 1.3 million people who had not had mental health problems before could be expected to need treatment for moderate to severe anxiety, and 1.8 million to need treatment for moderate to severe depression (O'Shea, 2020).

These are staggering figures, but we must look at them critically. There is on the one hand abundant evidence that many people have found it very difficult to deal with this crisis and that it has upset the balance of their lives completely. That is fully to be expected in the circumstances. Frontline workers, exhausted from dealing with the deaths and many potentially suffering PTSD, will certainly need extra support (Blackall, 2021). Those who are grieving over lost loved ones will need time to process their bereavement and complex grief. Women who have felt under pressure home-schooling their children and doing housework while holding down a job working from home, or who were victims of domestic violence in lockdown, will need adequate support to liberate themselves from this situation (Walter, 2021). Children who have lost their social networks at a vital stage in their development might need to be offered extra help. But these are all experiences that are situational and that we can do something about in real terms. They are not necessarily a reason for diagnosing mental illness. Here is an opportunity to change the mental health narrative about such human responses (Johnstone, 2000, 2020).

The crisis is showing us that, when people are under grave pressures, of course they experience feelings of anxiety, sadness, despair, helplessness and anger. It doesn't mean they have suddenly become ill with mental health disorders. It means that they are human beings responding in understandable, normal ways to a very difficult situation. Clearly people who were already on antidepressants or who were having a difficult time finding meaning in their lives or were being supported with existing mental health conditions will have been more vulnerable to the impact of the pandemic. Yet, interestingly, some of my clients with previous problems felt strangely relieved by the pandemic. They felt as if everyone else was suddenly on a level with them; their difficulties became validated and therefore easier to speak about.

Vos, in his review of the studies on the psychological impact of the pandemic, found that, more broadly in the general population, there was a whole range of causes for diminished mental health, which he summarised into nine specific factors (Vos, 2021, pp.114–115):

1. Reduced physical activity, which can itself lower mental and emotional wellbeing.
2. Loss of daily routine, affecting sleeping patterns and mood.
3. Social isolation, leading to boredom and fewer opportunities to release psychological and physical stress through leisure activities.
4. Loss of confidence due to social isolation particularly among single and socially marginalised people.
5. Financial worries and stress due to loss of income, business closures, unemployment and housing problems.
6. Overcrowding among large families with complex dynamics and no escape to alleviate the pressures.
7. Dwindling food supplies and lack of exercise leading to people losing the will to live.
8. Weakened immune systems due to the psychological stress caused by being confined in quarantine/lockdown.
9. Self-isolation leading to suicide or suicidal behaviour, because people stop feeling connected to others and may not see a future for themselves.

Vos estimated that, for every three deaths caused by the virus itself, there may have been another two caused by the lockdown, including failure to seek medical attention early enough for other serious medical conditions.

Most people recognised that lockdown, self-isolation and shielding for long periods had an intense knock-on effect on their mood. Many people reported having nightmares, especially at the start of the pandemic. Others reported losing their motivation to get up and get going because they were working from home. Parents were under particular pressure, trying to work from home while also home-schooling their children.

And there was evidence too that people were remarkably resilient. This was not a downward curve into some kind of mental health catastrophe. The UCL Covid-19 Social Study (Fancourt et al., 2021) carefully documented in monthly surveys the state of the nation's psychological wellbeing. Its reports showed how the levels of anxiety and depression went sky high at the start of the first wave of the pandemic, at the beginning of 2020, slowly reduced to a near normal level by August that year, when infection levels were at their lowest and lockdown was lifted, before rising again throughout the second wave and the return of lockdown. So, when the imminent threat eased and as life returned to normal, so did the nation's wellbeing. Another study, around the same time, documented the impact of people's coping strategies, and showed that not drugs, not appointments with the psychiatrist, not even counselling but ordinary social support was the most important factor in helping people recover mental equilibrium (Fluharty et al., 2020):

> People with greater use of problem-focused, avoidant, and supportive coping displayed more mental health symptoms, while greater use of emotion-focused coping was associated with fewer mental health symptoms. Symptoms decreased over time for all coping strategies, but only supportive coping was associated with a faster decrease in anxiety and depressive symptoms, indicating a potential protective effect of social support on psychological distress. (p.1)

It is clear that many people were plunged into existential crisis when, in so many ways, their normal expectations were unmet or put into question. People had to learn very hard lessons about how life goes: that we humans are not always able to control the forces of nature and their consequences. This may in some ways be a good thing: perhaps we have become more realistic, more aware that life involves deprivation and suffering and can't be expected to meet all our needs all of the time. In many people, the situation brought out huge resilience. But, before we can determine how this can be maximised, we need to understand the effects of the pandemic on people's faith in humanity and in life itself.

Broken connections

Most of the emotional and mental health problems caused by the pandemic have been related in some way to the fact that our usual frameworks of meaningful connections were suddenly broken apart and that we were not prepared for this. This was particularly true of children and teenagers who could no longer see their friends, their gang, their peers to make life interesting. It was also strikingly true for those who lived alone, or who were elderly, chronically unwell or disabled, most of whom have had to spend long months in almost total isolation. However, such disconnection has also been experienced as a positive thing by some people in some situations. Perhaps this has particularly been the case for people who had become over-connected in their lives. There certainly have been gains as well as losses in the pandemic. A team of researchers from a number of different universities have reminded us that we should not fall into the narrative of a pandemic mental health catastrophe (Bentall, 2021).

My life was certainly changed in many ways by the virus, and I would say that mostly these changes were positive. It certainly brought many difficulties into my life that had to be resolved: for instance, how to keep my business running, supporting all my staff members. It also brought some anxieties and deprivations, as well as a tangible fear of my own potentially impending mortality and new vulnerability. But it was also a great relief to stop commuting into London from my home in Sussex. As I started doing all my teaching, administration, therapy and supervision online, my everyday life became a great deal easier in the simple terms of logistics and I saved myself many train fares. Likewise, when air travel became almost impossible, I had to cancel numerous conference presentations and workshops that I had booked worldwide for 2020 and 2021 – trips to Russia, India, Iran and Australia, and various European venues. Most of these events were moved online, so overall, my life became calmer and more centred around its new focus in the home. I felt more able to spend time doing what I like doing.

I found that this had a very peaceful effect on me. I no longer struggled with the pressure to travel the world to spread the word or to accept every invitation I received. While invitations to speak at online events multiplied, it became much easier to say no, as there was not going to be a face-to-face encounter. It became more straightforward to guard my boundaries, as other people were already distant and kept out of my inner circle.

Like many other grandparents, I missed seeing my children, stepchildren, grandchildren and grand-dogs. That was an emotional and physical hardship that sparked a sense of being isolated and unimportant in their lives. It was especially difficult not being able to be with the grandchildren; I missed their warm and lively presence in my life. Seeing them online was just not the same as playing with them or hugging them. The way I dealt with this was to count my blessings that I could stay in touch via Zoom every week and by reminding myself how extra special it would be when we could finally meet again. I thought of all the people who had to say goodbye forever as they lay dying of the virus and I felt humbled. It helped that I have a very close relationship with my husband, and we were lucky enough to be able to adopt a puppy in lockdown, as did many thousands of other people. This provided plenty of occasions for cuddling and physical closeness. It made the isolation much easier, as it created a warm feeling of caring and being needed. It also helped that I was still very busy and very much required to continue working with colleagues, students and clients.

Having a philosophical mindset was also helpful. It always lifted my spirits to remind myself that this crisis was shared with every single person in the world and that we were working hard at solving the problems. Knowing the difficulties some people had to deal with helped keep my feet on the ground. I quickly realised that I was safe enough, locked away from human contact; things were not as bad for me as they were for a lot of other people. This made me aware that I could hardly count this experience as an existential crisis in my personal life. If it wasn't going to destroy my life or plunge me into grief or poverty, I sensed that I could cope with it with relative ease. It did stimulate me to think about the impermanence of my life in a new and more acute way and to become more reflective about my age and my growing dependency on my community around me.

This suggests that there have been mental and emotional gains for some at least, as well as losses in the pandemic. This also emerged from Vos's research:

> Many authors seem to paint the pandemic with a Janus face, and it is uncertain which will dominate. On the one face, there are those arguing how biopolitics undermines the material, psychological and social conditions of individual empowerment, democracy and revolution. On the other face, there are those saying that the pandemic is motivating people to reflect, criticise and rise against authoritarian governments. (Vos, 2021, p.72)

In other words, there was an effect of consciousness raising. We realised on the one hand that we were all in the same boat, but on the other hand discovered that we were not all in the same position on that boat. Some were travelling first class; others in steerage. I have already mentioned the poverty that struck those who lost their jobs, and the cramped living conditions for those who found themselves locked into small flats with their children, whom they were home-schooling. But the existential crisis was also fierce for those with pre-existing health conditions, who literally began to fear that their lives could be curtailed by simply going shopping. The phenomenon of 'shielding' was a peculiar experience that could easily lead to a sense of desperation and desolation and also to a feeling of constant alarm that sapped people's emotional stability. I was moved and saddened to hear about people who died of the virus alone, in their own homes, and who had not wanted to contact the health services in order not to be a burden or because they were afraid of dying in a hospital corridor. There was a lot of silent suffering that the world never witnessed.

I posted some YouTube videos reflecting on the paradoxes of the pandemic and people watched them more eagerly than other videos I had posted previously. It seemed as if people did really seek support and new ideas. It was pleasing to feel that I could contribute something, however small, to the wellbeing of others. The well-known saying that it is better to light a single candle than to curse the darkness was starkly in my mind.

Meaning-making from the pandemic

I became aware just how important it was to find ways to create meaning out of this disaster and to learn lessons that would allow us to live with more gratitude, understanding and care for each other afterwards. With many of my clients, the pandemic has been a time of intensity that showed up areas of difficulty that were normally hidden underneath the surface. Everyone needed to allow themselves a period of grieving when they realised they could no longer feel safe or meet with friends and family. We can't overcome crisis until we have faced the losses. But then it was my role to gently move them towards an appreciation of this opportunity to become aware of what they missed the most and to value the fact that they would, one day, get back to doing those things.

It is vital to admit that we are experiencing difficulties and to allow ourselves to feel the sadness about the harm done to us and the injuries we are suffering before we start trying to do something about it. But it is even more important not to let ourselves be defeated by this blow of fate, and rather to take our changed destiny by the horns and make it our own. It is important to shake off our blues and rediscover our capacity for making something of the troubles visited on us. It is important to invite ourselves back into the dance of life and rediscover hope.

Rebecca Solnit, writing from the US in April 2020, explored the experience of hopelessness that many in lockdown were reporting (Solnit, 2020). She captured eloquently the atmosphere of our awakening to the crisis in which we were plunged:

Disasters begin suddenly and never really end. The future will not, in crucial ways, be anything like the past, even the very recent past of a month or two ago. Our economy, our priorities, our perceptions will not be what they were at the outset of this year. The particulars are startling: companies… retooling to make ventilators, the scramble for protective gear, once-bustling city streets becoming quiet and empty, the economy in freefall. Things that were supposed to be unstoppable stopped, and things that were supposed to be impossible – extending workers' rights and benefits, freeing prisoners, moving a few trillion dollars around in the US – have already happened. (Solnit, 2020)

Solnit pointed out that normality had had to be abandoned for a 'new normal'. We discovered that our priorities in life shifted. Initially, we mainly just wanted to survive. This manifested very clearly in the scenes of panic-buying in our supermarkets during the first weeks of lockdown, when desperately anxious and insecure people bought particular products in order to hoard them, to shore up their existence. The idea of running out of essentials was on many people's minds: toilet paper, pasta, rice, flour and tinned goods were particularly prized. This was not greed, as many people thought; it was a simple human response to an extreme situation (Long & Khoi, 2020). When at risk, people's first instinct is to safeguard themselves and their loved ones, and so buying food was not a crazy thing to do. We also witnessed humanity returned to its very basics, as people fought over the last pack of toilet paper or tin of tomatoes, but this was not an expression of evil; it simply showed that, when in dire straits, people instinctively do what they think is necessary in order to survive.

We need to be realistic rather than judgemental about this and appreciate the psychological impact of fear on all of us ordinary people (McMullan et al., 2020, Shevlin et al., 2020). When we are suddenly confronted with death anxiety, we are bound to act emotionally and even violently if we feel our continued existence is at stake (Menzies & Menzies, 2020). In her article, Solnit referred to what happened in the aftermath of 2005 Hurricane Katrina, which flooded and destroyed large parts of New Orleans, so that many people died:

The mainstream media colluded in obsessing about looting in the aftermath of Katrina. The stock of mass-manufactured goods in large corporate chain stores seemed to matter more than people needing food and clean water, or grandmothers left clinging to roofs. Nearly 1,500 people died of a disaster that had more to do with bad government than with bad weather. (Solnit, 2020)

When life is in the balance, survival trumps moral correctness. When people feel their government is unreliable, they will take their own decisions where they feel it is necessary. In therapy sessions, clients regularly told me that they doubted the integrity and competence of government and drew comparisons between the UK and countries like New Zealand, which had locked down early and where deaths were few.

In early 2021, as the second wave of the virus was raging, although the vaccine was in its early days of being distributed and hope was definitely on the horizon, I participated in an extraordinary online panel, The Gaidar Forum 2021, organised by the Russian Presidential Academy of National Economy and Public Administration and the Moscow Institute of Psychoanalysis. It was an international gathering of psychiatrists and psychologists from Russia, the UK and the US, brought together to consider how we might create a better world after the pandemic, especially in terms of mental and emotional wellbeing. Thousands of participants attended. It was as if people were waking up to the importance of creating better relationships, not just in their own lives, but also at the level of states and nations. It is indeed what is needed at the end of a global crisis: a critical review of the situation that brought about the crisis and a constructive consideration of what new possibilities may now have become available and what new structures are now needed and wanted.

Managing our terror

What the Covid-19 pandemic did to many people is take away their sense of safety and certainty and fill them with alarm and terror – an experience that was new to many of us, forcing us to find new coping mechanisms. The theory of terror management (Greenberg et al., 2014; Harvell & Nisbett, 2016; Solomon et al., 2015) is inspired by the existential notion that human beings tend to deny death (Becker, 1971, 2011) in order to create a false sense of security. The terror management theory shows that we find new kinds of defences when faced with the reality of a death threat. Many people seek to affirm their self-esteem and thus to bolster their belief that they will survive. If challenged by, for example, being shown the facts about their personal risk level, they may use cognitive dissonance: they will store the contradictory information separately, in another compartment to their knowledge from their own experience, in an attempt to deny the problem and continue to believe that it doesn't apply to them.

When it becomes clear that their claims are mistaken and that they have built their safety on sand, they may be plunged into a sense of despair and discombobulation. People who previously thought themselves superior in some way and who imagined that this would protect them may find it much harder when they have to face the reality of their predicament. They may also deeply resent this happening to them and become quite angry, because their situation seems 'unfair'. Existential psychotherapist Irvin Yalom described such ways of defending against death anxiety as counterproductive because they stop us facing the reality of life itself. In his book *Existential Psychotherapy* (Yalom, 1980), he introduced the idea that people regularly turn to a number of defences against such experiences. Death anxiety is combatted by the individual either by thinking themselves so special that they will be spared or by seeking an ultimate rescuer – a figure who will save them from danger. Yalom's work with cancer patients made him aware that such defences are often seen as useless and counterproductive at the moment when a person is finally confronted with death, and are then regretted. It is often only when confronted with the reality of death that we realise we have wasted time trying to avoid reality, when we could have lived life to the full with our eyes open.

> Several of my cancer patients posed the same question. When speaking of their growth and what they had learned from their confrontation with death, they lamented, 'what a tragedy that we had to wait till now, till our bodies were riddled with cancer, to learn these truths'. (Yalom, 1980, p.165)

Yalom was to describe his own struggles in facing the reality of his death in another book, *Staring at the Sun* (Yalom, 2008) and the reality of experiencing the actual death of his wife, Marilyn, in a more recent book, *A Matter of Death and Life*, jointly written with Marilyn in her final months (Yalom & Yalom, 2021). In this last book, he writes of his own death anxiety that preoccupied him throughout much of his life. In an interview he gave to mark the publication of the book, he says (Jackson, 2021):

> The more regrets one has about life, looking back, the greater anxiety one has about dying… I can learn from my own life. As I look back on my life, as I've been doing this past year in my grief, I have virtually zero death anxiety. Whereas I had it so much earlier in my life. In *Staring at the Sun*, I wrote a whole book about it! But now I am old and I look back on my life, I don't have any regrets at all. I look at the books I've written, I married this extraordinary woman, had four children whom I love very much, I have lots of grandchildren, and I just have no regrets.

When we study Yalom's work, alongside that of philosophers like Kierkegaard (1954, 1980) and Heidegger (1927/1962, 1961, 1969), we realise that accepting the inevitability of death and of our continual state of existential insecurity is the route to regaining our footing.

This is exactly what Viktor Frankl, (1986, 2019) showed us when he wrote of his concentration camp experiences. As a psychiatrist and psychotherapist, he knew the importance of finding purpose, even when things seem utterly hopeless and therefore pointless. Speaking about the other men around him in the concentration camp, he says:

> Whenever there was an opportunity for it, one had to give them a why – an aim– for their lives, in order to strengthen them to bear the terrible how of their existence. Woe to him who saw no more sense in his life, no aim, no purpose, and therefore no point in carrying on. He was soon lost… We had to learn ourselves and, furthermore, we had to teach the despairing men, that it did not really matter what we expected from life, but rather what life expected from us. We needed to stop asking ourselves about the meaning of life and instead to think of ourselves as those who were being questioned by life – daily and hourly. Our answer must consist, not in talk and meditation, but in right action and right conduct. Life ultimately means taking the full responsibility to find the right answer to its problems and to fulfil the tasks which it constantly sets for each individual.
> (Frankl, 1985, p.84–85)

Faced with the ultimate threat to one's dignity, one's life, one's safety and one's future, there is no other way than to start creating meaning by finding a new attitude towards our fate. We can cultivate a philosophical or even stoical attitude towards the brevity of our existence. We can learn to appreciate the good things we can still find in the world we are in. We can learn to bring as much goodness as we can to other people around us. And we can learn to face our suffering with equanimity and courage. If we remain in a state of cognitive dissonance, we can do nothing, least of all make meaning from our existence; dissonance and defence make it impossible for us to learn. We have to face our troubles head on. We see this over and over again in the stories in this book: that true courage in facing our existential predicament is the key to being able to find a way to thrive on the experience (Beck et al., 2016; Bracken, 2002; Brown, 2012, 2015; Bugental, 1965; Craig, 1988; Ferrara, 1998).

Courage comes from living through our troubles with awareness and a willingness to cope and learn. Tim Hayward spent 10 days unconscious and close to death in intensive care due to Covid-19. His account (2021) is worth reading in this respect. His description of trying to make sense of his situation is excruciating and enlightening:

I spent 10 days unconscious in the ICU, but that's really the wrong
word. The drugs, the unfamiliar sensory input, the physical treatment of
my inactive body… 'delirium' during and after ICU is an unsurprising
side effect. Those days and a considerable period after were filled
with dreams… Men with rubber faces yell: 'Do you know where you
are?' and stuff things down my throat to the penetrating noises I will
later recognise as the pings and beeps of my own monitoring equipment.
Sounds quite amusing now, I know, but what's scary is that I doubt I'll
ever forget any detail of the dreams. I'm not sure I'll ever recover any of
the real experience that they overlaid. (Hayward, 2021)

Hayward concludes his piece with an insightful understanding that his ability
to describe what he went through is one of the reasons he hopes not to carry
long-term mental scars:

Unlike many who go through intensive care, I haven't displayed
symptoms of PTSD. Being asked to write this and being able to express
it, is one of the reasons I can hope that I won't. (Hayward, 2021)

The explorer Robin Hanbury-Tenison, now aged 84, also spent five weeks
in a coma in Derriford Hospital, in Cornwall, after contracting Covid-19. In
an article written about him for the Royal Cornwall NHS Trust (2020), he
recounted his awakening as a moment of almost bliss.

When all hope was lost, when family and friends feared the worst, I had
a breakthrough moment. Taken by the nurses, my guardian angels, to
Derriford's rehabilitation garden, I felt the warmth of the sun on my face
and I knew that I would live.

The rehabilitation garden was created with the express purpose of providing
Covid patients with a place where they could find a sense of healing and peace.
Lisa Niemand, Matron in the Critical Care Unit at Royal Cornwall Hospital,
said it was intended as:

… a place for healing and rehabilitation, not only physical but for the
mental and emotional self too, smelling different scents and the sound of
the breeze through the leaves. It gives people a grounding and a reminder
of what they have to aim for to keep them pushing through their recovery
and rehabilitation. There is no truer saying than 'the healing power of
nature'. (Young, 2020)

This dovetails with our existential model, which encourages people who are going through crisis to re-establish physical safety in nature, followed by reconnecting to trustworthy human relationships, followed by a retrieval of a sense of agency and personal worth and the setting of new purpose and direction in life.

As with other aspects of crisis, when meaning is torn apart at the seams and the fabric of one's life unravels, thread by thread, it is crucial to have an understanding of how we can rehabilitate our lives again. If we can do so, we will feel the return of a sense of hope.

Retrieving hope and meaning

When we begin to see that the pieces of our shattered life can be put together again, we begin to see the light at the end of the tunnel. It is vital that we don't go too fast or forget the territory we have just crossed with so much effort. It is also important not to idealise what came before our catastrophe or to try to rebuild our lives exactly as they were. The crisis has taught us courage and we need to have the courage to build our lives anew, rather than try to revert to how things were.

Solnit expressed it well in her Covid article (2020):

> Hope offers us clarity that, amid the uncertainty ahead, there will be conflicts worth joining and the possibility of winning some of them. And one of the things most dangerous to this hope is the lapse into believing that everything was fine before disaster struck, and that all we need to do is return to things as they were. Ordinary life before the pandemic was already a catastrophe of desperation and exclusion for too many human beings, an environmental and climate catastrophe, an obscenity of inequality. It is too soon to know what will emerge from this emergency, but not too soon to start looking for chances to help decide it. It is, I believe, what many of us are preparing to do.

It is easy to become convinced that there was a better world in the past. Our challenge is to accept today's challenges and create a better world for the future.

Here is our friend Joan, the nurse, again, writing for this book about his Covid experiences:

> The fear of Covid was the catalyst for me to become a volunteer in the Oxford trials to develop the vaccine. I did not want to live with Covid any longer than necessary and I reached the conclusion that the only way out of this pandemic would be with a vaccine. But being a volunteer has also

been a rollercoaster of emotions. My heart stopped every time a problem with the vaccine made the headlines, but at least it gave me hope and that hope was priceless. When they finally approved the vaccine and I actually held it in my hands, I cried. Being back working on the frontline has been the hardest thing I have done during my 23 years career in nursing, but it is also the thing I am most proud of. The impact on my mental health has been enormous, but thanks to my emotional awareness, which I learned through my previous crisis, and thanks also to the fantastic support of my psychologist, I have managed to keep a healthy mind.

We see how Joan learnt to hold that courage and transport it from one crisis to the next one. He also knew what he needed to do to stay sane and brave. Courage is not a one-off; it is an attitude that remains part of our process of living, a new backbone that remains with us.

This is what many of us who have been hiding from the challenges still need to realise – for there will be other pandemics, and there will be other crises related to climate change and other consequences of human meddling with nature. Before too long, there will be large areas of the earth that have become uninhabitable and new crises of migration of large populations will become a reality, because land is either too dry or flooded. We need to prepare ourselves for such eventualities. What we are learning is that life is precious and precarious. We should not think we can take our habitual mode of living for granted again. We will not be out of the woods for the foreseeable future and will face new crises again and again.

This is why finding meaning in crisis is so essential. We have to learn this skill when crisis strikes, so we train ourselves to be resilient on every future occasion when our courage is needed. Our lives will be far more profound and consequential if we are open to appreciating the dangers and difficulties, knowing we are equal to them and that we will be able to overcome them and appreciate the joys and treasures of everyday experience again. This is what many people discover after they have been through existential crisis: that they begin to appreciate the things they have been deprived of. As Camus remarked in his essay *Return to Tipasa* (Camus, 1942/1955):

In the middle of winter, I at last discovered that there was, within me, an invincible summer. (p.181)

If we let ourselves be touched deeply by our experience, we become much stronger for it. As Nietzsche wrote in *Thus Spake Zarathustra*:

… there is something in me that I call courage: it has always destroyed every discouragement in me… For courage is the best destroyer – courage that attacks: for in every attack there is a triumphant shout. (Nietzsche, 1883, p.177)

9

Living with existential courage

In these pages, I have proposed a systemic model for working with the individual in crisis that is based in structural existential analysis and takes into account the Four Worlds Model (van Deurzen & Adams, 2016) where we seek to understand how crisis affects the person at all levels. To enable a person to thrive from a crisis, they need to work on every dimension of their experience, mastering each well enough to reorganise their lives. This is usually done by observing, recognising, getting to know, then mastering, the opposing forces of the polarities at each level.

At the **physical** level, a person in crisis must find safety, by having shelter and finding comfort, so as to survive and hide away from further blows. We need good food and drink and lots of sleep, in order to be able to repair and heal body and mind, slow down and recover our sense of wholeness. Once we find our feet again, we can take ownership of this requirement and look after it carefully. Think of me, at the age of 10: the hospital kept me safe and sheltered me in my crisis, but afterwards I had to learn to think about how to manage that physical environment with circumspection.

At the **social** level, the task is to build new and stronger relationships, where trust is developed step by step. It is essential to learn to express emotions thoughtfully and only when we are ready to do so. We need to be able to take charge of the process of facing our losses, our grief and our doubts. We need to feel we still belong to a community and have a role to play in contributing something to it, even if we temporarily withdraw from it. If you think back to my own plight at the age of 10, my crisis precipitated my awareness of the tensions in the relationships in my family. It became vital for me to find new relationships in the world around me that I could build on to give me a sense of being appreciated.

At the **psychological** or mental level, we must retrieve and secure our capacity for clear thinking. This comes from retracing the past until it makes sense again and understanding how it links with the present. Then we can start to wonder about the direction we want to go. Taking responsibility for moving beyond the disaster is vital. Repairing and rebuilding a self comes with rebuilding our new life. This will transcend but never deny the catastrophe and the losses. This can only happen if we properly grieve for what has gone. For me, my existential crisis at the age of 10 was really the beginning of in-depth self-reflection. I started keeping a diary soon after this and became much more able to see my own impact on the world as well as the way the world affected me.

As we begin to rise from our crisis it becomes possible to address the **spiritual** or **philosophical** dimension of our experience. This is when we review past values that were shattered in the tragedy and realise what truly matters to us now, as we are emerging again. We can shape a stronger framework of meaning that holds together beyond cataclysm. It usually means going to the meta-level, where we begin to explore the universal forces at play in our lives. We wonder about what it means to be a human being and to exist, and we ask ourselves what our lives are for and can be used for. In my own existential crisis at 10, my world view was totally revolutionised. Previously, I had been made to believe that everything was good in my world and that life was exactly as it should be. I had also been led to believe I was basically safe. I learnt that life is not as simple as that and that unexpected events can transform everything, and that safety is very relative. I also learnt that people are never totally wrong or right, good or bad, and that we must be modest and humble in observing and encountering each other.

Figure 9.1 shows how these four levels overlap and intertwine, and how we might enhance our engagement at all levels to make our lives better. It also illustrates how we can gauge the enormity of an existential crisis by examining how many levels of a person's life have been affected or destroyed by an event. They will help us discover what enduring strengths can be found in each person's life that may be enhanced after crisis.

Owning our experience

A good example of supporting people in existential crisis is the work of existential therapists with offenders. The way we treat others is the way we treat ourselves. When we live in a world where we do damage, we become damaged too. Most offenders, despite their anger and beneath an attitude of nonchalance, aloofness or dispassion, experience suffering, loss, regret, isolation and often despair about themselves and the world. They may have cut themselves off from society or stopped seeking to make a positive contribution

Figure 9.1: Overcoming existential crisis

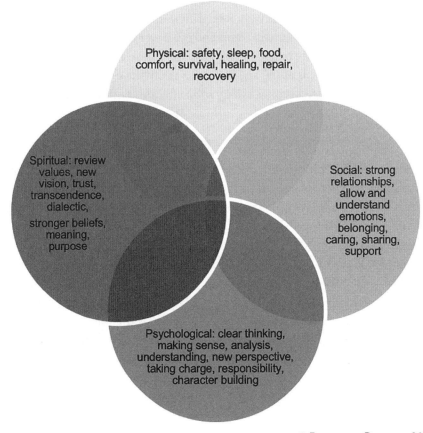

Physical: safety, sleep, food, comfort, survival, healing, repair, recovery

Spiritual: review values, new vision, trust, transcendence, dialectic, stronger beliefs, meaning, purpose

Social: strong relationships, allow and understand emotions, belonging, caring, sharing, support

Psychological: clear thinking, making sense, analysis, understanding, new perspective, taking charge, responsibility, character building

© Emmy van Deurzen, 2021

to it, but deep down they are people whose crises have left them scarred, isolated and stranded.

Siebrecht Vanhooren, an experiential-existential therapist in Belgium, works with offenders to help them understand the past events that led to their criminal behaviour and ultimately to their dysphoria and difficulty in facing their life's circumstances while incarcerated. His objective is existential in nature: to enable people to rise to the challenge of the bad things that have happened, take responsibility for them and learn from the experience to move on, beyond them, out of the trap they got caught in. In a long case study (Vanhooren et al., 2015), he describes his work with Diana, who had set fire to her boyfriend's flat and who had previously attempted suicide after a break-up. The work consisted of reviewing the past, including the index offences, in a calmly processing manner, looking at it from different angles, enabling her to grasp the reality of it, the reasons for it and the impact of it. Diana was thus enabled to own an experience she had previously sought to disown and distance herself from.

Vanhooren and his co-authors show that shifts occurred at all levels of Diana's life in this process, and they measured these with reference to the model described by Calhoun and Tedeschi (2013) in their three-factor model of post-traumatic growth. Diana showed a changed sense of self, changed relationships, and also a changed philosophy of life after the therapy.

> By processing the past in an experiential mode, she generated new meanings about herself, about others and about the meaning and purpose of her own life. Diana found new ways to meet her basic existential needs. She developed a more nuanced set of meanings and a richer palate of coping skills that enable her to live her life in a more meaningful and in a better adjusted way. (Vanhooren et al., 2015, p.4)

Such existential interventions make it possible for a person to stop blaming others or blaming themselves and start reflecting on what has actually happened and how their actions have created a crisis and have caused real damage to people's lives (including their own).

To further illustrate this process in practice, we can refer back to our EU citizens Joan and Lucie and remind ourselves of how they experienced devastation at all levels and what they did to rise from their crisis on each of those four dimensions.

1. **Physical** – Both felt insecure, unable to sleep and relax, and craved certain comfort foods and drinks. Both discovered how important it was to re-establish a good connection to their physical reality. They did this by feeding themselves better, by going out into nature, by physical exercise and by creating safety for themselves. They paid attention to bad habits and tried to replace them with better ones, in order to stay physically fit and be able to cope with the extra stress and be ready for the further battles ahead. All this took a lot of self-observation and a willingness to change.

2. **Social** – Both of them felt under attack and unwanted by many of the people around them, unable to rely on their previous sense of being liked and loved by others. They were each deeply affected by this and upset by the rejection. They both focused on improving their close relationships when they became aware that their partners were also suffering. They were willing to question their impact on the relationship and to realise they had to do something positive to maintain closeness, confidence and intimacy. Each of them realised how important and precious these relationships were

to them. Out of the crisis experience came a new comprehension of their spouses' experiences. Both learnt to focus on rebuilding trust with their spouse, instead of excluding them from their suffering. They also both learnt to take time away from destructive influences and not feel obliged to please everyone else.

3. **Personal** – Each of them went through a phase of low mood, when a tragic sense of doubt in themselves dawned upon them. They became aware of their vulnerability and had to notice that they were sometimes lacking in strength to withstand all these pressures. They learnt to be compassionate with themselves and to forgive themselves for messing up occasionally. Yet they were both also aware of how important it was to keep a clear head and keep working towards gathering fortitude. Each in their own ways began to search for methods in which they could get back to full mental and emotional strength and gain greater understanding of the situation they found themselves in. Each of them used self-development and self-care tools to enhance endurance and courage.

4. **Spiritual** – Each felt utterly bereft of their trust in humanity and society, let down and abandoned by their country and as if the world they had lived in before their crisis had been illusory or had now been totally changed. They each worked hard to make sense of what had happened and find meaning in their battle. They both understood that purpose and meaning are vital and they intentionally focused on those things that would make them feel they were living in the right way. They succeeded in forging new trust in life. They found ways of confirming the possibility of good things happening to them once more. They each found ways to change their life for the better, instead of remaining in a state of loss and despondency. Joan found meaning in actively contributing to the Covid vaccine trials and later on to working with Covid patients. Lucie left the rush and smoke of the city to move to the countryside and focus on creativity once again.

Their experience demonstrates very well that people are shaken awake rudely by their crisis, but that they can use their new awareness to start reflecting on life more vigorously. As we have seen, this is only possible if they are able to create safety and are also able to communicate securely with at least one person who can bear witness to their plight, accept it, validate it and help them understand it. This is what was so shockingly lacking in the veterans. When we can have physical and emotional safety and connectivity, we can find our bearings and begin to reconnect with new objectives and values. This is how we retrieve our appetite for continuing our life's journey, only now with a much more acute sense of direction and also of the potential threats ahead. We plunge in and immerse ourselves.

Social responses

These are the challenges for individuals in crisis. But we must not lose sight of the role of politics and society. If our institutions are not tuned into what happens to individuals, it becomes much harder to help them weather the hard times. If we don't support people, but diagnose them as having a mental illness instead, nobody will ever learn the human lessons of emotional and existential suffering. Society is rife with crises and disasters, many of them invisible to the eye. We encounter pressures and disappointments every day of our lives and some people live in circumstances that are impossible to sustain. It isn't enough to teach them to bear such challenges or be damned to becoming a mental patient. We must tackle the causes of these events in the outside world and provide more emotional support when bad things happen to people.

This is why it is so important for governments to begin valuing quality over quantity, wisdom over knowledge, collaboration over competition and kindness over warfare (Vos, 2020b). This isn't just about creating networks of support but about shifting the way in which we regard ourselves, each other and human existence: not as entities to be exploited or means to an end, but as valuable beings, each with a contribution to make to the wider world around us. If we want to be strong in a crisis, we must create such a society; one that is fair and strong and where people can earn their keep with satisfaction and dignity in a world of mutual respect, solidarity and safety. It means creating communities where there is open communication, where people are not punished, locked up or treated as mentally ill or insane when they fall out of step with the world because of an existential crisis. What we need is a society of solidarity and mutual support.

Life satisfaction in the UK has been steadily dropping for some time now. In January 2020, the Office for National Statistics (ONS, 2020) noted that life satisfaction scores, which have been measured in the UK for several years now, had dropped for the first time ever. The happiness measure had also dipped significantly. Anxiety ratings were rising. All this is very understandable, given the political, economic and social upheavals and uncertainties caused by Brexit and the Covid pandemic.

We also know from NHS Digital data (2019) that prescriptions for antidepressants and anxiolytics have been shooting up: 70.9 million prescriptions in 2018, compared with 36 million in 2008. To see the numbers of antidepressant prescriptions doubling in one decade tells us, first, that people feel under tremendous pressure, and second, that they are becoming increasingly dependent on drugs to cope with these stresses and strains.

It is high time we questioned the way we deal with this. We must start to acknowledge the role that society plays in this, rather than putting the onus on the individuals who are most vulnerable to pressure. For me, as an existential therapist, it is nothing new to see the problems people are experiencing as a response to the ills of society. Existential therapists speak of 'problems in living' instead of seeking to pathologise people's troubles. The Brexit debacle and the pandemic have given us an opportunity to see how large numbers of people respond in predictable and understandable ways to the woes of society. When they were put through the same loops of difficulties, many became trapped in emotional stress that made them seem mentally ill. In fact, they were just showing a human response to difficult circumstances. It is a large-scale experimental confirmation of the existential position on mental and emotional wellbeing.

I worked in the past with people like Thomas Szasz (Szasz, 1961, 1965/1988) and R.D. Laing (Laing, 1959, 1961, 1967), who made a very convincing case for the argument that society has looked at mental illness in the wrong way for far too long. They argued that, more often than not, their social, cultural, political, contextual and familial situations are what lead a person to a mental or emotional breakdown. Those who are most at risk are those who are most sensitive, for they will show up the fault lines of society before others do. But put anyone in an impossibly pressurised position for long enough and they will be shattered by events sooner or later. My own work has built further on these ideas for many years and I have formulated them in my books, proposing an alternative to psychopathological approaches to problems in living, especially so in *Everyday Mysteries* (2010), *Paradox and Passion* (2015a), and *Psychotherapy and the Quest for Happiness* (2009), and also in some co-authored books (van Deurzen & Arnold-Baker, 2005, 2018; van Deurzen & Kenward, 2005).

More recently, the movement of existential psychiatry and psychology has been transformed into a more pragmatic one that specifically aims to liberate people from their psychiatric diagnoses (Johnstone, 2000, 2014; Davies, 2013; van Deurzen, 2019a; Watson, 2019). And alongside existential therapy, there is now another framework for psychological interventions based in this view that it is often the unfair and imposing structures of society that cause the pressures that lead to emotional problems. This is called the Power Threat Meaning Framework (Johnstone & Boyle, 2018) and it is supported by the British Psychological Society. It is a very hope-giving step forward.

We need to start teaching people about adversity at a much younger age. It is as important for them to learn how to deal with existential crisis as it is for them to learn how to read and write and add up and how to stay physically healthy. Paul Wong, a positive existential therapist (Wong, 2009, 2021; Wong et al., 2021) advocates that we specifically educate the young about such things:

> Therefore, the cure for human suffering and the restoration of peace and happiness depends on the healing and transformation of brokenness to wholeness and oneness. Regarding the inner connections, the key to human happiness and mental health is learning how to maintain a dynamic balance between the heart's desires and the mind's rational judgement, between the dark and bright side of personality. (Wong, 2021)

If we learnt more about how human beings can rebalance their lives and rise to crisis, fewer people would need to resort to prescriptions for antidepressants. Somehow, we have wrongly come to expect that we will always be protected from troubles and that the world owes us prosperity and security and is obliged to provide us with a large dose of happiness. When things go awry, we expect to be able to pop a pill to heal our unease and distress, not realising we are started on a long road of psychological and medical dependency. We forget that life is hazardous and that we will fall ill sooner or later, that our working life can often exhaust and sometimes injure us, that we may lose our job, our home or our family due to events beyond our control. We forget that we can become isolated and rejected in the world and fall out with people we were close to. We forget that our time is measured, and that fate is not always friendly. We forget that things decay as well as grow. We forget about entropy, decline and deterioration. We forget that we will die and must make amends while we can.

We can make ourselves believe that life will continue in a safe and pleasant manner until something exposes the cracks in our illusions and self-deception. It is hard when this happens, and it often feels unfair. Yet, what we often fail to recognise when this happens is that we are being confronted with life as it actually is. Crises reveal the fault lines in our existence and their silver lining is that our eyes are opened to the injustices and difficulties we and others are confronted with. It offers us a chance to rethink our existence and *modus vivendi* and to question the structures of society. It makes us more aware of advantage and disadvantage. We have an opportunity to become part of the movement of progress and help change things for the better. It is often those who have suffered grave losses and injustices who are the driving force behind political and social improvements.

When we do not suffer such difficulties and problems, we slowly fall asleep. When things go too smoothly, we become superficial and inauthentic, believing ourselves to be deserving of exceptionalism and privilege. We become estranged from ourselves and each other. We become alienated from reality. It is in our suffering that we find the fight that will eventually get us back our freedom and depth of feeling. As Heidegger said: 'Only in communicating and in struggling does the power of destiny become free' (Heidegger, 1927/1962, p.384).

Only to the extent that we let ourselves be called by fate from our wishful thinking do we become capable of owning our existence to live it with deliberation and fortitude. Then it becomes possible to truly appreciate the vagaries of our lives and to feel thankful for them, no matter what happens to us. This is to become grateful for the being that is ours to hold preciously inside of us as long as we are alive.

> Original thanking is the thanks owed for being. That thanks alone gives
> rise to thinking of the kind we know as retribution and reward in the
> good and bad sense. (Heidegger 1954/1968, p.141)

The longest study on adult development ever carried out is the Harvard study, which stretched over more than 80 years. It systematically studied a group of male students at Harvard University in the US and boys of the same age from Boston's poorest neighbourhoods. It followed them up continuously, and included their wives, families and the next generations. It found that loneliness and isolation kill people; that connections with family, friends and community are vital. It isn't about quantity, but quality: the good life is built with good and meaningful relationships and having a sense of belonging and safety of abode (Waldinger, 2016).

When people who have been diagnosed with a particular kind of mental or emotional problem start talking to others with the same problem, they begin to think about why they have been labelled and isolated in this manner. They can begin to develop a different discourse about and understanding of the events leading up to their difficulties, and the road towards their liberation opens up for them. There is a dangerous place in our trials and tribulations where we become so harassed and victimised that we stop remembering that we can reclaim our authority and agency. If we hide from troubles for long enough, we get used to being in a one-down position. We lose track of our own authority. It is easy to become paralysed by this. When we start to notice our paralysis and begin articulating the problem, we immediately begin to reformulate our situation and start seeing ways of springing the trap open. We face facts. We befriend our anxiety and treasure its energy. We transform our experience by articulating what has happened to us and by lifting ourselves to a place from where we can oversee our circumstances; we refocus on the horizon, instead of hiding. Then we can see the landscape ahead, and change direction, start to breathe again and appreciate our new opportunities.

When people who are on the autism spectrum or have been labelled with various psychological difficulties, like dyslexia or dyspraxia, come together and compare notes about their living experience, they often discover that, although they may be different to 'normal' people, they also have specific abilities, gifts and strengths that come with their problems. The notion of neurodiversity can be very enabling in this respect (Tantam, 2012, 2014, 2018). It is hugely empowering to affirm who we are.

When refugees start talking to other refugees who are applying for asylum in the same country, they immediately begin to see that this is not just about them; it is not that they are not worthy of being accepted by their host country. They become more aware of dehumanising practices in their country of origin and also of those in the host country. They start articulating what is unjust in the way they are being dealt with. They can begin to think about how to liberate themselves from the effects of such inequitable treatment. They know they deserve to be treated as full and whole human beings, not as undesirables and outsiders who are surplus to requirements (Wilson, 2001). They may start to work together towards claiming back their humanity (Thompson, 2006; Tetlock, 1994; Wampole, 2016; Vos et al., 2019).

As Sartre said in his later work (Sartre, 1960/1982, 1983/1992, 1989/1992), we need to discover that transformation is brought about by praxis. Praxis is defined as reflective action, or active reflection. It is the process that enables us not to be totally absorbed in our difficulties. If we have a sense of overwhelming passivity and victimhood, it is hard to stand strong and find determination in the face of calamity and dispossession. When we find a way to act with greater awareness, we can get back to a position from which to transform our situation, at least to some extent. None of this happens by itself. We need to reclaim our autonomy and capacity for effecting change. When we have become disaffected and disenfranchised, we have to re-engage instead of disengaging. We have to remember once again how important our connective networks are to our emotional wellbeing.

Each time we manage to get safely through a crisis, through our own actions and with support from our friends, family, community and society, we learn that the vicissitudes of life are not to be feared and that our energies should not focus on avoidance and protection. Rather, we should meet life with openness, fortitude and an attitude of problem-solving and creativity. This is what I would define as existential intelligence: to love our lives and everything that life brings; to embrace the very contradictions of our existence and welcome truth and transparency. It is through a combination of feeling deeply and then articulating and understanding those feelings, so that we can collect them and reflect on them, that we become capable of acting with integrity, purpose and determination.

The German theologian, philosopher and mystic Meister Eckhart said that if you want to find the kernel of something you must break the shell. When our shell is broken in a crisis, we can see what is inside of us and also what is inside life itself. This is the silver lining of our crisis, but it is up to us to turn this to advantage, find our equilibrium, and rise from our ashes. We can only benefit from it, if we first manage to cope with it.

So, how do we do this?

Rising from crisis

In order to cope with crisis, we first of all have to survive it. This means we do have to protect ourselves and establish a zone of safety into which we can withdraw, heal our wounds and recompose ourselves.

Then we have to find others and convince them to help support and sustain us. This is best done in the spirit of generosity and mutuality. In that atmosphere, we can begin to communicate our plight calmly and soberly, articulating it for ourselves, so that we get clarity about it and can integrate it into our normal reality, instead of keeping it on the outside. Only then, when the situation becomes real to us and we can think about it, can we begin to find remedies.

As Sartre said in his essay 'What is literature' (Sartre, 1950/2001):

> A lucid view of the darkest situation is already, in itself, an act of
> optimism. Indeed, it implies that this situation is thinkable; that is to say,
> we have not lost our way in it as though in a dark forest, and we can on
> the contrary detach ourselves from it, at least in mind, and keep it under
> observation; we can therefore go beyond it and resolve what to do against
> it, even if our decisions are desperate. (p.289)

By describing our situation fully and carefully we make sense of it. We differentiate ourselves from our plight as we sketch out our predicament. We then become able to question our position. All this is only possible if we focus on the situation instead of hiding or fleeing from it. When we use our consciousness deliberately to focus our intentionality on finding a way out, we realise that our mind can always shine a light in the darkness. Faced with danger, we have to become attentive, resolute, determined and creative. We cannot rise from crisis by dulling ourselves down. So, here is how we sharpen up.

1. Formulate the problem clearly

When we become more attentive to what is happening to us, we can take ourselves back in hand and reunite with our inner authority. The act of formulating the problem is sufficient to switch us from passivity to activity. From the moment we get a grip on what is happening by telling a tale about it, summarising it, and exploring it, we problematise it – we make it into a puzzle that needs solving. So, instead of remaining enclosed in a reactive, confused state of mind that keeps us imprisoned in a state of feeling hurt and duped, we set ourselves on the trail of discovery.

This is how therapy works: we encourage people to frame their problems so that they get a hold of them and see them as something tangible that they can manipulate and grasp. Then, instead of feeling at the mercy of their difficulties or overwhelmed by their own emotions, people become enabled again, as they understand that change is possible and desirable. They get this simple truth: that we can choose to be in the situation and own our own existence.

But don't be too demanding of yourself about it. You may need to take time to ponder. We all need a phase in which we express our pain, our disappointment, our grief and our sorrow. It is a way of collecting enough frustration to build the energy to get cracking. The more we allow ourselves to feel the pain directly, the less we will be inclined to retaliate with aggression, passive aggression, cynicism or blaming tactics. The trick is to allow yourself to absorb the loss fully and appreciate all the inner sadness that is caused by it. Sit with that for a bit. It helps to have someone patiently sitting with you. Then we can dismiss the easy options of negativity and take time to think about a better response and a workable strategy. It is all too easy to get lost in the destructive practice of saying 'no' to everything. We have to say 'no' sometimes, to some things and some people, but we can only rejoice in life again when we learn to say 'yes' again.

2. Move from reactivity to activity

After we have told our story and formulated our problem, we can begin to come to terms with the realisation that this problem is ours – that we need to take ownership of it. As long as a person is reacting to a situation, they have not made it their own. It remains outside of them and they want to deny its reality or protest against it. They waste precious time and energy kicking against their fate. They complain about it endlessly. Just kicking against it, denying it, resenting it, or even cursing it will not change it. We need to start examining it and take a hold of it. As long as we remain focused on blaming and shaming, whether it be others or ourselves or even our situation, we keep ourselves imprisoned in precisely the same situation that is hurting us. As long as we remain focused on what is wrong, we ensnare ourselves in it and become identified with it. It is crucial to name the problem, but from there we need to move on to finding out what caused it, how we got caught up and lost in it and, most importantly, how we can remove ourselves from it. That requires determination, and often co-operation with others.

3. Conduct an inventory of your talents, skills and resources

We may need to remind ourselves that we are capable of being constructive rather than self-destructive or destructive when things go wrong for us. This starts with learning to take stock of your skills and talents for dealing with problems. What are your assets? What do you know about your own character that will help you through the crisis? What have you learnt from previous troubles and battles? How can you apply this knowledge to the current situation? What resources are available to you? Who are your potential allies? How can you connect with them? Who are your best supporters and what can you ask them to do or provide for you? What would actually be helpful to you, practically and concretely, and where and how can you obtain it? Where are the bibliographical or online sources of information that might guide you?

Do your research and make finding solutions your main objective for a bit. Join other people who are in a similar situation. Initiate an action group or a particular task group that can improve something in your situation and that of others. Put your heads together. When you do, think consistently in terms of what you can contribute and how you can help others. Shift the focus from your difficulties to the possible solutions. Use your plight to throw light for others in the future.

But in doing this, take cautious care of yourself. Not all contact with others will be supportive. Some of it will be undermining and, if so, it needs to be avoided. Our connections to others have to be managed with caution and our online presence has to be managed with especially great wariness.

4. Prepare for endurance and the long term

While we may need to collapse for a little bit, it is essential that we take ourselves in hand to gather the necessary strength for the battle ahead. We should not rush into our comeback but, rather, build it up slowly and carefully. It is at such low times that reconnecting with the widest protective circle around us is of the essence. This means going out into nature to be reminded that the natural environment is still out there, doing its job in recycling our earth and our air. Let the skies, the rivers, the woods, the sea, the meadows and the mountains remind you that life is still going strong and is right there on our doorstep for us to be part of.

Making an effort to create an atmosphere of calm and peace in our home is also conducive to feeling settled. When I work with people in crisis, I know they are on the right track when they decide to buy a plant or a new lamp or a comfy chair for their home, or when they spend a few hours decluttering or redecorating a room. When we are in trouble, it pays to spend a little bit of time ordering our physical environment to clear a space for peace of mind and safety. A little bit of nesting can work miracles. It signals that we are getting ready to go forth from a secure base.

Taking care consists of building ourselves up while staying safe and polishing up the good things still available to us. Eating foods that will nurture us better is a good way to prepare for the difficult tasks of repair ahead. These things are very personal and culturally specific, so think for yourself about what would make you feel better and then take the trouble to prepare it for yourself. Make it into a routine. Relish that moment of wholeness where you feel better, even just temporarily; learn to look forward to it and keep doing it. The more time we spend on such simple acts of self-nurturing, the better. Don't wolf and waste your appetite. Eat very slowly, paying lots of attention to every morsel. When you re-establish your secure base, wherever possible include the presence of a loved one – if not a person, then perhaps a pet or a plant (Charura & Paul, 2015).

Re-establish experiences of flow and good energy whenever possible (Csikszentmihalyi, 1990). Find music that used to please you in the past and listen to it again and again, but choose carefully and don't get drawn into music that is too moody or maudlin, or that takes you back with too much intensity to previous losses. Don't linger too long in melancholy remembering. Most of us have some old-time favourite movies that renew our vital energies. Fantasising about adventures and travels is a good thing for most of us. So, let yourself dream a bit – perhaps read a travel guide – but don't set off on any journeys just yet, as this can be a source of stress in itself. You need to concentrate on being who you are and where you are.

5. Establish an affirmative routine

When we commit to a reliable and affirmative routine, we create a stronger and more determined mindset every time we complete the actions we are committed to. I work on this every day. I wake at six o'clock and take time to think about the day ahead and consider what matters most for me to concentrate on in the coming hours. It is all about setting myself in the right mode of being, preparing myself mentally for what is to come and deciding in what order and in what ways I want to tackle the tasks and duties ahead of me. It is about sharpening your intentionality and reconnecting with your sense of direction, rather than about specifics. It is the opposite of worrying; as we contemplate the day ahead, we ask ourselves how we can make it a good day and actually enjoy our chores. Each and every one of us will do this differently. What matters is that we notice that we are setting out on a new day and a new adventure and that we give it our full attention, instead of wishing it away. This is about questioning our habits and taking charge of our own life, so we can relish every minute of it. It's about learning to savour our existence and using each day to change something for the better.

6. Learn to recognise, respect and name your feelings

Another thing we can learn to do is to listen to our own responses to things and people and to register and name our own feelings and make sense of them. Sometimes we may need to reflect for a bit before we understand why we feel as we do, but it always pays off to do so, when we have time, perhaps at the end of the day before going to bed. Take your feelings seriously, but never let them dictate your behaviour. Just venting feelings is not enough. We need to make sense of them and get to the bottom of why we experience things as we do. Talking to a partner about events and our reactions to them does not just help us clarify where we are and what we need to do next; it also brings us closer together. Carrying the weight of the world on his shoulders may have been fine for Atlas, but it is no good for ordinary humans. We are not superhuman and we must respect our own limits. It never pays off to deny or negate our feelings or put ourselves down for them. We have every right to feel as we feel, as long as we find a way to listen to ourselves compassionately and translate our feelings into thoughtful actions.

We need to protect ourselves from carrying too much stress and distress, self-reproach, frustrations, resentments or regrets. In a crisis it is so easy to seize up or become numb and just accept the status quo for too long. When you start to experience strong feelings that are bigger than you would normally be inclined to feel, don't just try to suppress them. There is no reason to be scared of your feelings. Your feelings are your guide and they are pointing you in the right direction. Teach yourself to write them down in a daily diary and discuss them with a partner or a close friend or perhaps even a therapist.

7. Join a community

There is nothing so conducive to finding new hope as finding like-minded people who are constructive in building a new future or overcoming problems. Many friendships have been forged during times of hardship. Co-operation is an art, and we need to learn to value each other's strengths and support each other at times of weakness and vulnerability. We can't all be good at everything, and offering some of the things we are good at to other people in exchange for them doing the same for us is the most wonderful human arrangement. It is the principle that community building is based on. Communities are crucial for our full functioning. When we all compete against each other, the world becomes a hectic and frantic place. When we can rely on others to make the most of the bit they are responsible for, while we make the most of what we have chosen as our responsibility, then we complete each other and the tasks are carried out more efficiently. Value yourself and each other in that process and everyone benefits.

8. Learn a new skill – or revive an old one

Learning new skills, especially a new language, a musical instrument, a craft, an art or a sporting activity, is very constructive and uplifting. This is not just about reconnecting to the plus sides of life but also about rebuilding self-esteem, self-respect and self-affirmation. It is about reclaiming our capacity for growth and education, despite, and perhaps especially because of, the crisis we find ourselves in. We are entitled to a growth spurt when we are spending so much time deeply in grief and mourning. So, start by allowing your curiosity to be triggered and try to find out new things about the situation you find yourself in. Then think about how you can add to that imaginatively.

In our ESSE service, we encouraged people to try many new ideas and many new practices. We are all different and we are the expert on what will do the trick for us. Some people get a real buzz out of discovering they can deal with such challenging activities as windsurfing, bungee jumping, abseiling, horse riding, mountain climbing, skiing, skating, caving or wild swimming. Somehow, having survived a crisis makes us braver. We feel our strength and we stop being quite so afraid of everything, because we sense that the worst has already happened.

Such heroics are not for everyone, however. Some people really need to keep things small and familiar. When they are prompted to think about activities that are soothing for them, they remember things they used to do in childhood that don't require huge energy and stamina, like jigsaw puzzles, colouring in, embroidery, knitting, building a model airplane from a simple kit, or even sculpting something out of playdough or whittling. When people rediscover such old and neglected skills, they often report a sense of calm and a rebuilding of confidence. Other people return to skills they only practised for a bit in the past and that they now want to hone. They may bring down from the loft or from the shed things that have long been broken and mend them. I knew someone who took his car apart when he was recovering from a crisis. Putting it back together again took long enough to help him slowly rebuild his trust in his own efficacy. Someone else carved out a canoe from a fallen tree trunk in his garden.

Another approach that can work, especially for those who feel that violence has been done to them, is to take up a martial art – judo, karate, kick boxing or self-defence classes, for example. Weight training works for some, dancing for others. Gentler but equally effective ways of re-energising and focusing energy include yoga, pilates, tai-chi, qigong, meditation and mindfulness. Find what works for you. It is the principle that matters: a person has to reactivate their personal capacity to make something of themselves and stop feeling as if they are being duped, molested and beaten. We can feel martyred for a bit, but then we have to find a retort or rejoinder to our sense of weakness and victimisation. We must step out of our corner, eventually and take the upper hand again.

9. Don't be a martyr

Martyrdom is a bad role to slide into, although many of us are inclined to do so. Suffering in silence is one of the worst ways of enduring, because it is not sustainable. Suffering must not become our new identity. If we get used to it, we will be expecting it and tolerating it for years to come. There are many reasons why people settle for silent martyrdom. Sometimes their families assigned them this role early on. Sometimes they are just too nice to fight back, or they think too lowly of themselves to feel entitled to anything better. Sometimes they think that good people suffer while bad people portion out suffering. But it isn't really like that. The world can beat you down, but it cannot keep you down, and it certainly cannot force you to be prepared to endure humiliation for the rest of your life. Be free in your own mind and never be afraid to show a bit of your power, especially when you have suppressed it for far too long.

10. Be decisive

We need to learn to step up to the plate and then keep stepping forwards. There is a hidden force in people who are decisive that everyone respects and that makes all the difference in how you will advance. This comes from having taken the time to reflect on what is the right way ahead, making your choice and setting out on the journey, staying on track and keeping up your tempo. There is tremendous empowerment in being decisive, especially if you feel you have been messed about. As we know, the best revenge for wrongs done to us is not to get angry but to get even. We can only do so if we set our sights on getting things right and we let go of our resentments. Unbroken commitment to forward motion and self-improvement create and facilitate accomplishments and triumphs.

Some people hesitate to conduct themselves in such a way, as they feel it may seem selfish. It's important to know the difference between being self-caring and resolute – i.e. doing what is right for us and necessary for our survival – and being egoistic and self-seeking – i.e. doing something that is purely for our own pleasure and advantage but may be harmful to others. It is often good to have a chance to speak with others about our decisions and make sure that our actions are good all round and are endorsed and validated by the people we value around us. If we are going to grow authoritative and strong-minded, we need to be clear sighted, and fair minded too. There is no need to guilt trip ourselves if what we aim for is of use and help to others. Once you have worked out what needs to be done, dare to be outspoken and self-assured. Then be definite and firm in your actions.

11. Find new meanings and purpose

Ultimately, overcoming hardship comes down to finding meaning in it, and focused action is one way of re-establishing meaning. I've returned to this a lot in this book, because it is so central. Keep reminding yourself that meaning comes from connectivity. This can be most easily achieved by creating new links and bonds and getting a more in-depth understanding of how the world fits together. As soon as we get a sense of being part of a network of meaning, it becomes far easier to see where we are, who we are and what direction we want to be heading.

There is a mutual reinforcement between the direction of our actions and the feedback we are getting by making these new connections in action. This means that we have found new purpose. This is the very opposite of accepting our fate passively. We find meaning when we get a bird's eye view of our situation and see how our experiences fit into a narrative that goes beyond ourselves. As soon as we begin to lift the veil and make sense of things that previously were a mystery, we begin to feel more in control and more able to intervene and change things for the better. This is exactly what all those who have thrived from their crises have been able to do. They have become more insightful and more actively engaged with their troubles. They have not given up but have become more ardent in their efforts to improve things for themselves and the world around them.

12. Stick with it

This brings us to the importance of commitment. Many people who falter and flail about in crisis continue to do so for longer than necessary because they fail to see the importance of committing to a constructive road ahead. They dart in many different directions and run out of breath. They flap about and become exhausted and despondent, because all roads seem to be blocked and nobody supports them.

Don't expect support; it is up to you to find your way around the obstacles and make alliances. Contemplate the problems, consider all the possible solutions you can think of, and keep going. Be creative and free-floating about it and eventually you will see your opening. You will know what attracts you and you will find your personal way of tackling the situation. Don't let other people tell you how you should do it. Nobody can do it for you or know what it is like for you. Sort it out for yourself, but always get as much information as possible, then get going and keep going.

Do not isolate yourself but rely on yourself to do most of the hard work and trust that you can get through, slowly but surely, step by step. Remember that progress often comes in stops and starts and is rarely as rapid as we would like it to be. Sometimes we take two steps forward and one step back. Be prepared for such patterns and for further problems on the road ahead. Life is never predictable; it will throw lots of curve balls at you. The best thing is to know and accept this, get into it and get good at playing the ball you are thrown or the cards you are dealt. Be consistent in your efforts and show conscientiousness, dedication and persistence in your practice. It's fine to sleep on the job once in a while, or to take a day off, so long as you keep up your commitment to progress.

13. Take courage from your fear

If this book has shown anything, it is that we should never fear change; we should learn to welcome and relish it. Change is the natural principle of life. It is the flowing river of vitality. Anything that is alive is continuously growing and expanding, or waning and decaying. Living things never stay the same from one minute to the next. We measure time by the changes in the universe and we measure our lives by the time that has passed and the things that have changed. There is no point in trying to stay the same or keeping things under control. Things and events are in motion, they always move on, and we have to move on with them. We cannot stop the tides of life or struggle against them; we have to learn how to go with them.

Of course, not all change is welcome. Crises are a sudden and often violent form of change that transforms everything we take for granted. But civilisations have been built on crises. It is crises that have forced people at all times in history to come up with new solutions and adapt to new situations. Many inventions and medical breakthroughs are a response to emergencies. They are arrived at through long experimentation and hard work, building on the work of previous generations, but they are frequently inspired by difficulties and problems that need solving. Medical progress arising from the two world wars was immeasurable. So too was technical progress (and, of course, military progress). As we have seen, human beings typically evolve in new directions after crisis, and if we can learn to make the most of that natural stage of transformative dynamism, we may even come to believe our crisis was for the best. Use its power and momentum.

Dare to engage with your predicament and stop fearing and fighting it. With the natural expansion you will feel when you dare to breathe again and meet the challenges, you will rediscover your capacity for self-reliance and contentment. There are few things better than to feel our whole being responding to an emergency in a way that makes us resilient and robust. We become toughened, like steel in a fire, our minds are tightened and our worldview is wised up by our letting go of some of our illusions and being able to face harsh realities. This stops us feeling afraid of the future or floundering about in uncertainty, and it might even make us itch for further challenges to continue building that strength and even greater capacity.

14. Share what you have learned

Once our cup is overflowing with this new verve and vivacity, it is important that we do not just keep it to ourselves. Use your insights and skills to support others in similar situations. Discover that you can be generous and supportive, nurturing and big hearted. Share as much as is possible without depriving yourself. The more you gain clarity about how life works and how you can build your inner powers to become more proficient in meeting existential crisis, the clearer you will see how your experience is connected to that of others. The crowning glory of surpassing existential crisis is that sense that we have learnt something invaluable about human existence, something that is of core importance and can never be taken away from us again. The deepening of our inner thoughts and confidence, the crystallisation of our wisdom and the gladdening of our heart will speak for themselves as we come to terms with an experience we thought would destroy us but that turned out to be the making of us.

* * * * * * *

And so, through crisis, we can find new understanding, new direction, a fresh sense of energy and a capacity for thinking more deeply and bravely about the things that truly matter. We will always mourn our losses and regret the wrongs done to us, but we will become emboldened with a renewed sense of purpose and much greater ability to adapt to whatever may come in the future.

Conclusions

What we learn from crisis

In crisis, as we have seen, we learn to be creative, because we have no other choice but to do things differently. A crisis is the end of the old and the beginning of the new way of doing things. We do not have to get it right straight away – it is a gradual adjustment; we do not have to prove anything or give a top-class performance. Going through crisis is a very personal experience in which we improvise and do things our own way. It is often not visible to others and, if we do well at it, it earns us no accolades. It does, however, sharpen our wits, our grit, our courage and our resilience. When we are at rock bottom, we discover that we are each responsible for creating, maintaining and honing our lives, day by day, whether we are observed or invisible to others.

Nobody is exempt from encountering such challenges at some point in their life. Nobody escapes such scary experiences that remind us that survival and good fortune are never guaranteed. In such encounters with destiny, we are confronted with our true character, its sharp edges and its weaknesses, and we are given a chance to develop into a kinder, stronger, fairer, wiser, more empathetic version of ourselves. It usually involves some redemptive experiences that can be very mundane, such as the elation we feel at discovering a bit of chocolate in a coat pocket when all we wanted was something sweet and the shops were closed. Or it may be the unexpected welling up of gratitude at the kind smile of the child who offers us their seat on the bus. We rediscover the importance of the small and simple things in life and the milk of human kindness.

This is a good time to get our priorities sorted out. We rediscover basic values, such as the satisfaction we can gain from planting a couple of tomato seeds in a pot on a window sill, tending them carefully, seeing them push out of the earth, grow leaves and then flowers, which swell and ripen into tomatoes that we eventually savour and devour. We are confronted with the importance of making good relationships with those near and dear to us. We learn to take responsibility for who we are and how we want to be in the world.

We discover that crisis is something we need to find a place for in our lives, instead of trying to avoid or deny it. We find that it teaches us many things, one of which is that we have to rise to it, with resilience, persistence and resourcefulness. Another is that we will carry the scars of such events ever after, but that our wounds will heal if we survive; the scars are not a disaster. I still carry the marks of my accident, of my migrations, of my flood, of my miscarriage, of my unfair dismissal, of my court case, of my divorces, of my cancer, of my Brexit and pandemic experiences, and a few other small crises besides. And I will, until the end, wear these scars with pride instead of with resentment. We never escape our human fate and, while we will sometimes be floored by a disaster, there is only one way forward and that is to learn to rise from it.

There are some great metaphors for such experiences: the phoenix rising from its ashes, the pearls that are produced by the oyster when grit gets into its shell, the diamonds that are formed by millions of years of carbon under pressure, the seeds buried in darkness, waiting to shoot new tendrils into the light. We are all familiar with these and other transformative concepts, such as the mutations of the caterpillar into chrysalis and butterfly. Change is never easy, and we should not expect it to lead to perfection, instant healing, redemption or restitution. The reality is often much more prosaic: after crisis, we continue the work of transformation for many years.

Beyond the crisis

Laure Ollivier-Minns illustrates this learning to adjust to a life of crisis and disappointment very well in a piece she wrote in a Facebook group on 'Loneliness through Brexit pain and lockdown' at the end of 2020. Her account sums up the tensions and paradoxes that continue to hurt, even after we rebuild our lives.

Laure is a French national who came to the UK more than three decades ago, in the mid-1980s, married a British citizen, had two British children and made the UK and the English language her own. When Brexit occurred, she decided to leave the UK at the end of 2018, because she no longer felt at home and had lost trust in the British government, the settlement scheme and the loss of her rights. She felt estranged by the way she was being treated by the UK authorities. She couldn't bear the idea of becoming an 'unworthy migrant' without a voice and decided to go back to her birth country. She felt betrayed and deceived by the government and robbed of her rights. To return to France, she had to deal with the complex paperwork involved in the process. She had to leave behind her grown-up British children and her British husband of 30 years, whom she divorced. These were hard, heart-rending decisions to have to take. The prospect of starting again, on her own, was clearly daunting, but she bravely affirmed her determination not to let her life be destroyed by the despair over Brexit. When the Covid-19 pandemic hit and borders closed, she realised she was now even more separated from her children. One crisis had merged into another. Here, with her kind permission, are her thoughts in the midst of the Covid-19 crisis:

> I am alone with my bewilderment, my anger, my disgust, my memories, my pain, my bitterness, my ordeals, my angst and my mourning… daily. But I somehow manage through my struggle with coming to terms with what is beyond our control, as we cannot stop the inevitable: a painful Brexit which is a crime against humanity.
>
> Coping in finding the balance between fierce activism and doing things I enjoy. I garden, I dance, I sing, I walk and I swim in the sea. In an attempt to have my needs met, this balance carries me through this pandemonium like riding waves, falling and rising again. I dig strength in unity, challenging what is wrong and in working together to bring better awareness.
>
> My social life and my friends, mostly online, make me cherish kindness and solidarity. No one should suffer in silence; we speak and share our words; we defend our values and defy the lies. The only positive thing in this Brexit shambles is to have met like-minded people who dare being outspoken. It helps to feel less alone even if the physical loneliness remains.
>
> Our second lockdown is ending in a couple of days… Will I dare go out believing in a life resembling the normal until curfew time? Small steps at a time… Tasting life but not in denial, nor in total oblivion, thinking protection.
>
> I found my refuge since my Brexodus; home is second to none and I am looking after it. Grateful to have this peaceful place to welcome my grown-up British children when they will be allowed to cross the Channel one day… I dream of future projects while multi-tasking several on the go. I am planning my building work and I look forward to a creative path again, grateful for this door opening at last, after several postponements.
>
> I shall continue to forge connections – aiming more on the French ground rather than online, despite my conflict with loyalty – some form of detachment is approaching but I know I will always keep a foot in the UK; part of me is left on that broken island… And I long to bring colours to a

grim landscape in our sick world and shape my feelings with clay. Mindful of nourishing hope in rebuilding, maintaining gratitude, and thirsty of soothing beauty in creativity, as well as looking for it around me.

Courage my friends! Unity in adversity is what is needed. Thinking of you.

It is clear that Laure embodies the paradox of existential crisis completely: pushed by circumstances, she chose to deal with the hardship of having to live in a separate country to her British children in a strong and determined fashion, but that has not made the pain disappear. She is courageous in rebuilding her life and does her utmost to create new connections and maintain old ones, where possible. But she still feels the sharp sting of loneliness, because of her separation from her loved ones, caused by the dual curses of Brexit and Covid-19. She is becoming stronger day by day but is nevertheless acutely aware that this fate should not have befallen her. It feels as if something went desperately wrong in her life and that an injustice was done to her. She is using her own resources to work through her anger and bitterness, developing resilience, rebuilding her life and keeping hope alive. Like many others, she has learnt to use media with care and caution.

Immersing yourself in fake news and becoming constantly exasperated about the wrongs being done to you is mad-making, and having constantly to justify yourself is exhausting. Cutting yourself off and living in fantasy instead of with facts and reality are equally wrong. There is a way of mediating the news coming in from the outside world that allows you to manage it. You have to observe your own responses and figure it out by trial and error.

In the same way, you figure out how to foreground love in your life – not just the love we have for our families but the love we have for all the objects, animals, places, people and ideas that matter to us. Love is truly the earth on which we build our safety, especially when safety has become temporarily unavailable. To create that sanctuary and find that solace, we have to know what are the things that we love, and we have to learn to love ourselves first and foremost. During the Brexit years, so many of the five million EU citizens in the UK felt hated and discarded and began to feel not just unwelcome but unworthy. So many struggled with maintaining a simple, basic dose of self-care, self-esteem, self-worth and self-love. In our ESSE clinic, we taught so many people how to retrieve a sense of self-compassion and accept that they were valid, good people who were being made to feel surplus to requirements, but who mattered. But we also helped them see that, while they had no responsibility for their plight, they had complete responsibility for their response to it. Many discovered they could always learn to respond better.

The same happened in the pandemic. Some people, who had to self-isolate because of their age or because of their particular vulnerability, began to doubt their value to society. They perceived, like the five million EU citizens, that society was affording them less value than it afforded other people. Many took it all very personally, especially those who weren't surrounded by caring and loving family members. They began to feel as if they were a burden to society and fell into a state of despondency before they re-emerged and began to find ways to enjoy life and think about who they were and how they were actually making a difference for the better to the world. Those who survived realised the importance of making the most of life while we still have it.

Making sure the existential crisis doesn't harm us but heals us

Existential crises, as we have seen, affect every element of our existence. We have to relearn to keep ourselves safe and find out what that entails, at so many levels. We also have to relearn the importance of human cooperation and kindness. The existential crises we suffer help us scoop out our integrity and plumb the depths of our personality. Ultimately, the experience calls on us not just to reshape our own existence and remodel ourselves but also to reflect on our reasons for living and our ways of being.

We discover that life is of value, that we have to live well and with mutuality and generosity, sensitivity and understanding. Life loses its shine as soon as we become casual or dismissive about it. In the same way, life loses its meaning if we become hateful and negative in relation to other people. We have to create what is right and good and get better all the time at discarding what is wrong and bad for us.

Thus, living through existential crisis teaches us the ultimate lesson: that life is precious, that death is inevitable and that making the most of the few years we have received as a gift is by far the most important thing for us to concentrate on. We also find that the things we have in common need attending to. We need to look after the planet and all the creatures and elements that are part of it and live on it. We need to support each other without becoming discouraged. We need to shine our light and add positives and love at every opportunity.

And then we come to realise that, when crises do hit us, we do not fold and falter. We do not let ourselves fall down but we re-assemble, re-group, reflect, retrieve our strength and rise until we overcome and transcend what has initially felt impossible to encompass. Our trials and tribulations are what make us who we become and the ways in which we deal with them set out a new path for the future. To thrive from existential crisis is to face reality and all its hidden dangers and to be undaunted. It is to live with existential courage. It is to say to ourselves that we will do our best and keep going until we see a light on the horizon. It is not to allow ourselves to give up or baulk at the task before us. It is not to expect to be saved or to be given exemptions. It is to stop doing special pleading and trying to escape from the danger. None of us is excused from such challenges. All of us are tested and must find the key to our own resilience and resourcefulness.

Learning that we have the inner strength and the talents required to do this is one of the great gains of rising from crisis. Those who have done so will forever be changed for the better. They will be less likely to complain or expect life to be easy and predictable. They have acquired a capacity for almost relishing their struggles and exertions. They are recognised and marked out by their capacity for courage and for compassion for others.

But it is crucial to remember that crisis is never just the problem of a single individual. Crisis is never solitary. We may be thrown apart from other people in crisis, but we discover that in our hearts we long to belong with them. Our experience of catastrophe connects us up particularly to all those fellow humans who have been through crisis, loss and calamity before us and all those who will come after us. We recognise the signs and become tearful inside at seeing someone else suffering a similar plight.

Overcoming our crisis requires a supreme effort in putting ourselves above that plight, so that we learn to lift ourselves up and grow strong. Like seedlings, we learn to seek the light, and, in this process, we understand something about the tasks of humanity: to solve problems and withstand difficulties and transform adversity into opportunity. We recognise that those who have surmounted crises and have distilled the essence of that experience become a voice for change, for understanding and survival. They always know that thriving on crisis is a communal human endeavour that restores interconnectivity.

We are alone when exposed to the initial shock, but we discover solidarity and support and co-operation along the way and acquire a new level of dignity and wisdom. We become united with all those others who have lost their voice and have suffered or have become a minority. We recognise wrongs; we identify with the injustice. We know that feeling of isolation and loss of power in our bones. We want it sorted. When we find our human voice and sing in harmony, we find our vital energy and personal dynamism.

When we do so, we rise.
We rise when we affirm our right to life and dignity.
We rise when we find alliances.
We rise when we take responsibility and change things.

We rise when we remember who we are and what we are capable of.
We rise when we take heed and re-establish vital concord.
We rise when we see the similarities as well as the differences.
We rise when we learn self-compassion and compassion for our
     fellow travellers.

The voices of the people

When the second wave of the pandemic reached the UK, I posted an open question on social media asking people how they were coping with Covid and a world in turmoil: 'How do you cope with adversity and existential crisis?'

Immediately the responses flooded in. Here are some of the things people wrote:

I focus on what is true and good: head bumps from cats
hot earl grey tea and biscuits
finally retrieving that peanut stuck in your tooth
the dog snoring
seeing democracy prevail
buying a new book
going to bed early to read
putting on fireplace-warmed pants and socks
going to sleep in newly-clean bed sheets.

Exercising, dancing, yoga, reading, walking in nature, stroking a cat, helping somebody, gardening, drumming, singing.

Knitting. Grooming horses, singing/playing in our band while care home residents join in the chorus; walking in lovely countryside; gardening; hot bubble bath; swimming in peace; riding out in the winter sunshine; dancing; cycling; real ale, good wine and gin.

Working with wood. Cutting and splitting logs/timber. Stacking it even better. So satisfying.

Sweeping the drive. Cleaning.
Walking. When I can. As far as I can.

Fast motorcycle ride. Riding bike.

Stargazing! There is something massively peaceful about being alone, outside in the still, dark skies with no company other than the stars above!

Watching craft programmes. Creating a Lego model.

Haircut and blow dry.

Specifically the top drawer of my dishwasher. Putting all the cutlery in serried ranks… Knowing I can control this little thing makes me okay with not being able to control everything.

Collecting and sorting seeds.

Doing the washing. I love sorting it into piles and watching it somersault in the machine and drier.

Working the heavy bag in the Gym, and the whole ritual that goes with it. First, it's wrapping up my hands, to ensure they are protected, yet it allows me to feel the impact, and then the glove wraps go on and then the gloves themselves: protection and strength.

Cross-stitching, colouring, walking in nature, playing with a puppy, photography, guitar playing, cooking with a podcast on, boxing, belly laughing over something stupid (usually me).

Gregorian chant. Sorting out spices or buttons. Knitting.

Fast descent on skis or snowboard. The sun in my face and on the snow. Blue sky.

Painting walls. DIY.

Baking is my absolute joy… the pleasure of creating something out of basic ingredients, while spreading a cloud of heat and fragrant promises of sweet treats. I also love my produce to be relished and savoured.

I put my mindful music on to go to sleep - the shipping forecast with a classical background, bird song, sound of the sea, it helps to detox from the day and helps lull me into restorative sleep.

I go out in nature and observe the subtle seasonal changes. I find that very grounding and soothing and it brings me much joy. I also garden and grow veg. Sowing seeds brings me hope.

I watch funny home videos of my six-month-old grandson's reaction to his first experience of taste and being startled by his mother's laughter. It gets me every time I watch it, all my happy hormones are instantly activated.

I go outside at night and see a multitude of stars, with no light pollution, and know this turbulent time will pass.

I go into my little urban garden before dawn in all seasons and sit quietly watching the light change and waiting for the first birdsong of the day.

Hope is the main thing that keeps me going; I have a non-religious faith that things will be okay, change isn't always a bad thing. I believe no matter how hard life gets, or what we endure, holding onto hope will help us survive.

Gaining a new understanding of our financial world… I found it essential for me to anchor myself in fields other than humanity and religion when Covid struck in January. Taking a deep dive into economics and science is what I craved for and needed.

I decided to consciously turn to the insight and wisdom of those who have spent years in prison or in truly life-death situations. All of them speak of still being able to experience transcendence, beauty, grace, joy in being alive in those imprisonments. I found that so extraordinary and humbling and helpful.

I remain anchored to my faith and prayer. Because truly when all is stripped from us it is this courageous faith that will keep us going. No matter how little it is, this little plus little plus little equals to Big.

I'm chronically sick, I've been 90% housebound for years. When I'm able to, I craft and sew, low-energy stuff that brings me joy.

I just dance in my kitchen on techno sets or record silly videos of me dancing and share it on social media, which elicits fun chats and virtual connections with my friends.

Those often very small acts of innocent kindness and generosity, of welcome and hospitality, imperfect, humble, often entirely spontaneous in their emergence.

Drawing the curtains to keep this dangerous new world at bay. Lighting candles against the evil spirits. Racing away on a ferry to a country that feels safer. Riding a horse through a stream in a country park: deliberately slowly, hearing the water splashing under the hooves.

As we can see, people have plenty of ways to make themselves feel happy and safe again. When we can harvest all this silent wisdom, the world comes together in joy and hope. The more of these moments of goodness we can create for ourselves, the better. If we can share them, better still. But there is always a risk that, by focusing on feeling better, we forget to pay attention to the wider perspective. The political, social, historical, philosophical and ontological aspects of crisis deserve to be minded and mined as well. The lessons that need to be learnt from what went wrong are every bit as important as our capacity to get back on top of things. If we don't learn those lessons, catastrophes will continue to happen. And, while existential crises will bring positive transformation to many of us, we should never gratuitously invite disasters that can be avoided or idealise the experience. Let us not forget those millions of people whose lives were taken in the pandemic, and the many millions who, like the EU citizens in the UK, are casualties of political, social and other man-made crises, as their lives are turned upside down and their very sense of self and worthiness is assaulted.

My personal reminder for managing life through the Covid pandemic was as follows:

Be calm, composed and collected.
Stay close, courteous and connected.
Be courageous, constructive and reflective.
Dare to be creative while being self-protective.
Commit, be consistent and conscientious.
Co-operation and kindness beat competitiveness.
Change is inevitable and necessary.
When afflicted, weep deeply whilst sheltering.
Retain the good, discard the dispensable.
Conscious choices bring contentment.
If you're caring, compassionate and charitable
Confidence will crown life eventually
With truth, transparency and clarity.

Coda

People will find their own way, their own solutions to their existential crisis. We all have to learn to ride the rollercoaster of our emotions. We take permission from the special circumstances to do things differently; we become both more self-indulgent and more mindful of others. We think a lot about past times, when things were easier. But, as we unweave our past lives, we also have an opportunity to retrieve from them what is most important and to discard what has become outdated and redundant. We learn to keep the good and make a new start. We learn to appreciate the good times and value what continues to be positive in our lives. With some further reflection we also learn how to redress the balance that was disturbed by our challenges. If we have any sense, we teach ourselves to savour what we still have, although our losses may be great and grave. We save what we can save. You never know if things will get better or worse; things grow and develop as well as decay and perish.

We look after our bodies and our physical existence, especially in nature. We reach out to others and consider what we can add to the world. We mould ourselves into better mental and emotional shape: we build new backbone and strength of character that will remain part of us as long as we live.

We face facts and seek truth; we learn to befriend and treasure our anxiety. We recognise that anxiety is the provider of vital energy. We find new purpose, so that we can direct that energy wisely and use it to the full. We learn to breathe more deeply, appreciating the life that rushes through us. We discover our courage, and we renew our commitment to the values that guide us. We place our faith in these. We accept that life is full of problems and disappointments, but that we have the strength to solve these problems and find new projects to aspire to and accomplish.

We embrace existence in all its contradictions, for that is how we rise from adversity: by holding the paradox and finding its dialectic to guide us. We welcome the fact that we have been opened up and have become transparent to ourselves, that we can no longer hide behind our masks and pretences. We are beginning to see that our Northern Star is inside us and always with us, yet it points us to something well beyond and outside of us. We do not own the universe, but we are always part of it.

We remember to be free, to be strong, to feel deeply and sleep long when possible. We know that to be well we have to be true, face facts, keep safe, be creative and become what we are capable of becoming.

Crisis confronts us with what is beyond us and reminds us that we are smaller than we thought. It teaches humility. We know, in our bones, that we are ultimately intertwined with what Bohm called the implicate order of the universe (Bohm, 1980/2002).

An existential crisis, in the final analysis, brings us closer to understanding the meaning of our existence, as we open our hearts, count the cost of our losses and come home to ourselves, knowing that our pain has led to a profound sense of awe and wonder.

References

Adams, M. (2018). *An existential approach to human development: Philosophical and therapeutic.* Palgrave Macmillan.

Adams, R. (1972/2018). Watership Down. Penguin Random House.

Aho, K. (2021). The uncanny in the time of pandemics: Heideggerian reflections on the coronavirus. *Journal of the Society for Existential Analysis*, *32*(1), 5.

Akhtar, S. (1999). *Immigration and identity: Turmoil, treatment, and transformation.* Jason Aaronson.

Albright, M. (2018). *Fascism: A warning*. William Collins.

Angelou, M. (1978). And still I rise. In M Angelou, *And still I rise*. Random House.

Anonymous. (2021, January 20). This is what it is like to be an intensive care unit nurse right now. *The Guardian*. www.theguardian.com/commentisfree/2021/jan/20/intensive-care-nurse-eu-europeans-health-britain?CMP=Share_iOSApp_Other

Arendt, H. (1943). We refugees. In *The Jewish writings: Hannah Arendt* (J. Kohn & R.H. Feldman, Eds.). Schocken Books.

Arendt, H. (1964). *Eichmann in Jerusalem: A report on the banality of evil* (2nd revised ed.). Penguin.

Arendt, H. (1973). *Crises of the republic*. Penguin.

Arendt, H. (1951/1979). *The origins of totalitarianism*. Harvest Books.

Arendt, H. (1958/2018). *The human condition* (2nd ed.). University of Chicago Press.

Arnold-Baker, C. (2020). *Motherhood as an existential crisis*. Palgrave Macmillan.

Banks, J.A. & McGee Banks, C.A. (2001). *Handbook of research on multicultural education.* Wiley.

Barnett, L. (2009). *When death enters the therapeutic space: Existential perspectives in psychotherapy and counselling*. Routledge.

Barrett, W. (1962/1990) *Irrational man*. Anchor Books.

Baumeister, R.F. (1991). *Meanings of life*. Guilford Press.

Baumeister, R.F. (2005). *The cultural animal: Human nature, meaning, and social life.* Oxford University Press.

Bazzano, M. (2013). *Spectre of the stranger: Towards a phenomenology of hospitality*. Sussex Academic Press.

Beck, J.G., Chanoff, S. & Chanoff, D. (2016). *From crisis to calling: Finding your moral center in the toughest decisions*. Berrett-Koehler Publishers.

Beck, J.G. & Sloan, D.M. (Eds.) (2012). *The Oxford handbook of traumatic stress disorders*. Oxford University Press.

Becker, E. (1971). *The birth and death of meaning: An interdisciplinary perspective on the problem of man*. The Free Press.

Becker, E. (2011). *The denial of death*. Free Press Paperbacks.

Beech, J. (2020, November 24). Settled status: Are your EU workers ready or at risk? *Personnel Today*. www.personneltoday.com/hr/settled-status-are-your-eu-workers-ready-or-at-risk/

Bemak, F., Chung, R.C.Y. & Pedersen, P. (2003). *Counseling refugees: A psychosocial approach to innovative multicultural interventions*. Greenwood Publishing Group.

Benedi Lahuerta, S. & Iusmen I. (2019). Exploring EU nationals' vulnerability in the context of Brexit: The case of Polish nationals. *Journal of Ethnic and Migration Studies, 47*(1), 284-306.

Bentall, R. (2021, February 9). Has the pandemic really caused a 'tsunami' of mental health problems? *The Guardian*. www.theguardian.com/commentisfree/2021/feb/09/pandemic-mental-health-problems-research-coronavirus?fbclid=IwAR0MjFqUWQz2TI_bqx3zhQgMGIt6RtyWh07-AmAzaUB9vpw-12SckLIyRgQ

Berry, J.W. & Kim, U. (1988). Acculturation and mental health. In P.R. Dasen, J.W. Berry & N. Sartorius (Eds.), *Health and cross-cultural psychology: Toward applications* (pp.207–236). Sage.

Bhugra, D., Craig, T., & Bhui, K. (Eds.). (2010). *Mental health of refugees and asylum seekers*. Oxford University Press.

Blackall, M. (2021, February 8). We get daily abuse: UK frontline workers on the Covid second wave. *The Guardian*. www.theguardian.com/world/2021/feb/08/we-get-daily-abuse-uk-frontline-workers-on-the-covid-second-wave?CMP=Share_iOSApp_Other

Blackwell, D. (2005). *Counselling and psychotherapy with refugees*. Jessica Kingsley Publishers.

Bohm, D. (1980/2002). *Wholeness and the implicate order*. Routledge.

Bonanno, G.A. (2004). Loss, trauma, and human resilience: Have we underestimated the human capacity to thrive after extremely aversive events? *American Psychologist, 59*, 20–28. doi:10.1037/0003066X.59.1.20

Bonanno, G.A. (2010). *The other side of sadness: What the new science of bereavement tells us about life after loss*. Basic Books.

Boss, M. (1979). *Existential foundations of medicine and psychology*. (S. Conway & A. Cleaves, Trans.). Northvale: Aronson.

Boyle, M. & Johnstone, L. (2020). *A straight talking introduction to the Power Threat Meaning Framework*. PCCS Books.

Boyles, J. (2017). *Psychological therapies for survivors of torture*. PCCS Books.

Bracken, P. (2002). *Trauma: Culture, meaning and philosophy*. Wiley.

Brophy, J. (2019, December 23). Brexit and mental health: Are you coping? *The Parliament Magazine*. www.theparliamentmagazine.eu/articles/opinion/brexit-and-mental-health-are-you-coping

Brown, B. (2012). *Daring greatly*. Penguin.

Brown, B. (2015). *Rising strong*. Vermilion.

Brown, D.E. (2017). *Human universals* (2nd ed.). McGraw Hill Education.

Bugental, J. (1965). *The search for authenticity: An existential-analytic approach to psychotherapy*. Holt, Rinehart & Winston.

Bulman, M., & Bussy, C. (2019, January 5). 'They say we'll be fine. We are already not fine': EU nationals 'suicidal' as no-deal Brexit looks increasingly likely. *The Independent*. www.independent.co.uk/news/uk/home-news/eu-nationals-brexit-suicidal-mental-health-anxiety-depression-uncertainty-a8698216.html

Calhoun, L.G. & Tedeschi, R.G. (1989). Positive aspects of critical life problems: Recollections of grief. *Omega: Journal of Death and Dying, 20*(4), 265–272.

Calhoun, L.G. & Tedeschi, R.G. (2013). *Posttraumatic growth in clinical practice*. Routledge.

Camus, A. (1942/1955). Return to Tipasa. In *The myth of Sisyphus and other essays*. (J. O'Brien, Trans.) Hamish Hamilton.

Charura, D. & Paul, S. (2015). *Love and therapy: In relationship*. Karnac Books.

Children's Commissioner for Wales (2021). *Coronavirus and me: Nation-wide survey for children and young people in Wales*. Children's Commissioner for Wales. www.childcomwales.org.uk/coronavirusandme/

Clarkson, P. (2006) *The bystander. (An end to innocence in human relationships*?) Wiley.

Coates, S. (2018, December 12). Brexit: Suicide warning if exit turns chaotic. *The Times*. www.thetimes.co.uk/article/brexit-suicide-warning-if-exit-turns-chaotic-rjlhwb2n0

Connor, K.M. (2006). Assessment of resilience in the aftermath of trauma. *Journal of Clinical Psychiatry, 67*(suppl 2), 46–49.

Connor, K.M. & Davidson, J.R. (2003). Development of a new resilience scale: The Connor–Davidson Resilience Scale (CD-RISC). *Depression and Anxiety, 18*(2), 76–82. https://doi.org/10.1002/da.10113

Cooper, M. (2008). *Essential research findings in counselling and psychotherapy: The facts are friendly*. Sage.

Cooper, M. (2015). *Existential psychotherapy and counselling: Contributions to a pluralistic practice*. Sage.

Cooper, M. (2017). *Existential Therapies* (2nd ed.). Sage.

Corbett, L. & Milton, M. (2011). Existential therapy: A useful approach to trauma? *Counselling Psychology Review, 26*(1), 62–74.

Craig, E. (Ed.). (1988). Psychotherapy for freedom: The Daseinsanalytic way in psychology and psychoanalysis. (Special; issue). *The Humanistic Psychologist, 16*(1).

Csikszentmihalyi, M. (1990). *Flow: The concept of optimal psychology*. Harper Collins Publishers.

Danesh, A.H. (2019) *Exploring Iranian Political Refugees' Experiences in Britain. The phoenix rises from the ashes: An existential-phenomenological study*. Doctoral thesis. Middlesex University.

Davidson, S. & Seyler, F. (Eds.). (2019). *The Michel Henry reader*. Northwestern University Press.

Davies, J. (2013). *Cracked: Why psychiatry is doing more harm than good*. Icon Books.

de Beauvoir, S. (1948/2018). *The ethics of ambiguity*. (B. Frechtman, Trans.). Open Road Media.

de Beauvoir, S. (1954/2005). *The mandarins*. HarperCollins.

de Board, R. (2014). *The psychoanalysis of organizations*. Routledge.

de Jong, E.M., Ziegler, N. & Schippers, M. (2020). From shattered goals to meaning in life: life crafting in times of the COVID-19 pandemic. *Frontiers in Psychology, 11*: 577708. doi: 10.3389/fpsyg.2020.577708.

de Wind, E. (1947/2020). *Last stop Auschwitz*. Penguin.

Denham, A.R. (2008). Rethinking historical trauma: Narratives of resilience. *Transcultural Psychiatry, 45*(3), 391-414.

du Plock, S. (2010, April 17). *Trauma in the relational world: An existential perspective.* [Presentation]. British Psychological Society, Division of Counselling Psychology Conference.

Eger, E. (2017). *The choice*. Penguin Random House.

Eilk, S. (2012). *Iran-Turkey relations, 1979-2011: Conceptualising the dynamics of politics, religion and security in the middle-power state*. Routledge.

Emotional Support Service for European Citizens in the UK (ESSE). (2020). *Service audit: Internal report*. ESSE.

Fancourt, D., Bu, F., Mak, H.W., Paul, E. & Steptoe, A. (2021). *Covid-19 social study: Results release 31*. University College London. www.covidsocialstudy.org/results

Fanon, F. (1963). *The wretched of the earth* (C. Farrington, Trans.). Penguin Modern Classics.

Ferrara, A. (1998). *Reflective authenticity*. Routledge. Ford

Field, T. & Lamplugh, D. (2010.) *Bully in sight*. Success Unlimited.

Fluharty M., Bu F., Steptoe, A. & Fancourt, D. (2020, November 10). *Association of coping strategies with mental health trajectories during the first twenty-one weeks of Covid-19 lockdown*. Preprint. https://doi.org/10.31234/osf.io/hy5wb

Frank, A. (2007). *The diary of a young girl* (O. Frank & M. Pressler, Eds; S. Massotty, Trans.). Puffin Books.

Frankl, V.E. (1978). *The unheard cry for meaning*. Simon & Schuster.

Frankl, V.E. (1984). *Man's search for meaning* (revised and updated ed.). Washington Square Press.

Frankl, V.E. (1985). *Psychotherapy and existentialism: Selected papers on logotherapy*. Simon & Schuster.

Frankl, V.E. (1986). *The doctor and the soul: From psychotherapy to logotherapy* (3rd ed.). (R. Winston & C. Winston, Trans.). Vintage Books.

Frankl. V.E. (2019). *Yes to life, in spite of everything*. (J. Young, Trans.). Penguin Random House.

Freedom from Torture. (2017, March 24). *Freedom from Torture welcomes UN decision to maintain independent expert on Iran*. www.freedomfromtorture.org/news/freedom-from-torture-welcomes-un-decision-to-maintain-independent-expert-on-iran

Freeman, M. (2005). *Human rights*. Polity Press.

Fromm, E. (1941/2001) *The fear of freedom*. Routledge Classics.

Fromm, E. (1956/1995). *The art of loving*. Harper Collins.

Fromm, E. (1993) *The art of being*. Constable & Robinson.

Gandhi, M.K. (2001). *An autobiography: The story of my experiments with truth*. Penguin Books.

Gentleman, A. (2019). *The Windrush betrayal: Exposing the hostile environment*. Guardian/ Faber Publishing.

Gerrity, E., Keane, M.K. & Tuma, F. (eds.) (2012). *The mental health consequences of torture*. Springer Science & Business Media.

Grayling, A.C. (2018). Foreword. In E. Remigi, D. Williams, H. de Cruz, S. Pybus, C. Killwick & P. Blackburn (A. Harrey, Illus.). *In limbo too: Brexit testimonies from UK citizens in the EU*. CreateSpace Independent Publishing Platform.

Greenberg, J., Koole, S.L. & Pyszczynski, T.A. (Eds.). (2014). *Handbook of experimental existential psychology.* Guilford Press.

Grinberg, L. & Grinberg, R. (1989). *Psychoanalytical perspectives on migration and exile.* Yale University Press.

Grover, N. (2021, January 12). Nearly half of NHS critical care staff report PTSD, depression or anxiety. *The Guardian.* www.theguardian.com/society/2021/jan/13/nhs-icu-staff-ptsd-severe-depression-anxiety?CMP=Share_iOSApp_Other

Hakim Dowek, N. (2019) *A phenomenological exploration of the lived experience of being bi-rooted/poly-rooted, the reciprocal relations between those roots and their impact upon the sense of self.* Doctoral dissertation. University of Middlesex/New School of Psychotherapy and Counselling.

Hakim Dowek, N. (2020). The bi-rooted migrant: An existential journey. In M. Bazzano (Ed.), *Re-visioning existential therapy: Counter-traditional perspectives* (pp.158–167*)*. Routledge.

Handlin, O. (1973). *The uprooted.* Little, Brown & Company.

Harkness, C. (2018). *The nature of existence: Health, well-being and the natural world.* Red Globe.

Harmand, J., Ashlock, L. & Miller, T. (1993). Treating post-traumatic stress disorder among Vietnam combat veterans: An existential perspective. *Journal of Contemporary Psychotherapy*, *23*(4), 281–291.

Harvell, L.A. & Nisbett, G.S. (Eds.). (2016). *Denying death: An interdisciplinary approach to terror management theory.* Routledge.

Harvey, S.B., Hatch, S.L, Jones, M., Hull, L., Jones, N., Greenberg, N., Dandeker, C., Fear, N.T. & Wessely, S. (2012). The long-term consequences of military deployment: A 5-year cohort study of United Kingdom Reservists Deployment to Iraq in 2003. *American Journal of Epidemiology*, *176*(12), 1177–1184.

Hatherley, S. (2019, December 17). Lithuanian woman who didn't feel welcome after Brexit committed suicide, inquest hears. *Southern Daily Echo.* www.dailyecho.co.uk/news/18103679.lithuanian-woman-didnt-feel-welcome-brexit-committed-suicide-inquest-hears/

Hayes, H. (2007). An existential perspective on migration, settlement and the meanings of home. *Existential Analysis, 18*(1), 2–16.

Hayward, T. (2021, January 22). Covid and me: Ten days on life support. *The Financial Times.* www.ft.com/content/2b0dbba3-6fe8-4c2d-8cca-90e87261d436

Health Foundation (2020a). *Generation COVID-19: Building the case to protect young people's future health.* The Health Foundation.

Health Foundation. (2020b, May 20). *Emerging findings on the Impact of Covid-19 on black and minority ethnic people.* www.health.org.uk/news-and-comment/charts-and-infographics/emerging-findings-on-the-impact-of-covid-19-on-black-and-min

Heidegger, M. (1927/1962). *Being and time* (J. Macquarrie & E. Robinson, Trans.). Harper & Row.

Heidegger, M. (1954/1968). What is called thinking? (J. Glenn Gray,Trans.). Harper & Row.

Heidegger, M. (1961). *An introduction to metaphysics* (R. Manheim, Trans.). Doubleday.

Heidegger, M. (1969). *Identity and difference* (J. Stambaugh, Trans.). Harper & Row.

Heim, E., Maercker A. & Boer, D. (2019). Value orientations and mental health: A theoretical review. *Transcultural Psychiatry*, *56*(3), 449–470.

Henry, M. (1993). *The genealogy of psychoanalysis* (D. Brick, Trans.). Stanford University Press.

Henry, M. (2008). *Material phenomenology* (S. Davidson, Trans.). Fordham University Press.

Henry, M. (2012). *Barbarism* (S. Davidson, Trans.). Continuum.

Hill, A. (2021, January 18). One in four UK young people have felt 'unable to cope' in pandemic. *The Guardian*. www.theguardian.com/society/2021/jan/19/one-in-four-uk-young-people -have-felt-unable-to-cope-in-pandemic?CMP=Share_iOSApp_Other

Hinde, N. (2019, October 2). One man's psychosis was triggered by 2016 Brexit result, says his doctor. *Huffington Post*. www.huffingtonpost.co.uk/entry/mans-psychosis-was-triggered- by-outcome-of-eu-referendum-says-doctor_uk_5d91c4e6e4b0019647ab3e02

Hoffman, E. (2011). *Lost in translation: A life in a new language*. Vintage.

Hoffman, L., Cleare-Hoffman, H., Granger, N. & St John, D. (2020). *Humanistic approaches to multiculturalism and diversity*. Routledge.

Hoffman, L., Yang, M., Kaklauskas, F.J. (Eds.). (2009). *Existential psychology east-west*. Universities of the Rockies Press.

Home Office. (2020, January 16). *EU settlement scheme statistics, December 2019: Experimental statistics*. https://assets.publishing.service.gov.uk/government/uploads/system/uploads/ attachment_data/file/857589/eu-settlement-scheme-statistics-december-2019.pdf

Husserl, E. (1927/1971). Phenomenology. In, 'Phenomenology', Edmund Husserl's article for the Encyclopaedia Britannica (1927): New complete translation by Richard E. Palmer (R.E. Palmer, Trans.). *Journal of the British Society for Phenomenology, 2*(2), 77–90.

Husserl, E. (1983*). Ideas pertaining to a pure phenomenology and to a phenomenological philosophy* (F. Kersten, Trans.). First Book.

Huston, N. (2002). *Losing north: Essays on cultural exile*. McArthur & Co.

Iacovou, S. (2015). *The impact of active service on the intimate relationships of ex-servicemen: An existential-phenomenological study*. Doctoral dissertation. Middlesex University.

Iversen, A., Dyson, C., Smith, N., Greenberg, N., Walwyn, R., Unwin, C., Hull, L., Hotopf, M., Dandeger, J.R. & Wessely, S. (2005). 'Goodbye and good luck': the mental health needs and treatment experiences of British ex-service personnel. *The British Journal of Psychiatry, 186*(6), 480–486.

Jackson, C. (2021). The more regrets one has about life, looking back, the greater anxiety one has about dying. *Therapy Today, 32*(3), 24–29.

Jacobsen, B. (2006). The life crisis in an existential perspective: Can trauma and crisis be seen as an aid in personal development? *Existential Analysis, 17*(1), 39–54.

Jaspers, K. (1951). *The way to wisdom* (R. Marsheim, Trans.). Yale University Press.

Jaspers, K. (1969). *Philosophy* (E.B. Ashton, Trans.). University of Chicago Press.

Johnston, J. (2020, January 14). Lib Dem peer compares post-Brexit Britain to Nazi Germany during Lords Debate. *PoliticsHome*. www.politicshome.com/news/article/lib-dem-peer- compares-postbrexit-britain-to-nazi-germany-during-lords-debate

Johnstone, L. (2000). *Users and abusers of psychiatry: A critical look at traditional psychiatric practice* (2nd ed.). Routledge.

Johnstone, L. (2014). *A straight talking introduction to psychiatric diagnosis*. PCCS Books.

Johnstone, L. (2020, September 3). Does Covid-19 pose a challenge to the diagnoses of anxiety and depression? A psychologist's view. *BJPsych Bulletin*. First view. https://doi. org/10.1192/bjb.2020.101

Johnstone, L. & Boyle, M. with Cromby, J., Dillon, J., Harper, D., Kinderman, P., Longden, E., Pilgrim, D. & Read, J. (2018). *The Power Threat Meaning Framework: Towards the identification of patterns in emotional distress, unusual experiences and troubled or troubling behaviour, as an alternative to functional psychiatric diagnosis.* British Psychological Society.

Jones, E., Wessely, S. (2005). *Shell shock to PTSD: Military psychiatry from 1900 to the Gulf War.* Psychology Press.

Joseph, S. (2011). *What doesn't kill us: The new psychology of posttraumatic growth.* Basic Books.

Kafka, F. (2009). *The trial.* (M. Mitchell, Trans.). Oxford World Classics.

Kästner, E. (1928/2015). *Emil and the Detectives.* (E. Hall, Trans.). Puffin Books.

Kästner, E. (1949/1985). *Lottie and Lisa.* Puffin Books.

Kastrup, B. (2009). *Rationalist spirituality.* Iff books.

Keane, T.M., Scott, WO,. Chavoya, G.A., Lamparski, D.M. & Fairbank, J.A. (1985). Social support in Vietnam veterans with posttraumatic stress disorder. *Journal of Consulting and Clinical Psychology, 53*, 95–102.

Kierkegaard, S. (1940). *Stages on life's way.* (H. Hong & E. Hong, Eds. &Trans.). Princeton University Press.

Kierkegaard, S. (1954). *Fear and trembling and the sickness unto death* (W. Lowrie, Trans.). Princeton University Press.

Kierkegaard, S. (1980). *The concept of anxiety.* (R. Thomte, Trans.). Princeton University Press.

Kierkegaard, S. (2000). Either/or, a fragment of life II. In H.V. Hong & E.H. Hong (Eds.). *The essential Kierkegaard.* Princeton University Press.

Kim, Y.Y. (1988). *Communication and cross-cultural adaptation: An integrative theory.* Multilingual Matters.

Kim, Y.Y. (2001). *Becoming intercultural: An integrative theory of communication and cross-cultural adaptation.* Sage.

Kim, Y.Y. (2005). Adapting to a new culture: An integrative communication theory. In W. Gudykunst (Ed.), *Theorizing about intercultural communication* (pp.375–400). Sage.

King, M.L. (2019). *Strength to love.* Beacon Press.

Klein, N. (2008). *The shock doctrine: The rise of disaster capitalism.* Allen Lane.

Klein, N. (2014) *This changes everything: Capitalism vs. the climate.* Simon & Schuster.

Krystal, H. & Niederland, W. (1968). Clinical observations on the survivor syndrome. In H. Krystal (Ed.). *Massive psychic trauma.* International Universities Press.

Lago C., Charura D. (Eds.) (2021). *Black identities and white therapies: Race, respect and diversity.* PCCS Books.

Laing, R.D. (1959). *The divided self.* Penguin.

Laing, R.D. (1961). *Self and others.* Penguin.

Laing, R.D. (1967). *The politics of experience.* Penguin.

Lennart, C. (1957). *Roosje's eyes (De ogen van Roosje).* AAM Stols.

Linley, P.A. & Joseph, S. (Eds.). (2004). *Positive psychology in practice.* Wiley.

Long, N.N. & Khoi, B.H. (2020). An empirical study about the intention to hoard food during COVID-19 pandemic. *EURASIA, 16*(7), em1857.

Low, A. (2017, February 9). In some respects the Brexit referendum was a violation of human rights. *LSE*. https://blogs.lse.ac.uk/europpblog/2017/02/09/brexit-referendum-human-rights/

Madison, G.A. (2009). *The end of belonging: Untold stories of leaving home and the psychology of global relocation*. Madison.

Magomed-Eminov, M.S. (1997). Post-traumatic stress disorders as a loss of the meaning of life. In D.F. Halpern & A. Voïskunskii, *States of mind: American and post-Soviet perspectives on contemporary issues in psychology* (pp.238–252). Oxford University Press.

Mandela, N. (1995). *The long walk to freedom: The autobiography of Nelson Mandela*. Abacus.

Marcel, G. (1965). *Being and having: An existentialist diary.* (K. Farrer, Trans.). Harper & Row.

Marcel, G. (2001) *The mystery of being.* (Vols. 1 & 2). (G.S. Fraser, Trans.). St. Augustine's Press.

Maslow, A.H. (1970). *Motivation and personality*. Harper & Row.

Maslow, A.H. (1973). *The farther reaches of human nature*. Penguin.

May, R. (1967). *Psychology and the human dilemma*. W.W. Norton & Co.

May, R. (1969a). *Love and will*. W.W. Norton & Co.

May, R. (1969b). *Existential psychology*. Random House.

May, R. (1977). *The meaning of anxiety*. W.W. Norton & Co.

May. R. (1983). *The discovery of being*. W.W. Norton & Co.

May, R. (1999). *Freedom and destiny*. W.W. Norton & Co.

May, R. & Yalom, I.D. (2013). Existential psychotherapies. In R.J. Corsini & D. Wedding (Eds.). *Current psychotherapies* (10th ed.). Thomson/Brooks/Cole.

May, R., Angel, E. & Ellenberger, H.F. (1958). *Existence*. Basic Books.

McCormack, L. & McKellar, L. (2015). Adaptive growth following terrorism: Vigilance and anger as facilitators of posttraumatic growth in the aftermath of the Bali bombings. *Traumatology, 21*(2), 71–81.

McMullan, L., Duncan, P., Hulley-Jones, F. & Blight, G. (2020, July 22). The psychological toll of coronavirus in Britain: A visual guide. *The Guardian*. www.theguardian.com/world/ng-interactive/2020/jul/22/psychological-toll-coronavirus-britain-visual-guide-anxiety-mental-strain?CMP=Share_iOSApp_Other

Meichenbaum, D. (2006). Resilience and posttraumatic growth: A constructive narrative perspective. In L.G. Calhoun & R.G. Tedeschi (Eds.), *Handbook of posttraumatic growth: Research & practice* (pp.355–367). Lawrence Erlbaum Associates Publishers.

Membrecht, S. (1963). *Waiting for the sun* (*Wachten op de Zon*). Contact.

Membrecht, S. (1965). *Leaping into the net* (*De Sprong in het Net*). Contact.

Menzies, R.E. & Menzies, R.G. (2020). Death anxiety in the time of COVID-19. *Cognitive Behaviour Therapist, 1*, 13.

Midgley, M. (2004). *The myths we live by*. Routledge.

Miller K. & Rasco L. (Eds.). (2004). *The mental health of refugees*. Lawrence Erlbaum Associates.

Minton, S.J. (2016). *Marginalisation and aggression from bullying to genocide*. Sense Publishers.

Moran, D. (2000). *Introduction to phenomenology*. Routledge

Moran, L. (2020, February 8). It's shameful that one in three EU children has been refused permanent residency. *The Independent*. www.independent.co.uk/voices/brexit-eu-nationals-settled-status-boris-johnson-a9323556.html

Morrice, L. (2011). *Being a refugee. Learning and identity: A longitudinal study of refugees in the UK.* Trentham Books.

Nagel, T. (2012). *Mind and cosmos.* Oxford University Press.

Neimeyer, R.A. (2006). *Lessons of loss* (2nd Ed.). Routledge.

Neimeyer, R.A. (2011a). *Grief and bereavement in contemporary society.* Routledge.

Neimeyer, R.A. (2011b). Reconstructing meaning in bereavement: Summary of a research program. *Estudos de Psicologia (Campinas) 28*(4): 421–426. DOI:10.1590/S0103-166X2011000400002

Neimeyer, R.A. (2015). *Techniques of grief therapy.* Routledge.

Nelson, T.D. (2016). *Handbook of prejudice, stereotyping, and discrimination* (2nd ed.). Psychology Press.

NHS Digital. (2019). *Prescription cost analysis - England, 2018.* https://digital.nhs.uk/data-and-information/publications/statistical/prescription-cost-analysis/2018

NHS Digital. (2020). *Mental health of children and young people in England, 2020. Wave 1 follow up to the 2017 survey.* https://files.digital.nhs.uk/AF/AECD6B/mhcyp_2020_rep_v2.pdf

Nietzsche, F. (1883–85/1997). *Thus spake Zarathustra.* Wordsworth Editions.

Nietzsche, F. (1886/2010). *Beyond good and evil.* (R.J. Hollingdale, Trans.). Penguin Books.

Nietzsche, F. (1889/2012) *Twilight of the idols.* CreateSpace Independent Publishing Ltd.

Norcross, J.C. (1987). A rational and empirical analysis of existential psychotherapy. *Journal of Humanistic Psychology, 27*, 41–68.

Nussbaum, M. (1994, October 1). Patriotism and cosmopolitanism. *Boston Review.* http://bostonreview.net/martha-nussbaum-patriotism-and-cosmopolitanism

O'Carroll, L. (2020, February 17). Italian man, 95, resident in the UK for 68 years, told to prove it. *The Guardian.* www.theguardian.com/uk-news/2020/feb/17/italian-man-95-resident-in-uk-for-68-years-told-to-prove-it

Office for National Statistics (ONS). (2020). *Coronavirus and anxiety, Great Britain: 3 April 2020 to 10 May 2020.* www.ons.gov.uk/peoplepopulationandcommunity/wellbeing/articles/coronavirusandanxietygreatbritain/latest

Orcutt, H.K., King, L.A. & King, D.W. (2003). Male-perpetrated violence among Vietnam veteran couples: Relationships with veteran's early life characteristics, trauma history, and PTSD symptomatology. *Journal of Trauma Stress, 16*(4), 381–390.

O'Shea, N. (2020). *Covid-19 and the nation's mental health.* Centre for Mental Health.

Ossebaard, H. & Maalste, N. (1999). The Bastiaans method of drug-assisted therapy. *Bulletin of the Multidisciplinary Association for Psychedelic Studies (MAPS) 9*(2), 3–9.

O'Toole, F. (2018). *Heroic failure: Brexit and the politics of pain.* Apollo Books.

Overland, G., Eugene Guribye, E. & Lie, B. (2014). *Nordic work with traumatised refugees: Do we really care?* Cambridge Scholars Publishing.

Pagnol, M. (1988). *Jean de Florette & Manon of the Springs* (W.E. Van Heyningen, Trans.). North Point Press.

Papadopoulos, R.K. (1999). Storied community as secure base: Response to the paper by Nancy Caro Hollander 'Exile: Paradoxes of loss and creativity'. *British Journal of Psychotherapy, 15*(3), 322-332.

Papadopoulos, R.K. (2001). Refugees, therapists and trauma: Systemic reflections. *Context, the Magazine of the Association for Family Therapy, 54*(April), 5-8.

Papadopoulos, R.K. (Ed.). (2002). *Therapeutic care for refugees: No place like home.* Tavistock Clinic Series. Karnac

Park, C., Aldwin, C., Fenster, J. & Snyder, L. (2008). Pathways to posttraumatic growth versus posttraumatic stress: coping and emotional reactions following the September 11, 2001, terrorist attacks. *The American Journal of Orthopsychiatry, 78*(3), 300–312.

Peterson, C.P. & Seligman, M.E.P. (Eds.). (2004). *Character strengths and virtues: A handbook and classification.* Oxford University Press.

Petersen, C., Maier, S.F. & Seligman, M.E.P. (1995). *Learned helplessness: A theory for the age of personal control.* Oxford University Press.

Powdthavee, N., Plagnol, A., & Frijters, P. (2019). Who got the Brexit Blues? The effect of Brexit on subjective wellbeing in the UK. *Economica, 36*, 471–494.

Quinn, B. (2017, June 24). Sleepless, anxious, depressed: EU citizens in the Shadow of Brexit. *The Observer.* www.theguardian.com/politics/2017/jun/24/eu-citizens-shadow-brexit-sleepless-anxious-depressed

Razouk, P. (2015). *The Iran-Iraq War.* Harvard University Press.

Refugee Council. (2021). *Mental health support for refugees and asylum seekers.* Refugee Council. www.refugeecouncil.org.uk/our-work/mental-health-support-for-refugees-and-asylum-seekers/

Remigi. E. & Martin V. (Eds.) (G. Harrey, Illus.). (2017). *In limbo: Brexit testimonies from EU citizens in the UK.* CreateSpace Independent Publishing Platform.

Remigi, E., Martin V. & Sykes, T. (Eds.). (2020). *In Limbo: Brexit Testimonies from EU citizens in the UK* (2nd Ed.). Spokesman Books.

Remigi, E., Williams, D., de Cruz, H., Pybus, S., Killwick, C. & Blackburn P (G. Harrey, Illus.) (2018). *In limbo too: Brexit testimonies from UK citizens in the EU.* CreateSpace Independent Publishing Platform.

Rosen, M. (2021). *Many different kinds of love: A story of life, death and the NHS.* Ebury Press.

Royal College of Psychiatrists (2021, April 9). *Country in the grip of a mental health crisis with children worst affected, new analysis finds.* Royal College of Psychiatrists. www.rcpsych.ac.uk/news-and-features/latest-news/detail/2021/04/08/country-in-the-grip-of-a-mental-health-crisis-with-children-worst-affected-new-analysis-finds

Royal Cornwall NHS Trust. (2020, September 11). *Covid survivor's Cornish climb for critical care garden.* www.royalcornwall.nhs.uk/covid-survivors-cornish-climb-for-critical-care-garden/

Runciman, D. (2018). *How democracy ends.* Profile Books.

Sadavoy, J. (1997). Survivors: A review of the late-life effects of prior psychological trauma. *American Journal of Geriatric Psychology, 5*(4), 287–301.

Said, W.E. (1994). Reflections on exiles. In M. Robinson (Ed.). *Altogether elsewhere: Writers on exiles* (pp.137–149). Faber & Faber.

Said, W.E. (1999). *Out of place: A memoir.* Granta Books.

Samasundaram, D. (2010). Complex mental health problem of refugees. In D. Bhugra., T. Craig. & K. Bhui (Eds.). (2010). *Mental health of refugees and asylum seekers.* Oxford University Press.

Sample, I. (2020, December 27). Covid poses 'greatest threat to mental health since second world war': UK's leading psychiatrist predicts impact will be felt for years after pandemic ends. *The Guardian.* www.theguardian.com/society/2020/dec/27/covid-poses-greatest-threat-to-mental-health-since-second-world-war

Sanderson, C. (2020, December 11). Michael Rosen: 'I don't think I realised until maybe August, how ill I'd been'. *The Bookseller.* www.thebookseller.com/profile/michael-rosen-i-don-t-think-i-realised-until-maybe-august-how-ill-i-d-been-1230607

Sartre, J.P. (1938/1962). *Nausea.* Penguin Books.

Sartre, J.P. (1939/1962). *Sketch for a theory of the emotions.* Methuen.

Sartre, J.P. (1943/1956). *Being and nothingness: An essay on phenomenological ontology* (H. Barner, Trans.). Philosophical Library.

Sartre, J.P. (1948). *Anti-Semite and Jew.* Schocken Books.

Sartre, J.P. (1950/2001). *What is literature?* (B. Frechtman, Trans.). Routledge.

Sartre, J.P. (1952/1963). *Saint Genet, actor and martyr.* (B. Frechtman, Trans.). Braziller.

Sartre, J.P. (1960/1982). *Critique of dialectical reason.* (A. Sheridan-Smith, Trans.). Verso/NLB.

Sartre, J.-P. (1963). Foreword. In: Fanon, F. (1963). *The wretched of the earth* (C. Farrington, Trans.) (pp.7-31). Penguin Modern Classics.

Sartre, J.P. (1983/1992). *Notebooks for an ethics.* (D. Pellaner, Trans.). University of Chicago Press.

Sartre, J.P. (1989/1992). *Truth and existence.* (A. van den Hoven, Trans.). University of Chicago Press.

Schneider, K.J. (1999). *The paradoxical self: Toward an understanding of our contradictory nature* (Revised ed.). Humanity Books.

Schneider, K.J. (2009). *Awakening to awe: Personal stories of profound transformation.* Jason Aronson.

Shevlin, M., McBride, O., Murphy, J., Gibson Mellor J., Hartman, T.K., Levita, L., Mason L., Martinez, A.P., McKay R., Stocks T.V.A., Bennett, K.M., Hyland P., Karatzias T. & Bentall, R.P. (2020). Anxiety, depression, traumatic stress and Covid-19-related anxiety in the UK general population during the Covid-19 pandemic. *BJPsych Open, 6*(6): e125.

Sisto, A., Vicinanza, F., Campanozzi, L., Ricci, G., Tartaglini D. & Tambone V. (2019). Towards a transversal definition of psychological resilience: A literature review. *Medicina, 55*(11), 745. https://doi.org/10.3390/medicina55110745.

Smith, D.L. (2011). *Less than human: Why we demean, enslave, and exterminate others.* St. Martin's Press.

Smith, D.L. (2019). How media makes, ignites, and breaks ideology. In C. Fox, J. Saunders (Eds.), *Media ethics, free speech and the requirements of democracy* (pp.183–202). Routledge.

Smith, D.L. (2020). *On inhumanity: Dehumanization and how to resist it.* Oxford University Press.

Snyder, C.R. & Lopez, S.J. (2005). *Handbook of positive psychology.* Oxford University Press.

Solnit, R. (2013). *The faraway nearby.* Granta Publications.

Solnit, R. (2020, April 7). The impossible has already happened: what coronavirus can teach us about hope. *The Guardian.* www.theguardian.com/world/2020/apr/07/what-coronavirus-can-teach-us-about-hope-rebecca-solnit?CMP=Share_iOSApp_Other

Solomon, S., Greenberg, J. & Pyszczynski, T. (2015). *The worm at the core: On the role of death in life.* Random House.

Solomon, Z., Mikulincer, M. & Habershaim, N. (1990a). Life-events, coping strategies, social resources and somatic complaints among combat stress reaction casualties. *British Journal of Medical Psychology, 63*(Pt 2),137-48. doi: 10.1111/j.2044-8341.1990.tb01607.x.

Solomon, Z., Waysman, M. & Mikulincer, M. (1990b). Family functioning, perceived social support and combat-related psychopathology: The moderating role of loneliness. *Journal of Social and Clinical Psychology, 9,* 456–472.

Stanley, J. (2018). *How fascism works: The politics of us and them.* Random House.

Strangor, C. (2016). The study of stereotyping, prejudice, and discrimination within social psychology: A quick history of theory and research. In T.D. Nelson (Ed.), *Handbook of prejudice, stereotyping and discrimination* (2nd ed.) (pp.1–26). Psychology Press.

Stolorow, R.D. (2015). A phenomenological-contextual, existential, and ethical perspective on emotional trauma. *Psychoanalytic Review, 102*(1), 123–138.

Stolorow, R. (2016). Pain is not pathology. *Journal of The Society for Existential Analysis, 27*(1), 70–77.

Sue, D. (2015). *Counseling the culturally diverse: Theory and practice.* John Wiley & Sons.

Sundararajan, L. (2014). Indigenous psychology: Grounding science in culture, why and how. *Journal for the Theory of Social Behaviour, 45,* 64–81.

Szasz, T.S. (1961). *The myth of mental illness.* Harper.

Szasz, T.S. (1965/1988). *The ethics of psychoanalysis: The theory and method of autonomous psychotherapy.* Syracuse University Press.

Tantam, D. (2012). *Autism spectrum disorders through the life span.* Jessica Kingsley Publishers.

Tantam, D. (2014). *Emotional well-being and mental health: A guide for counsellors and psychotherapists.* Sage Publications.

Tantam, D. (2018). *The interbrain: How unconscious connections influence human behaviour and relationships.* Jessica Kingsley Publishers.

Taylor, C. (2018a). *The ethics of authenticity.* Harvard University Press.

Taylor, C. (2018b). *A secular age.* Belknap Press.

Taylor, H. (2015). *Refugees and the meaning of home: Cypriot narratives of loss, longing and daily life in London.* Palgrave Macmillan.

Tedeschi, R.G. & Calhoun, L.G. (1996). The Posttraumatic Growth Inventory: Measuring the positive legacy of trauma. *Journal of Traumatic Stress, 9,* 455–471.

Tedeschi, R.G. & Calhoun, L.G. (2004). *Posttraumatic growth: Conceptual foundations and empirical evidence.* Lawrence Erlbaum Associates.

Tedeschi, R.G., Shakespeare-Finch, J., Taku, K. & Calhoun, L.G. (2018). *Posttraumatic growth: Theory, research, and applications.* Routledge.

Tetlock, P.E. (1994). Political psychology or politicized psychology: Is the road to scientific hell paved with good moral intentions? *Political Psychology, 15,* 509–529.

Thompson, S. (2006). *The political theory of recognition: A critical introduction.* Polity Press.

Tillich, P. (1951–63). *Systematic theology.* (Vols. 1–3). University of Chicago Press.

Tillich, P. (1952). *The courage to be.* Yale University Press.

Tillich, P. (1954). *Love, power and justice.* Oxford University Press.

Tolkien, J.R.R. (1968/2005). *The lord of the rings.* HarperCollins.

Tribe, R. (1999). Therapeutic work with refugees living in exile: Observations on clinical practice. *Counselling Psychology Quarterly, 12*(3), 233–243.

Tsai, J., El-Gabalawy, R., Sledge, W., Southwick, S. & Pietrzak, R. (2015). Post-traumatic growth among veterans in the USA: Results from the National Health and Resilience in Veterans Study. *Psychological Medicine, 45*(1), 165–179.

UN Convention against Torture. (1984). *United Nations convention against torture and other cruel, inhuman or degrading treatment or punishment (UNCAT).* www.ohchr.org/EN/ProfessionalInterest/Pages/CAT.aspx

UNHCR. (2002). *Refugee resettlement: An international handbook to guide reception and integration.* Victorian Foundation for Survivors of Torture (VFST) & UNHCR.

UNHCR. (2014). *Convention and protocol relating to the status of refugees.* www.unhcr.org/uk/1951- refugee-convention.html

van der Veer, G. (1998). *Counselling and therapy with refugees and victims of trauma: Psychological problems of victims of war, torture and repre*ssion. Wiley.

van Deurzen, E. (2009). *Psychotherapy and the quest for happiness.* Sage.

van Deurzen, E. (2010). *Everyday mysteries: A handbook of existential psychotherapy* (2nd ed.). Routledge.

van Deurzen, E. (2012). *Existential counselling and psychotherapy in practice* (3rd ed.). Sage.

van Deurzen, E. (2014). Structural existential analysis (SEA): A phenomenological research method for counselling psychology. *Counselling Psychology Review, 29*(2), 70–83.

van Deurzen, E. (2015a). *Paradox and passion in psychotherapy* (2nd ed.). Wiley.

van Deurzen, E. (2015b). Structural existential analysis: A phenomenological method for therapeutic work. *Journal of Contemporary Psychology, 45,* 59–68

van Deurzen, E. (2018a, July 16). Brexit feels like an experiment to test our sanity. *The New European.* www.theneweuropean.co.uk/top-stories/brexit-feels-like-an-experiment-to-test-our-sanity-1-5609487

van Deurzen, E. (2018b). *Has Brexit driven us all mad?* Voices for Europe. https://voicesforeurope.com/has-brexit-driven-us-all-mad

van Deurzen, E. (2018c). *The existential and emotional impact of Brexit.* British Psychological Society. www.bps.org.uk/blogs/european-semester-psychology-2018/existential-and-emotional-impact-brexit

van Deurzen, E. (2019a). Problems in living: An existential perspective. In Watson, J. *Drop the disorder: Challenging the culture of psychiatric diagnosis* (pp.54–66). PCCS Books.

van Deurzen, E. (2019b, May 7). Brexiter psychosis: Delusions, self-deception and Britain's political disorder. *Byline Times.* https://bylinetimes.com/2019/05/07/brexiter-psychosis-delusions-self-deception-and-britains-political-disorder/

van Deurzen, E. (2019c, 4 October). *Brexit and mental health: How are you coping?* [Paper presentation]. European Parliament. www.europarl.europa.eu/unitedkingdom/en/media/past-events/european-parliament-events-2019/mentalhealth.html

van Deurzen, E. (2020) Rising from a shattered life: Psychotherapy and existential crisis. *Grief Matters: The Australian Journal of Grief and Bereavement, 23*(1), 25–30.

van Deurzen, E. & Adams, M. (2016). *Skills in existential counselling and psychotherapy* (2nd ed.). Sage.

van Deurzen, E. & Arnold-Baker, C. (2005). *Existential perspectives on human issues.* Palgrave Macmillan.

van Deurzen, E. & Arnold-Baker, C. (2018). *Existential therapy: Distinctive features.* Routledge.

van Deurzen, E. & Arnold-Baker, C. (2019). Existential phenomenological therapy illustration: Rahim's dilemma. In van Deurzen, E., with Craig, E., Schneider K., Längle, A., Tantam, D. & du Plock, S. *Wiley world handbook for existential therapy* (pp.181–197). Wiley.

van Deurzen, E., with Craig, E., Schneider K., Längle, A., Tantam, D. & du Plock, S. (2019). *Wiley world handbook for existential therapy*. Wiley.

van Deurzen, E. & Iacovou, S. (2013). *Existential perspectives on relationship therapy*. Palgrave Macmillan.

van Deurzen, E. & Kenward, R. (2005). *Dictionary of existential psychotherapy and counselling*. Sage.

Vanhooren, S., Leijssen, M. & Dezutter, J. (2015). Post-traumatic growth during incarceration: A case study from an experiential-existential perspective. *Journal of Humanistic Psychology, 58*(2), 144–167.

Vos, J. (2017). *Meaning in life: An evidence-based handbook for practitioners*. Macmillan.

Vos, J. (2019). A review of research on existential-phenomenological therapies. In van Deurzen E., Craig, E., Längle, A., Schneiderm, K.J., Tantam, D. & du Plock, S. *Wiley world handbook of existential therapy* (pp.592–614). Wiley Blackwell.

Vos, J. (2020a). *Analysis of emotional words on social media: Internal report*. ESSE Emotional Support Service for European Citizens in the UK.

Vos, J. (2020b). *The economics of meaning in life: From capitalist life syndrome to meaning-oriented economy*. University Professors Press.

Vos, J. (2021) *The psychology of Covid-19*. Sage.

Vos, J., Cooper, M. Correia, E. & Craig, M. (2015). Existential therapies: A review of their scientific foundations and efficacy. *Existential Analysis: Journal of the Society for Existential Analysis, 26*(1), 49–69.

Vos, J., Roberts, R. & Davies, J. (2019). *Mental health in crisis*. Sage.

Vos, J., Tantam, D. & van Deurzen, E. (2020). A Brexistential crisis? *The Psychologist, 33*, 10. https://thepsychologist.bps.org.uk/brexistential-crisis

Waldinger, R. (2016, January 25). *What makes a good life? Lessons from the longest study on happiness*. Ted Talk. www.youtube.com/watch?v=8KkKuTCFvzI

Walter, N. (2021, February 28). Guilt and fury: How Covid brought women to breaking point. *The Observer*. www.theguardian.com/lifeandstyle/2021/feb/28/mums-women-coronavirus-covid-home-schooling-inequality#_=_

Wampole, C. (2016). *Rootedness: the ramifications of a metaphor*. The University of Chicago Press.

Watson, J. (2019) *Drop the disorder! Challenging the culture of psychiatric diagnosis*. PCCS Books.

Wertz, F.J. (2016). Outline of the relationship among transcendental phenomenology, phenomenological psychology, and the sciences of persons. *Schutzian Research: A Yearbook in Lifeworldly Phenomenology and Qualitative Social Sciences, 8*, 139–162.

Wilson C. (2001). *The outsider*. W&N

Wong, P.T.P. (2009). Positive existential psychology. In S.J. Lopez (Ed.), *Encyclopedia of positive psychology* (Vol. 1) (pp.361–368). Wiley Blackwell

Wong, P.T.P. (Ed.). (2012). *The human quest for meaning: Theories, research, and applications* (2nd Ed.). Routledge.

Wong, P.T.P. (2021, January 5). *What is existential positive psychology? Why is it necessary for mental health during the pandemic?*. www.drpaulwong.com/what-is-existential-positive-psychology-why-is-it-necessary-for-mental-health-during-the-pandemic/

Wong, P.T.P. & Wong, L.C.J. (Eds.). (2006). *Handbook of multicultural perspectives on stress and coping*. Springer.

Wong, P.T.P., Mayer, C.-H. & Arslan, G. (Eds.). (2021). COVID-19 and existential positive psychology (PP 2.0): The new science of self-transcendence. Research topic. *Frontiers.* www.frontiersin.org/research-topics/14988/covid-19-and-existential-positive-psychology-pp20-the-new-science-of-self-transcendence

Woodhouse, P. (2009). *Etty Hillesum: A life transformed*. Bloomsbury.

Yalom, I.D. (1980). *Existential psychotherapy*. Basic Books.

Yalom, I.D. (1989). *Love's executioner and other tales of psychotherapy*. Bloomsbury.

Yalom, I.D. (1992). *When Nietzsche wept*. Harper-Collins.

Yalom, I.D. (1996). *Lying on the couch*. Basic Books.

Yalom, I.D. (2001). *The gift of therapy*. Harper-Collins.

Yalom, I.D. (2008). *Staring at the sun*. Piatkus.

Yalom, I.D. & Yalom, M. (2021). *A matter of death and life: Love, loss and what matters in the end*. Piatkus.

Young, L. (2020, September 12). Coronavirus patient to scale Brown Willy for Royal Cornwall Hospital. *The Packet*. www.falmouthpacket.co.uk/news/18715278.covid-patient-scale-brown-willy-royal-cornwall-hospital/

Name index

A

Adams, M. 1, 21, 92, 94, 154
Adams, R. 90
Aho, K. 138
Akhtar, S. 107, 110
Albright, M. 5, 28
Angelou, M. ix
Anonymous 135, 137
Anouilh, J. 89
Arendt, H. 5, 126–127
Aristotle 94
Arnold-Baker, C. 1, 92, 95, 98, 129–130, 160

B

Balzac 90
Banks, J.A. 110
Barnett, L. 92
Barrett, W. 92
Baumeister, R.F. 103–104, 110
Bazzano, M. 110
Beck, J.G. 123, 149
Becker, E. 92, 128, 147
Beech, J. 22
Bemak, F. 110
Benedi Lahuerta, S. 28
Bentall, R. 143
Berri, C. 91
Berry, J.W. 110
Bhugra, D. 110, 112, 127
Blackall, M. 135, 140
Blackwell, D. 110
Bohm, D. 97, 184
Bonanno, G.A. 110
Borgognoni-Holmes, G. 24
Boss, M. 94

Boyle, M. 160
Boyles, J. 110
Bracken, P. 149
British Psychological Society 160
Brophy, J. 125
Brown, B. 95, 149
Bugental, J. 149
Bulman, M. 125
Busy, C. 125

C

Calhoun, L.G. 21, 118, 157
Camus, A. 88, 94, 152
Casale, R. 24, 25, 66
Charura, D. 106, 167
Children's Commissioner for Wales 140
Cicero 88
Clarkson, P. 22
Clegg, N. 24, 25
Coates, S. 125
Connor, K.M. 119
Cooper, M. 98
Corbett, L. 111, 119
Craig, E. 149
Csikszentmihalyi, M. 167

D

Danesh, A.H. 112, 126–132
Davidson, J.R. 119
Davidson, S. 97
Davies, J. 160
de Beauvoir, S. 21, 30, 88, 94
de Board, R. 95
de Cruz, H. 32

Subject index

A

ability 5, 19, 119, 173
abuse 3, 34, 114, 121,
   sexual, 129
absurdity 3, 121, 124, 125
accent 34, 39
accident 8–10, 16, 80, 87, 92–93
action 66, 67, 79–80, 130, 171
   humanitarian, 55–56
   importance of, 3, 119
   meaningful, 149, 166–68
   reflective, 163
   transform into, 40
activity 79, 165, 169
   physical, 141
adaptability 7, 36, 79, 108, 115, 132, 172–73
alienation 120
ambiguity 107
anger 40–43, 60
   transformation from, 50, 73,
   trauma-related, 121–23, 155
anxiety 20, 33, 55
   of Covid-19 134–36, 140–42
   of death 148
   managing, 77, 117, 162, 184
   and panic attacks 41, 71
aspiration 104
assumption
   of safety 92
attention 183
   medical, 136, 141
   mindful, 167–68
attitude 79, 149, 155, 163
Auschwitz 84
authenticity 105–56, 109

availability
   of support 52, 85 139, 166–67
avoidance 163
awareness 36, 43, 76, 90, 149
   of responsibility 3, 8
   self-, 114, 152, 158, 163
   social, 154, 176

B

beliefs
   challenged, 4, 95, 113, 132
   religious, 97
   rights and, 39
   values and, 54, 98
bi-rooted 106–7, 115
blame 76, 82, 130
   self-, 69–70
body 43, 85, 101, 104
   connection with, 113
   healing 80, 136, 154
   and stress 73
boundaries 16, 143
breakdown 4, 38–56, 160
Brexit 6, 20–37, 175–77
   benefits of, 52–55, 76, 176
   campaign against, 72
   impact on relationships 48
Brexiteers 41
bullying 28–29
bystander 22

C

capacity
   emotional, 83, 86, 123–24, 145, 169–70

*Case Studies in Existential Therapy:
Translating theory into practice*

Edited by Simon du Plock

ISBN 978 1 910919 28 6

The ethos of existential therapy is that practitioners seek to co-create a therapeutic alliance with clients that emphasises 'being with' rather than 'doing to'. Trainees and practitioners alike are therefore eager to have access to accounts of what senior practitioners do in their day-to-day practice. Also, it is rare that books both show the reader what the therapist does and explicitly relate this to cutting-edge thinking in theory.

Case Studies in Existential Therapy is designed to address both these gaps by providing, through the medium of the case study, a platform for leading practitioners in the existential therapy community to show how they are applying their own innovations in theory to enrich their practice. Each of the contributors describes a specific innovation in theory, and then brings this to life in an account of their engagement with a specific client. Every chapter concludes with a Question and Answer section in which the author reflects on the significance of their work in dialogue with the editor.

This is a book both for students of therapy and for the experienced practitioner keen to expand their repertoire. It will also be of interest to the psychologically minded general public.